R.K. Narayan

And His

Social Perspective

R.K. Narayan

And His Social Perspective

S.R. Ramteke

ATLANTIC
PUBLISHERS & DISTRIBUTORS (P) LTD

ATLANTIC
PUBLISHERS & DISTRIBUTORS (P) LTD

7/22, Ansari Road, Darya Ganj, New Delhi
Tel.: +91-11-4077 5252, 2327 3880
E-mail: orders@atlanticbooks.com
Web: www.atlanticbooks.com

Published by Atlantic Publishers & Distributors (P) Ltd 2024

Printed & bound in India by Atlantic Print Services

PREFACE

R.K. Narayan has carved a niche for himself in the galaxy of Indo-Anglian novelists. Simple and unpretentious, he has shun publicity in life, and yet a number of doctoral dissertations have come out evaluating the creative work he has produced. The present book is based largely on the thesis entitled 'Society and the individual in the Novels of R.K. Narayan : A study in Interaction,' for which I obtained Ph.D. from Nagpur University in 1988. However, much of it is amended, recast, and deleted which was found to be irrelevant in the present set up.

It is worth appreciating that Narayan's major characters make some efforts at self-assertion, though feeble and half-hearted in the traditional and orthodox milieu who are otherwise, for most part of their lives, seen complacently moving along the predetermined mechanical track for pre-ordained life-roles, completely resigning to their fate. How can they help it? Thanks to the 'creator' that made them so! It is really shocking to find that they lack scientific approach to deal with the problems they face. The futility writ large on their faces with no energy and will-power left, and placing themselves entirely in the hands of fate has shaken me to the core. All it has roots in Hindu ethos which Narayan too could not shake off, however detached he sounds himself in his work : the aspect, worth delving deep, warrants due attention.

I fall short of words to express my gratitudes for constant encouragements and guidance, to my teacher and guide, Dr. V.R. Kanadey, Professor and Former Head, Department of English, Nagpur University. It is a matter of pride for me to keep myself in his debt for his invaluable 'Foreword' to the book. Dr. K.J. Purohit, a litterateur of great repute, Mumbai, has inspired me a lot. His encouragement immensely helped me in my present endeavour. I am greatly indebted to him.

During the course of my work I have received guidance, love

and co-operation in abundant measure. It is with great pleasure that I record my obligations to Dr. Pankaj Chande, Dean, Faculty of Arts, Nagpur University, and now Vice Chancellor, Kavi Kalidas Sanskrit University, Ramteke and to Dr. T.G. Meshram, Head, Post Graduate Department of Sociology, Nagpur University, Nagpur. Dr. M.R. Somkuwar, Shri Marotrao Kamble, Shri S.K. Kamble, and Shri R.S. Ramteke have been, as usual, unfailing sources of help and encouragement. I am grateful to them.

I am thankful to the authorities of the Library of Nagpur University and also that of Dr. Babasaheb Ambedkar College, Bramhapuri, where I am teaching, for their prompt and generous service.

Grateful acknowledgements are also due to Dr. Shamim Mamdani for her assistance in checking and proof reading; to Sanghamitra, my wife, for her invaluable help in preparing the Select Bibliography. I shall be ungrateful if I forget the timely help rendered by my loving daughters Kiran and Pradnya, without which it would have been difficult to prepare the Index.

M/s Atlantic Publishers and Distributors, New Delhi, deserve special thanks for their prompt service in bringing out the book in its present form.

S.R. RAMTEKE

FOREWORD

The emergence of Mulk Raj Anand, R.K. Narayan and Raja Rao during the thirties constitutes a historic landmark in Indian English fiction. They were a product of a significant historical phase in India's struggle for independence. It would, however, be a narrow reading of history if they were sensitive witnesses to an essentially revolutionary phase of Indian society during which an ancient and spiritual India was trying to come to terms with the modern values of a scientific and industrial world. Their fiction, each in its own characteristic way, reveals the stresses and strains of this great upheaval.

R.K. Narayan's fiction attempts to comprehend, though in a low key, the clash of deep-rooted values of Indian culture with these of the modern West. His fiction reflects, again through the lives of ordinary lower middle-class people in South India, the slow erosion of Indian traditions caught up in the crucible of change. His small towns of Malgudi has today rightly acquired a classic significance.

Not surprisingly, therefore, R.K. Narayan's fiction has attracted considerable critical attention both in India and abroad. Considering, however, some of the repetitive criticism of Narayan's work, it would seem redundant to have one more similar book on his novels. But the present work by Dr. S.R. Ramteke is not a mere repetitive addition to the corpus of Narayan's criticism. For one thing, it is not merely a conventional evaluation of Narayan's literary achievements.

Dr. Ramteke's work is a bold study of Narayan's fiction that challenges the commonly held notions about his work. Perhaps it is harsh, but certainly not unsympathetic, and at no point loses its essential objectivity.

It may sound harsh primarily because excessive praise for Narayan's achievement has precluded scholars from attempting a realistic assessment of his work. To cite just one example, we find this view which asserts that "they [his characters] are in the Upanishadic tradition, moving from the unreal to the real, from darkness to light, and from death to immortality." There is no dearth of such enthusiastic effusiveness in Indian English criticism. Perhaps a secret wish to see Indian authors among the world class writers seems to be at work behind such excesses of criticism.

A favourite assessment of Narayan is that Malgudi is a microcosm of India. At best a half-truth, such a judgement ignores the fact that Narayan only depicts the Hindu society to the exclusion of large parts of the complex Indian reality. Further, even within this circumference, Narayan's fiction tends to ignore the numerous aspects of the central conflict in Hindu Society which springs from the doggedly persistent inequalities of caste, not to speak of the dire poverty and misery of its teeming millions. The inner contradictions of Hindu culture as reflected in the fabric of the Malgudi society have seldom been examined in depth, and Narayan's response to these internal conflicts has received even less attention.

Dr. Ramteke's work brings this aspect of Narayan's fiction under the microscope and analyses his attitude to these cultural contradictions and conflicts. To this end he has critically evaluated over a dozen of Narayan's novels. Perceptive readers may suspect a certain ideological orientation in his thesis, which, given his background and experience, seems inevitable. Nevertheless, he has carefully avoided being carried away by it.

Dr. Ramteke's systematic study throws up several startling revelations which, I am sure, will interest both the ordinary students of Narayan's fiction and the more serious scholars and researchers.

DR. V.R. KANADEY

CONTENTS

Preface *v*

Foreword *vii*

Introduction *xi*

1. NOVELS EVALUATED 1—95

I. Swami and Friends 1

II. The Bachelor of Arts 6

III. The Dark Room 12

IV. The English Teacher 20

V. Mr. Sampath 28

VI. The Financial Expert 39

VII. The Waiting for the Mahatma 47

VIII. The Guide 54

IX. The Man Eater of Malgudi 64

X. The Vendor of Sweets 73

XI. The Painter of Signs 80

XII. A Tiger for Malgudi 89

2. NARAYAN'S CONCEPTION OF INDIVIDUAL 96—109

3. NARAYAN'S CONCEPTION OF SOCIETY 110—150

I. Social Values 110

II. Economic Aspect 117

III. Social Vision 126

IV. Cultural Aspect 134

4. **CONCLUSION** **151—182**
(Comparison with Dr. Mulk Raj Anand and Dr. Bhabani Bhattacharya)

Select Bibliography 183

Index 190

INTRODUCTION

Rushipuram Krishnaswami Narayan is highly acclaimed as a detached observer of life. The reader is easily led to accept him to be so for his so-called objective and beguiling presentation. And doubtless he is a novelist par excellence. However, if one goes through his novels and personal life the record of which we find authentically maintained in his Memoir *My Days*, there is hardly any difficulty in ascertaining the fact that Narayan lays bare his mind in all its true spirit. In fact, this is not the case with Narayan alone to be singled out for recording his mind's view. It is as much so with novelists like Defoe, Richardson and even James Joyce who appear to keep themselves out of the action they narrate. "In fact they betray their opinion on the characters and situations and — in as much as every novel is an extended metaphor of the author's view of life — on the life itself. They do so by the very choice of the characters they write about, the thoughts and feelings they give them, and the behaviour and motives they attribute to them."[1]

Every novelist then, gives us in his novels his own personal idiosyncratic vision of the world. The mind of man is a complex phenomenon. It is always in the process of change. It acts and reacts to the events and the situation around him. It all depends how one develops his mind right from his childhood. The vision of life is certainly enlarged and broadened in case of those who came out of their surroundings and develop rapport with eminent personalities of diverse faiths rooted to different soils. Here the faith and beliefs one inherits hardly matter, for they never stick to their age-old beliefs and myths and legends of the communities they belong to. The writings of Dr. Mulk Raj Anand and Dr. Bhabani Bhattacharya will sufficiently prove this beyond doubt. On the contrary, Narayan's is a vision of a man who has never set his foot outside the province, or the intimate circle for that matter, till about forty years of his life. Narayan's vision of the society as we find in *Malgudi* is the outcome of his intimate familiarity and involvement only with the people of his community. He is brainwashed as it appears, to accept without questioning, the things he learnt from his grandmother, the commanding figure of the family, to whom no one, not even Narayan could dare ask questions. It is but natural, therefore, that Narayan remains confined to the myth and legends of the Hindu religion which he inherits, however detached he may appear to be in his writings. At certain times he appears reluctant to accept the things as it so happens when he looses his dear wife Rajam and he is suggested to go in for psychic communion with the spirit of his dead wife but then the ideas so engraved and stored in his sub-conscious level, suddenly come up to grip his mind and he falls back to his former position leaving everything to its fate. So are the characters in his novels.

Born in 1907 in an upper middle class Brahmin family of Madras, Narayan sees South Indian as a fundamentally conservative Hindu society which he realistically presents in most of his Novels and Stories with the lower middle class common man as his base. The imaginary town that he creates and calls Malgudi has all the qualities of a society Narayan dwells in, and he depicts it with a keenly observant eye. "Its members are neither too well off not to know the rub of financial worry, nor too indigent to be brutalized by want and hunger."[2]

R.K. Narayan is not a social critic as such nor is he interested in propagating any ideas. But the stories of his Malgudi novels reveal that Narayan makes his common man hero aware of his talents and potentialities which help him rise above his so-called destined role in the society. That he falls back to his former position, has roots in Hindu culture which has so great an impact that neither Narayan nor his characters have been able to shake themselves off the irrational social customs and superstitions.

It is in this light that Narayan's contribution claims serious attention which it has not so far received in the measure it deserves. Narayan's individuals moving under the prevailing social customs and traditions revolting and accepting defeat in the end with the sense of resignation is thus, the subject of the present study.

Narayan was not a brilliant student as such. He somehow managed to pass his B.A. from Maharaja College, Mysore. His further education being discontinued, Narayan had to become a newspaper reporter to support his family. His business was to gather Mysore city news and send it to a newspaper called, *The Justice* published in Madras. Its aim was to promote the cause of the non-Brahmins who suffered from the domination of the minority Brahmin class in public life, government service and education.

Narayan is now a prolific and eminent writer. He has published over a dozen novels, two-hundred short stories and four books of non-fiction. Narayan's mother tongue is Tamil, he has settled down in Mysore where the regional language is Kannad, and he writes in English. K.R. Shrinivas Iynger rightly observes :

> "Whereas Anand finished his Education in Cambridge and London, Narayan had his Education entirely in South India. He is of India, even of South India: he uses the English language much as he used to wear dhoties manufactured in Lancashire—but the thoughts and feelings, the stirrings of the soul, the wayward movements of the consciousness, are all of the soil of India, recognizably autochthonous. He is one of the few writers in India who take their craft seriously, constantly striving to improve the instrument, pursuing with a sense of dedication.[3]

With Graham Greene's recommendation Narayan's first novel "*Swami & Friends*" saw the light of the day in 1935. Then appeared in quick succession two more novels: *Bachelor of Arts* (1936), and *The Dark Room* (1938). The end of the IInd War meant the return of spring to Narayan, and we see *The English Teacher* (1945), *Mr. Sampath* (1949), *The Financial Expert* (1952), *Waiting for the Mahatma* (1955), *The Guide* (1958) and *My Dateless Diary* (1960). He has also collected two volumes of his short stories *An Astrologer's Day and Lawlay Road* and a volume of his weekly causeries, *Next Sunday* (1960). Then appeared *The Painter of Signs* (1972), and *A Tiger for Malgudi* (1982). Narayan also published shortened prose versions of the ancient epics *The Ramayan* and *The Mahabharat. Gods, Demons and Others, A Horse and Two Goats* and *My Days : A Memoir* also add to the valuable contributions by R.K. Narayan. It is quite natural, therefore, that there are a number of literary awards and distinctions to his credit : *National Prize* of Indian Literary Academy (1958), *Sahitya Academy Award* on *The Guide* (1960), *Padma Bushan* (1964), *National Association of Independent School Award* (1965), *D.Litt.*, by University of Leeds (1967), followed by Delhi University (1973).

Narayan is no original thinker; he has no independent philosophy to propagate in his novels. He largely subscribes to the Hindu ideals enshrined in the ancient Hindu scriptures. What makes him original is his down to earth interpretation of Indian ideals : 'Varnashram Dharma' or a man's role and duties according to his place in a scheme of castes and also according to his stage of life; Karma or the principle of deeds and their consequences which are worked out both in this life and in successive births until the ultimate release, moksha; a hierarchy of values generally classified as Dharma or right action, artha or worldly interest, and Karma or human love, and a cyclically ordered time and universe encompassing these values. Not all Hindus would hold these beliefs in their scriptural form to the same extent, nor would they apply them to all situations, yet they are constantly referred to and they are taken for granted in many Hindu institutions and rituals. A product of the Hindu high caste family, Narayan shares the beliefs, superstitions, traditions, customs and rituals in Indian life. He admitted to Ved Mehta "his inability to write novels without Krishna, Ganesh, Hanuman, astrologers, Pundits and devadasis or temple prostitutes, and explained his point of view by adding in his characteristic humble way that in any case that has turned out to be his India."[4]

It is, therefore, little surprising that Hindu myths and ideals have gripped Narayan's mind so much that he naturally takes them up for themes in most of his novels. Ours has been a traditional society, admitting and absorbing all change. The huge mass of myths and legends that we have accumulated through centuries has become the common repository of the people of the land. These myths and legends and our religious and culutral heritage have shaped our mind and imagination, behaviour pattern and general attitude to life. This influence is so deeply engraved that it finds unconscious expression in the very aspect of his novels. William Walsh is worth quoting when he says : "The religious sense of Indian myth is part of Narayan's grip of reality, of his particular view of human life and his individual way of placing and ordering human feeling and experience."[5]

Malgudi is deeply traditional and caste ridden. Here arranged marriage is a common phenomenon and horoscopes are often compared. This happened in Narayan's own life. Narayan married Rajam in spite of the fact that their horoscope did not agree. The astrologer of the girl's side had predicted that Narayan would prove a widower, but he was defeated by Narayan's own pundit who at the sight of rupees was all praise for Narayan's horoscope. Narayan lost his wife after five years, and this confirmed Narayan's belief in horoscopes all the more. Chandran in *The Bachelor of Arts* does not marry the girl he loves because the horoscopes do not tally. This problem crops up in *The Financial Expert* as well. The astrologer who thinks that the horoscopes of Balu and Brinda do not match, is dismissed with a fee of Re. one, whereas the one who testifies that the horoscopes match perfectly, is rewarded with a fee of Rs. seventyfive.

Varna Vyavastha that has come down to us from generations together has not freed Hindu mind, and that is realistically portrayed by Narayan in many of his novels. Raju's mother in *The Guide* is first sympathetic towards Rosie, but she changed her attitude completely when she learns that Rosie belongs to the dancing girl's class. Shrinivas's wife in *Mr. Sampath* does not take food cooked by a non-Brahmin. So is the case with Savitri in *The Dark Room* who refuses to eat in the house of Mary and Ponni the low caste couple. It is difficult for Jagan (*The Vendor of Sweets*) to accept a non-Hindu girl as his daughter-in-law. Raman's aunt in *The Painter of Signs* decides to go on a pilgrimage when she learns that Raman is going to marry a Christian girl. It is also equally true that Chandran (*The Bachelor of Arts*), Mali (*The Vendor of Sweets*), Raman (*The Painter of Signs*) and Raju (*The Guide*) give a jolt to the established customs of the Hindu society.

Mahatma Gandhi is brought in to address the Malgudians. The atmosphere becomes cheerful no doubt, but Shriram's Granny appears restless at the idea that Gandhi spoils the sanctity of their temples by allowing the untouchables to pray to their gods. The chairman of the Municipal Committee appears red with anger when Gandhi beckons an urchin of a sweeper to sit on his divan. A large section of the population is thus kept away from the main stream of life. They are treated by the caste Hindus far worse than animals. Their abodes are no better than pigsties. It is really horrifying that the Untouchables receive inhuman treatment and are continuously exploited at the hands of the high castes. Bhabani Bhattacharya rightly observes, "Society, rural society (and nine-tenths of India was rural) was sick with taboos and inhibitions of its own making; the iniquities of caste and untouchability; the ritualism that passed for religion; the wide-flung cobweb of superstitious faith. It was all an outgrowth of centuries of decadence."[6]

In this traditional set up are seen clerks, doctors, tutors, school and college students, housewives, shopkeepers, film actors, artists, sculptors, journalists, astrologers, archaeologists and printers. Rich persons and beggars and untouchables are no doubt present, but they are pushed to the background. Narayan's chief concern is with middle class people he is intimately familiar with. The characters are invariably common men with a marked potential for the uncommon, trying to win attention for themselves. How do such men struggle towards maturity — such maturity as they can achieve within the accepted religion and social framework — that seems to have been Narayan's pre-occupation enacted in a succession of novels with different degrees of success. The major characters that we come across in the *Malgudi Circle* belong to higher strata of society. Hence he has no difficulty in presenting them in their true spirit.

Most of his characters are innocent at large pitted against an unsympathetic environment. They are traditional and superstitious. They believe that everything on earth is preordained and that no amount of human efforts can ease the situation. The heroes of his novels do not control the events but events control them. They are helpless creatures torn by desires and tossed this way and that by the caprice of fortune. Chandran, *The Bachelor of Arts*, who is intensely in love with Malthi, cann't marry her because the horoscopes do not agree. He leaves home and becomes a sanyasi. In *Mr. Sampath* Narayan sees the world as being controlled by blind and unpredictable forces. *Mr. Sampath*, the cunning rogue who dominates the story, is also forced by the circumstances to leave Malgudi forever. *The English Teacher*, after the death of his wife, finds solace in the world of spirits, and Raju, the Guide, dies a ruined man not because he wanted to die, but circumstances so conspire that the only alternative before him is to become an unwilling martyr. Briefly, the heroes of Narayan depend upon chance or luck for their happiness or unhappiness; if things go contrary, they run away and sometimes even become sanyasi. Largely, they accept defeat and find happiness in submission to traditional force of the society. Rajiv Taranth rightly observes: "From average to the extraordinary and back again to a more poignant state of average — seems to be the recurrent movement in terms of interacting characters in the majority of Narayan's novels."[7]

Sampath starts as a printer, becomes producer-actor, finds disaster overtaking his film-company and ends as a forlorn person whose real job is to be a printer. Chandran in *Bachelor of Arts* moves from a busy normalcy through infatuation to dejection, tries sanyas for a short time and settles down into sober state of regained ordinariness, happily looking forward to his marriage with Susila as per the wishes of his parents. In *The Dark Room* the movement from the normal to the abnormal and back to normal is seen both in Ramani and his wife Savitri.

In Narayan's novels there is generally a flight, an uprooting, a disturbance of order — followed by a return, a renewal, a restoration of normalcy. Swami, Chandran, Savitri, Margayya's son Balu all run away but later come (or are brought) back. Shrinivas returns to his paper, Margayya to his knobby trunk, Natraj to restored quiet of his office. Shriram and Bharathi are back in Malgudi, and Susila herself, defying death (if at all one believes) is with Krishna again.

The characters are dissatisfied either with their own self or with the world around them. Whether it is Raju of *The Guide*, Sampath of *Mr.*

Sampath, Swami of *Swami and Friends*. Natraj of *Man Eater of Malgudi* or Ramani of *The Dark Room*, all of them share the same qualities, have the same approach towards life and the world and at the end fall short of nothing but reality. As Dr. Badal observes: "Narayan's characters are typically Malgudians rooted in the age-old local traditions. His characters belong to Malgudi. His Sampaths and Chandrans do not play their part, but live, move in and out, talk and laugh, and then disappear only to appear again and again in the familiar sights."[8]

Growing frustration sometimes makes his characters rebel against the social customs and traditions. The traditional religious values and the modern approach cannot go hand in hand. Hindus are deeply traditional, and the onslaught of science and scientific advancement have confused them considerably. They are reluctant to forgo their age-old beliefs and established social values however harmful they are for the proper growth of their individuality. It so happens because their minds are trained to accept puranic stories right from childhood. In such a social set up with new values and new approaches clapping all around, many of them find themselves in a dilemma. Unable to get along with the old values, they develop rebellious attitudes and try to assert their individuality. For example, Chandran (*The Bachelor of Arts*) renounces the earthly world out of sheer reluctance to its irrational and ridiculous nature of social customs, but finally returns to his family, marries in the same old traditional way and settles down in life. Savitri's high caste (*The Dark Room*) creates a deeply psychological barrier between herself and Mari and Ponni of the lower caste, who rescue her from drowning. She too in her attempt to assert her individuality leaves her husband, though in the end she has no other alternative left but to accept defeat in life. She returns home to her unrepentant husband.

Though the characters make certain attempts to go against the prevailing social customs and traditions, they simply cannot shake them off. They cannot stand the collective force of the society as a whole. The result is, they accept defeat, remorse comes, and they find happiness in submission. Narayan does not seem to approve of their attitude or any kind of rebellion on their part. There is a marked attack on sentimentality in almost all his novels. Chandran is able to lead his life properly and seriously when he overcomes sentimentality that causes frustration in his life. Savitri returns to her husband and children when she comprehends the actual situation and realises the futility after her escape from home. Ravi and Raju are not able to cope with and rise above cheap sentimentalism and hence one of them goes mad and the other is led to end his life abruptly. Margayya survives the shocks of life possibly because he has sufficient fund of common sense and practical wisdom in him.

R.K. Narayan is not a didactic novelist. However, he has an extra-ordinary power of evoking a sense of propriety in life. Though not a critic of society, he is certainly a critic of conduct. There emerges a definite view or vision of life from each of his works. To Narayan life is not normally either an elysium or a vale of tears. Toeing the same line of approach Shrinivas in *Mr. Sampath,* "perceived a balance of power in human relationships. He marvelled at the invisible forces of the universe which maintained this subtle balance in all matters; it was so perfect that it seemed to be unnecessary for anybody to do anything."[9]

There is nothing wrong with this type of vision so for as Narayan's middle class people are concerned; rather it seems advantageous to the members of the class and the caste to which Narayan belongs. But the view is totally irrelevant and meaningless when one comes to take up the life of the underdogs. In Malgudi we rarely come across a labourer or a coolie. No doubt there are poor men like the cart-boy in *Swami and Friends,* and the taxi driver in *The Guide,* but they are all good innocent people trying to earn an honest livelihood. And Narayan wisely leaves them alone showing no sympathy at all for the miserable lot of the have-nots. His main concern is with the middle class people he is intimately familiar with. Poverty and privation never touch them. His is a world of sunshine and laughter, a happy warm and compassionate humanity under whose shade eccentric individual polish their absurdities. Narayan's is the art of resolved limitation. He is content like Jane Austin with his 'little bit of ivory just so many inches wide'; he would like to be a detached observer to concentrate on a narrow scene to sense the atmosphere of the place to show a small group of characters in their oddities and angularities :

> "His province was the South Indian middle class which he knew how to handle in fiction. He was a product of the Hindu middle class, sharing the beliefs, superstitions and the prejudices of his class, in a small town and viewing its goings on with sympathy but also with a keen eye for the comic in life around him, and so he had qualified himself to be a writer of his own class and the provincial town."[10]

There is nothing in his work of the angry reformist feeling which informs the fiction of Mulk Raj Anand, with his passionate concern for the villagers, with the ferocious poverty and the cruelties of caste, with orphans, untouchables, urban labourers. Narayan's work contains no scalded sense of social injustice, no anguish, no colonial indignation and yet Narayan is clearly an Indian as any other writer. His is a realistic portrayal of Hindu ethos.

No doubt in *Waiting for the Mahatma* Narayan touches the problem of untouchability the Mahatma has taken up for social amelioration in the country. Gandhi's stay at a small hut in the sweeper's colony situated for away from the mainstream of life, points to the fact. But it is a pity that the same Mahatma has nothing concrete to offer to uplift them in the society and bring them at par with the high caste. His only advice to the untouchables and also to the million others of the miserable lot, is to have an implicit faith in God and everything will be alright. His leaving them to their fate, and himself enjoying the privileges and liberties of the high caste, does not appeal to a fair and just mind.

Woman's secondary position in the society has unnerved Narayan as well, and he depicts it realistically in many of his novels. In his autobiographical book *My Days* Narayan writes : "Man assigned her a secondary place and kept her there with such subtlety and cunning that she herself began to lose all notion of her independence, her individuality, stature and strength."[11] Bullying husbands like Ramani and meek wives like Savitri (*The Dark Room*) are a common feature of our traditional society. Woman is a helpless creature to be guarded by her father as a child, by her husband in her youth, and by her son when she is old and a widow.

Narayan moves with the passage of time. He candidly confesses: "I suppose, I have moved along with the times. This girl in my new novel, Daisy in *The Painter of Signs* is quite different; not only is she not dependent on man, she actually has no use for them as an integral part of her life."[12]

From the suffering helpless Savitri (*The Dark Room)* to Bharati (*Waiting for the Mahatma*) and then to Daisy in *The Painter of Signs*, Narayan has shown the rise of individuality in woman. Rosie in *The Guide* obviously belongs to a new class of women who have an opportunity to be released from the conventional confinement to join colleges and universities in order to acquire a formal education, a right so far denied to women in general. Rosie is a master's degree holder despite the fact that she belongs to the lower stratum of society. She marries Marco, a research scholar who is no match to her. However, it is her art that she is dedicated to, and throughout the novel she makes everything subservient to that. Neither marriage nor love counts, not even money nor fame. She likes to be with artists and tries to go after perfection. In her dedication to art there is an undercurrent of sincerity, for she does not allow herself to be sold to the highest bidder nor does she like to remain within the four walls of the house. She leaves her husband and comes to Raju because she thinks he will guide her to be a dancer. When she finds he is making use of her only to make money, she feels choked up, thinks of her husband, and finally leaves everything behind to follow her art as a dancer.

Likewise Daisy in *The Painter of Signs* attaches no sentiments to married life. A girl's running away from the family, her education at a missionary organization, her acceptance of a social work, and her living all by herself are some of those phenomena which would not be tolerated in an orthodox Hindu family. She carves out her separate identity, devotes herself whole-heartedly to the cause of family planning. In Daisy, Narayan has viewed perhaps the model of women who would be prospering after the women's lib-movement.

The conflict between the old and the new generation crops up in many of his novels. It starts right from his childhood days when Swami (*Swami and Friends*) unable to face his father, runs away from his home. There is a difference of opinion between Chandran (*The Bachelor of Arts)* and his parents. He too runs away when he finds that he can't marry the girl he loves owing to the impediment of the horoscopes. Contrary to the wishes of his mother, Raju (*The Guide*) accepts Rosie in his house. Jagan (*The Vendor of Sweets*) has to go out in to wilderness owing to the differences with his son Mali who has brought in Grace from America. Margayya and his son, Balu (*The Financial Expert*) have also contempt for each other. Ironically, it is Balu who becomes an instrument for the ruin of Margayya's financial edifice in the end. Raman's aunt (*The Painter of Signs*) goes on pilgrimage when she learns that Raman proposes to marry Daisy, a Christian girl. One thing that appears common in each case is that the people of old generation have stuck to the old social values which, the younger ones feel, have choked them resulting in frustration in life. Sometimes it is the old ones who go out in wilderness, unable to bear the pangs in their heart. On some other occasions we find the younger ones, leaving their homes in protest against the traditional values their forefathers have held so dear in their lives.

The spiritual aspect that has troubled Narayan after the death of his dear wife, has found full expression in *The English Teacher*. The death filled Narayan with profound sorrow. What a horrible shock to a person, planning to settle his married life so blissfully, should be separated from his beloved wife in such a cruel way! He comes to believe that death is not the end of everything because the human personality has several other planes of existence. What follows such a critical event is the ordeal of consciousnss or a gradual awakening on the part of the protagonist to the need for acceptance of life in spite of all its trials and tribulations. Like Narayan, Krishna follows a temporary psychic communion with the spirit of his dead wife.

That an intelligent, sensitive and sceptical man like Krishna in *The English Teacher*, should have recourse to spiritualism testifies to the general attitude of the people. Of course, the ultimate truth, what we come to recognise as one of the profound constituative insights, has dawned upon Krishna in the end. "There is no escape from loneliness and separation"....I told myself often, "wife, child, brothers, parents, friends.... We come together only to go apart again. It is one continuous movement."[13]

Narayan is opposed to the present system of education. He appears to be in favour of 'Leave alone system' of the ancient time, which we find, expressed in *The English Teacher.* Narayan writes : "My outlook on education never fitted in with the accepted code at home. Since revolt was unpractical, I went through it all without conviction, enthusiasm, or any sort of distinction."[14] Narayan wanted to be free and read what he pleased and not be examined at all. As a result, he had to make several unsuccessful attempts to cross his intermediate and B.A. Exam. before he graduated himself in 1930 from Maharaja's College, Mysore.

Narayan is essentially ironic in his treatment of the characters in his novels. He is keenly aware of the fundamental, irremedial incongruities which life and world are constantly confronting us with. He is also active to the facts that there is no possibility at all of reconciling the opposites which every facet of his experience brings to his knoweldge. He, therefore, accepts the reality as it presents before him.

Narayan's genius, essentially comic, proves itself inadequate to the task of handling tragic characters and their conflicts and dilemmas. His strength lies in quick observation and ironic recording of human oddities and eccentricities rather than in sustained exploration and searching examination of tragic conflicts. He fails to give an adequate picture of the agonised feelings of either Rosie or Marco after they part their ways. The point has been well made by Dr. Gutpa when he observes : "It is my strong suspicion that Narayan, who is so eminently capable of skimming the surface of life and capturing the idiocies and idiosyncracies of the men and women of his fictional world, just seems to shrink from the responsibility of delving deep into their hearts and souls when they are caught in the grip of tragic emotions."[15]

Narayan also lacks the flair for imagination and passion for the profundities which Raja Rao offers or the kind of verbal exuberance and hearty gusto characteristic of Mulk Raj Anand. It is also true that his works lack the emotional and humanitarian appeal as we find in the novels of Dr. Mulk Raj Anand and Bhabani Bhattacharya. What is really worthwhile to note in Narayan is that he obeys what has been described as the first rule of all imaginative composition, that he stays within the range of his imaginative inspiration.

Narayan is highly spoken of as a detached observer of the frailties and follies of human nature and action. However, literature cannot be said to be detached and objective like the physical sciences. "It shows a concern", as Northrop Frye has remarked, "over the situation of man in society, his place in the universe and his ultimate destiny. The humanities and social sciences show a similar concern, but literature does this through an intense vision. Literature is not detached but concerned. It deals with what is there in terms of what man wants and does not want."[16]

Narayan too admits this in an interview that the writer is a spokesman of the community in which he lives and of himself, and to him absolute freedom of spirit matters most. A well known critic V. Pandurang Rao is therefore absolutely right when he observes : "Narayan is a writer with a full commitment to certain spiritual and religious values and ideas, with which Indians are normally familiar. Narayan's vision is essentially moral, for the problems he sets himself to resolve in his novels are largely ethical."[17]

What Narayan aims at in his expression is grace and ease rather than artificial glow and picturesqueness. His style is lucid, and as is said of Thackery, words seem to flow from his pen without any effort like snow water upon the mountain sides. Narayan has the gift of healthy, refreshing invigorating humour, compassionate, sympathetic and even profound. He entertains us with the pure mirth of the lower middle class comedy in contemporary South Indian life. In opposition to Anand who is forthright and committed with a raucous unromantic voice, Narayan's easy and spontaneously comic expression hypnotizes us into an acceptance of the *status quo* in social life, thereby upholding the chief assumptions that lie at the heart of Hindu religion.

Notes and References

1. Allen Walter, *The English Novel*, Introduction (A Penguin International Edition), pp. 16-17.
2. William Walsh, *R.K. Narayan : A Critical Appreciation* (New Delhi: Allied Publishers Pvt. Ltd., 1983), p. 36.
3. K.R. Shrinivas Iynger, *Indian Writing in English* (New Delhi : Sterling Publishers Pvt. Ltd., 1983), p. 359.
4. G.B. Baghmar, *R.K. Narayan : The Novelist* (The Ph.D. Thesis submitted to Nagpur University, Nagpur, 1981), p. 359.
5. William Walsh, R.K. Narayan, *A Critical Appreciation* (New Delhi : Allied Publishers Pvt. Ltd., 1983), pp. 166-167.
6. Bhabani Bhattacharya, *Music for Mohini* (New Delhi : Orient Paperback, 1952), pp. 67-68.
7. Quotation by Dr. R.K. Badal, *R.K. Narayan : A Study* (Bareilly : Prakash Book Depot, 1976), p. 13.
8. *Ibid.*, p. 7.
9. R.K. Narayan, *Mr. Sampath* (Delhi : Hind Pocket Book, 1979), p. 76.
10. Dr. K.N. Joshi and B. Shymla Rao, *Studies in Indo-Anglian Literature* (Bareilly : Prakash Book Depot, 1979-80), p. 127.
11. R.K. Narayan, *My Days* (Mysore : Indian Thought Publication, 1979), p. 119.
12. S. Krishnan, *A Day With Narayan* : 'Span' (Vol. XVI, April, 1975), p. 127.
13. R.K. Narayan, *The English Teacher* (Mysore : Indian Thought Publication, 1981), p. 203.
14. R.K. Narayan, *My Days*, p. 53.
15. G.S. Balram Gupta, *The Journal of Indian Writing in English* (Vol. 12, Jan. 1984, No. 1), p. 19.
16. Northrop Frye, *The Critical Path* (Bloomington : Indian University Press, 1971), p. 91.
17. V. Pandurang Rao, *The Art of R.K. Narayan*, Journal of Commonwealth Literature, No. 5, July 1968, pp. 99-100.

CHAPTER 1

NOVELS EVALUATED

I. Swami and Friends

R.K. Narayan made a modest beginning of his career as a novelist with *Swami and Friends* published in 1935. It was Graham Greene without whose recommendation to Hamish Hamilton, Narayan's career as the novelist would have ended abruptly for want of the publisher, then and there, and the fame and popularity that he now enjoys as an eminent and prolific writer would have been a distant possibility. Graham Greene wrote : "It was Mr. Narayan with his *Swami and Friends,* who first brought India, in the sense of the Indian population and the Indian way of life, alive to me.... Swami is the story of a child written with complete objectivity, with a humour strange to our fiction, closer to T. Checkov than to any English writer, with the same underlying sense of beauty and sadness."[1]

Born and brought up in a conservative Hindu family Swaminathan has to move within the strict orthodox atmosphere at home, and it has a large bearing on his raw mind, which is unmistakably seen when he is alone or in the company of his friends. Swami's family, neither indigent nor too well-off, is profoundly unified in its assumptions about the ends and means of life. This naturally leaves a little scope for a boy like Swaminathan to shape his mind as he desires. His relations with his doting granny and to a lesser extent with his constantly exasperated father, Swami's friendships, his quarrels, and his dislike for homework and also the system of examinations in school, his running away into wilderness, make up what seem the fairly orthodox material of a school story. We find Naryan more or less in the same set up as Swami is, for Swami is nothing but the projection of his own self which Narayan accepts with characteristic fact, to begin, that process of communicating the life of Malgudi, which will continue with more and more complex effect throughout his oeuvre.

Swami and Friends is an interesting account of the school life of Swaminathan and his friends. The narration is autobiographical in the sense that, like Narayan, Swami the protagonist of the novel, shuddered at the very thought of school. However, he kept on going till he was dismissed first from the Albert Mission School, then from the Board High School, the atmosphere of which, together with strict home discipline under his orthodox father, forced him to leave Malgudi only to return a day or two after, with a remarkable change of heart. The mental make up that he has formed at home and the surrounding atmosphere right from his childhood, is one which has an imprint of Hindu culture, the instances of which we come across in the characterization of Swami in the novel.

While it is admitted that Mr. Ebenezar's references to Hindu gods were provocative, but one should not deny them as completely baseless in that many of the Hindus are steeped in so much superstition and make believe that they worship any rock, which to them, appears as an emblem of God's presence. And it is in the name of God and religion that the high caste hypocrites have exploited and pushed the gullible masses to their miserable plight. The references to Hindu gods by Mr. Ebenezar, the script teacher in Albert Mission School, are indeed thought provoking :

> " Can they bless you? No. Can they take you to heaven? No, why? Because they have no life. What did your gods do when Mohammed of Gazni smashed them to pieces, trod upon them, and constructed out of them steps for his lavatory."[2]

Reaction of Swami's father to the references is quite in keeping with Hindu culture of which he has been the product. In his letter to the Headmaster of Albert Mission School, Swami's father writes, "I hear that he (Ebenezar) is always most insulting and provoking in his references to the Hindu religion. It is bound to have a bad effect upon the boys."[3]

The child is imitative by nature. The power of imitation is found to be very high in him. He watches with curiosity the goings on in the house and imbibes whatever he comes across. The stories which are told to him about ghosts and demons, gods and goddesses, hell and heaven have a great bearing upon the raw mind of the child. William Walsh rightly observes: "Our minds are trained to accept without surprise characters of godly or demoniac proportion with actions and reactions set in limitless worlds progressing through an incalculable time-scale."[4]

A coachman's process of minting high currency has easily caught Swami's attention, who made all out efforts to acquire six pies demanded by him. He also remembered Ebenezar's saying in the class that God would readily help those that prayed to Him. This had a desired effect on him. Swami secured a small cardbox, placed in it a couple of pebbles and covered them with fine sand and leaves. He carried the box to the pooja room in which a few framed pictures of gods hung on the wall. Swami stood before the gods and with great piety, prayed to them to convert the pebbles into two three pie coins. With closed eyes he muttered : "Oh, Shri Rama! Thou hast slain Ravana though he had ten heads, can't you give me six pies?"[5]

Swaminathan was dismissed from the Board High School. Now that he had nowhere to go, he remembered his home, a place which contained his father, a stern, stubborn father, and that tyrant of a headmaster that forced him to leave Malgudi. He wandered lonely in the dead of night when his mind was gripped with fear. He heard strange voices calling him by name. He stopped and looked about. It appeared to his mind that an immense monster was crouching with its immense black legs wide apart and its shadowy arms joined over its head. It now swayed a little. He dared not take his eyes off it for fear that it might pounce upon him. A little later, when the first shudder of fear subsided, he saw a little more clearly and found that, "the monster consisted of massive tree trunks and their top branches."[6]

Swami is very much afraid of gods and he does nothing which may insult them. To his shock when Swaminathan found that the pebbles, leaves and the sand were still there without any expected change even after ten minutes, he was filled with rage. He wanted to abuse the God, but at the same time he was terribly afraid, lest he would incur God's wrath. Nonsense ideas touched his mind: "They (gods) might make him fail in his examinations, or kill father, mother, granny or the baby."[7] With a feeling of regret, Swaminathan picked up the box, the sand, the leaves and the pebbles that were crushed, crampled and kicked a minute ago in wild rage, and buried the box reverentially.

Swaminathan allowed the events to control him, and placed himself in the hands of circumstances. An ant which he placed in the boat that he made of paper and let it go along swift current of the stream, resembles the life of man in Hindu culture. It's fate is anybody's guess. When it passed under a tree, a thick dry leaf fell down and upset the boat. Swaminathan ran frantically to the spot to see if he could save at least the ant which he placed in the boat. He peered long into the water, but there was no sign of the ant. The ant, that helpless creature which was left to its fate, must have met its end.

In an hour of distress, every Indian prays to God to bring him out of difficulty. Not only that, whatever happens in his life, he attributes it to God's will. Narayan depicted this mentality in the character of Swaminathan. He left Malgudi and wandered aimlessly without any specific destination. When he was completely exhausted, he collapsed like an empty bag in wilderness. He did not know what to do. He felt completely lost with no hope to return to Malgudi, his mind turned to divine help. Swami prayed to all the gods that he knew, to take him out of that place. He promised them offerings, two coconuts every Saturday to the elephant faced Ganpati, a vow to roll barebodied in dust, beg and take the alms to the lord of Tirupati. He fell unconscious and was brought back to Malgudi with changed heart of submission and regret for what he had committed.

Both Swaminathan and his friend Rajam, chief characters in the novel, belong to the Brahmin caste. However, there is a marked change in their outlook. Swami is brought up in a Hindu orthodox family, steeped in superstitions and blind beliefs. He is set in contrast with the character of Rajam, the son of the Superintendent of Police. He rebukes Swami in no uncertain terms when the latter narrates how he is cheated by the coachman : "We Brahmins deserve that and more," said Rajam, "in our house my father does not care for New-moon days and there are no annual ceremonies for the dead."[8]

Rajam was brought up in a modern family, his father being the Superintendent of Police. However, he too could not completely free himself from the impact of Hindu culture. The stories of hell and heaven had a great bearing upon his mind. When his friends came to him, he gave a hair-raising account of hell which made them shudder. It may be that he narrated the story of hell only to impress upon his friends to leave the enmity that they fostered amongst them. Rajam continues: "it was written in the Vedas that a person who fostered enmity should be locked up in a small room after his death. He would be made to stand, stark naked, on a pedestal of red hot iron. There are behives all round with bees as big as lemons. If the sinner stepped down from the pedestal, he would have to put his foot on immense scorpions and centipedes that crawled about the room in hundred."[9] A shudder went through the company of his friends whose minds were trained that way from childhood.

Swami, the chief protagonist who is seen rushing along the trodden path within the accepted social framework finds himself frustrated at the orthodox ways at home and the social surroundings in which he lives. His running away from home, though not surprising has unnerved his parents considerably. Their efforts, later on, to patch up differences, brainwashing him to accept and maintain the religious sanctity of home, bear fruit, and the family disorder in terms of the conflict between the old and the new that has set in, has been restored. Narayan is certainly opposed to any kind of sentimentalism on the part of his protagonist, for he himself perhaps likes to be within the traditional set up the high caste people have so labouriously built up. Any kind of change therein is opposed, to maintain *status quo* in social life.

Though restricted in range and scope, *Swami and Friends* has in it two important motifs which Narayan is to deal with in his later novels. Swami is not the only protagonist to run away from home, Chandran in *The Bachelor of Arts*, Savitri in *The Dark Room*, Shriram in *Waiting for the Mahatma*, and Mali in *The Vendor of Sweets* all follow suit only to return home completely resigned to their fate. Secondly, rudimentary religious ritual designed to produce money is the first sketch of Margayya's more elaborate plans and more excruciating ordeal in *The Financial Expert*.

The world which begins to be delicately established in *Swami and Friends* is both ancient and modern. Swami is presented with all his fears of ghosts and demons, hell and heaven, gods and retribution, with Rajam showing a modern trend of outlook.

Notes and References

1. Graham Greene, Introduction to *Bachelor of Arts* (Pocket Book Edition, London, 1951), p. 7.
2. R.K. Narayan, *Swami and Friends* (Mysore : Indian Thought Publication, 1971), p. 5.
3. *Ibid.*, p. 6.
4. William Walsh, *R.K. Narayan : A Critical Appreciation* (New Delhi : Allied Publishers Pvt. Ltd., 1983), p. 16.
5. R.K. Narayan, *Swami and Friends*, p. 70.
6. *Ibid.*, p. 158.
7. *Ibid.*, p. 71.
8. *Ibid.*, p. 109.
9. *Ibid.*, p. 46.

II. The Bachelor of Arts

R.K. Narayan's *The Bachelor of Arts*, again with Graham Greene's recommendation, was published in 1937.

It is the story of a 'Bachelor' destined to lead a well settled married life after much aimless wandering as a Sanyasi. His final return to Malgudi is symbolic of the strength and sustenance of the traditional values and the age-old customs being upheld and scrupulously followed by his parents. Chandran's impulsive renunciation of the world and the veneration he receives from the villagers, betrays his imperfect personality. However, his renunciation though a temporary phase of his life, can be looked upon as a revenge on the society and the circumstances in which he is placed. In the end, Chandran's submission to his fate, is but the reality, we observe in Hindu culture which is perfectly in keeping with Narayan's comic philosophy of life.

Irrational and ridiculous nature of social customs has been realistically presented in the novel, with great precision, in a completely detached manner, for which Narayan is so highly acclaimed. The formalities like the matching of horoscopes, etc. that precedes the marriage ceremony quite upset the mind of Chandran, the chief character in the novel, who gets infatuated with Malthi. That the initiative in the matter should come only from the bride's people makes him very uneasy. To top it all, when Chandran finds that his mother is very keen in following the time-honoured customs, he reacts sharply : "To the dust pots with your silly customs."[1] The rigidity of caste system prevalent in the society troubles his mind. Chandran fears that perhaps his parents would not allow him to marry the girl he loves. He blows out the lamp and sits in his chair completely absorbed in the thoughts: "Suppose, though unmarried, she belonged to some other caste? A marriage would not be tolerated even between sub-sects of the same caste. If India was to attain salvation these watertight divisions must go — Community, Caste, Sects, Sub-sects and still further divisions."[2]

Chandran felt very indignant and he resolved to set an example himself by marrying this girl (Malthi) whatever her caste or sect might be: an appreciable stand in complete contrast with the old social values upheld by his parents.

Chandran's father did not appear to place active obstacles in Chandran's way. However, Chandran wanted to be free to arrange his life as he pleased. But when he found that his parents had upperhand in almost every matter he asked indignantly : "Why should we be cudgelled and noseled by our elders?... Why can't we be allowed to arrange our lives as we please? Why can't they leave us to rise or sink on our own ideals?"[3]

However, it was Chandran's father who took initiative in sending one Mr. Sastrigal — keeping aside the time honoured custom — to the house of the bride to bring about the settlement. Horoscopes were exchanged. But the bride's father D.W. Krishnan Iyer was so orthodox in his attitude that he rejected the marriage proposal outright, saying that Chandran's horoscope was ill-matched. "I know a little of astrology myself. I am prepared to overlook many things in a horoscope. I don't usually concern myself with the factors that indicate prosperity, wealth, progeny, and all that. I usually overlook them. But I do feel that we can't ignore the question of longevity. I know hundreds of cases where the presence of Mars in this house...I can tell you that...." He hesitated to say it. "It kills the wife soon after the marriage. He said, when pressed by Chandran's father."[4] Love marriages are a distant possibility under such circumstances. K.R. Shrinivas Iynger is right when he says : "With rigid caste prohibitions to be respected and difficult astrological hurdles to be crossed, how can there be 'love marriages' in India?"[5]

Chandran lost his temper. Choking his emotions, he wrote a letter to Malthi, which he called a simple, matter of fact piece of writing. That the letter remained undelivered was a different matter. But it shows the struggle amongst the young people of modern generation against the orthodox nature of Hindu culture.

Chandran insisted on being sent to Madras when he failed in his attempt to marry the girl he loved. He wandered aimlessly for serveral days. He soon realised the futility of his aimless wanderings. He became homesick. But the thought of Malthi and the rigid social custom made him furious. And he took to the life of a Sanyasi, the only thing possible short of committing suicide. Narayan's comments on his renunciation are thought provoking. He says: "It was an alternative to suicide. Suicide he would have committed but for its social stigma. Perhaps he lacked the barest physical courage that was necessary for it. He was a Sanyasi because it pleased him to mortify his flesh. His renunciation was a revenge on society, circumstances, and perhaps, too, on destiny."[6]

Chandran's remorse for what he has committed is best known through his own words: "Sitting in the dark, he subjected his soul to a remorseless vivisection. From the moment he had donned the ochre cloth to the present, he had been living on charity, charity given in mistake, given on the face value of a counterfeit. He had been humbugging through life. He told himself that if he were such an ascetic he ought to do without food or perish of starvation. He ought not to feed his miserable stomach with food which he had neither earned nor, by virtue of spiritual worth, deserved."[7]

In a family completely steeped in superstitions and blind beliefs Chandran was in a sense modern in his outlook. One day at day break Chandran caught a thief who was stealing Jasmine flowers from the garden. Surprisingly the thief turned out to be a middle aged man, bare-bodied with matted hair wearing only a loin cloth of ochre colour, indicating that he was a Sanyasi. See how Chandran reacts to the orthodox and superstitious nature of his mother. On seeing the thief, mother screamed, "Oh, hold him, hold him." She was shaking with excitement. "Take him away and give him to the police." Chandran said to the thief, "You wear the garb of a Sanyasi, and yet you do this sort of thing!" "Is he a sanyasi?" Mother asked, and noticed the colour of the thief's loin-cloth. "Ah, leave him alone, let him go." She was seized with fear now. The curse of a holy man might fall on the family. "You can go, Sir," she said respectfully. Chandran was cynical. "What, Mother, you are frightened of every long hair and ochres dress you see."[8]

The dialogue makes it clear that the womenfolk in a Hindu family nurse a fear in their mind that the Sanyasi is blessed with strange and unseen power which might curse their family. The moment Chandran's mother sees the thief's ochre-coloured dress, she gets frightened and pleads with Chandran to leave the holy man. Not only that, she allows the thief-turned-sanyasi to take as many flowers as he wants saying that there couldn't be a better way of worship than giving flowers to those who really worship.

The priest has been portrayed as hypocrite and greedy extracting huge amount of money from the gullible masses. In the novel *The Bachelor of Arts*, we come across one Mr. Ganpaty Sastrigal, who after retiring from government service settles down as a general adviser, officiating priest and rituals and a match-maker. It is intersting to note that he confined his activities only to a few rich families in the town. They know that they are cheating the masses, and yet they do it in the name of religion and God, one of the safest way to convince the gullible folk.

Dowry is another social evil Naraya touches upon in the novel. It is the elders who are bent upon perpetuating this evil despite the hue and cry being made from time to time by rationalists. Chandran's parents are apparently seen to have been least interested in dowry but they have been inwordly craving for that. Their greed is exposed through the character of Chandran's mother who says: "My father gave seven thousand in cash to your father, and over two thousand in silver vessels, and spent nearly five thousand on wedding celebrations. What was wrong in it? How are we any the worse for it? It is the duty of every father to set some money apart for securing a son-in-law. We can't disregard custom".[9]

Chandran did not like his mother's attitude. He became uneasy and sharply reacted: "Don't talk like that, Mother. I shall never forgive you if this marriage does not take place through your bickerings over the dowry and the presents."[10]

Chandran wanted that there should not be unnecessary expenditure in the form of dowry and presents at the wedding ceremonies. He made it clear that "it was all irrational extravagance and that the total expenses for a marriage ought not to exceed a hundred rupees."[11]

In the caste-ridden Hindu society, arranged marriages are the only possibility. They hold a belief that the marriages are made in heaven, and that it is all settled already, the husband of every girl and the wife of every man. It is in nobody's choice. However irrational it may appear, but the belief still holds the water and the practice is continued even today. For one reseason or another, obstacles are often put in the way, and the love marriages get broken. Narayan reveals the irrational attitude through Chandran's mother : "It is all a matter of fate.... You can marry only the person whom you are destined to marry and at the appointed time. When the time comes, let her be the ugliest girl, she will look all right to the destined eye."[12]

Even D.W. Krishnan, the bride's father holds the same belief when he says in his letter to Chandran's father: "However, we can only propose. He on the Trupati Hills alone knows what is best for us."[13]

One of the themes deftly and thoroughly worked in the novel is the domestic one. Family is supposed to be the sacred institution of the Hindus which enfolds both the ultimate and immediate texture of experience. It is, as Narayan says, the duty of the women to translate and refine the principles of orthodoxy and correctness into codes and etiquettes covering the basic drives for food, shelter, sex, and company, and Chandran's mother is shown to be doing exactly the same thing for her family. Under such circumstances one can understand the position of Chandran and his younger brother too, when the question of his marriage is brought up. Chandran's younger brother Seenu cannot even bring himself to voice the matter to his brother. As for Chandran, it is impossible for him to address the girl he has fallen in love with, directly.

Chandran, the chief character in *The Bachelor of Arts*, though comparatively modern in his outlook, could not completely shake himself off the time-honoured customs and traditions. At times he felt indignant at the irrational ways of his parents. The circumstances forced him even to leave home and try sanyas for a time being perhaps as a revenge on the social values prevalent in the society. But the tremendous impact of the Hindu ethos that he swallowed during his childhood surfaced again and he realised the futility of his action to fight against the traditional force. The novel depicts individual freedom simmering into revolt but voluntarily coming to terms with the traditional norms.

Chandran's father appears helpless before the accepted norms. He lacks courage to stand by his son. It is but natural for a person steeped in tradition to follow the accepted social values. He remains a passive onlooker when Chandran's mother allows the thief to go away seeing him in the ochre-coloured dress for fear that he may curse her family. Well, Chandran's father shows a considerable sympathy when he sees the miserable, lovelorn face of his son. He sets aside the established social custom and sends one Ganpaty Sastrigal to bride's parents initiating the marriage proposal for Chandran's sake.

Chandran is essentially a free spirit hedged round by rules and restrictions both in the college and at home, while Veerswami and Mohan on the one hand, Malthi, and later Susila on the other, help him in realising his aspirations and their limitation. Realising the futility of his aimless wandering, he accepts the wishes of his parents to marry Susila, a girl selected by them. After graduation we find Chandran searching for a job which he fails to get. On the advice of his friend, Mohan, he acts and makes up his mind to accept the job of a reporter of *The Daily Messenger*. Then, with the help of his uncle at Madras, he gets the agency of the paper to support his family. One may recall here Narayan's own experience as a news reporter for a paper called *The Justice*. Chandran plungs himself whole-heartedly in building up and raising the circulation of *The Daily Messenger*, and settles in life comfortably with his family and friends.

The Bachelor of Arts depicts the old social values questioned every now and then by people with modern and rational approach towards life. Persons like Chandran, have failed to achieve the desired goal. They have to accept defeat in life, firstly because their minds have been trained to accept and obey the elders in the family and the society in which they live, secondly, if at all they like to bring about some changes in the accepted social norms, their half-hearted efforts fall miserably short; and they simply could not withstand the collective force of the traditional society. Except a few like Chandran, all others see to it that the accepted social norms are kept intact, for the *status quo* is always advantageous to the religious old folk and they try their utmost to maintain it at all costs. What Narayan's protagonists want to achieve, in the words of Chandran, is a life free from distracting illusions in the Indian tradition; the freedom from hysterics is the cool qualification introduced by Narayan. At first the intention is obscure, buried under the habits of ordinary life, personal responsibilities and since this is India a heavy inherited burden. The novel plots the rise of this intention into awareness, its recognition in a crisis of consciousness and then its restoration as it happens in the case of Chandran, the protagonist of the novel.

Notes and References

1. R.K. Narayan, *The Bachelor of Arts* (Mysore: Indian Thought Publication, 1979), p. 70.
2. *Ibid.*, p. 56.
3. *Ibid.*, p. 71.
4. *Ibid.*, pp. 87-88.
5. K.R. Shrinivas Iynger, *Indian Writing in English* (New Delhi : Sterling Publishers Pvt. Ltd., 1983), p. 366.
6. R.K Narayan, *The Bachelor of Arts*, p. 108.
7. *Ibid.*, p. 111.
8. *Ibid.*, p. 43.
9. *Ibid.*, pp. 84-85.
10. *Ibid.*, p. 84.
11. *Ibid.*, p. 85.
12. *Ibid.*, p. 158.
13. *Ibid.*, p. 86.

III. The Dark Room

The Dark Room, first published by Macmillan in 1938, is thematically more sombre with a marked leaning towards symbolism, satire and melancholy. It is the story of conjugal conflict, with three principal characters — Savitri, the traditional wife silently sobbing and suffering, Ramani, the callous and philandering husband, and Shantabai the coquettish woman — taken together, represent a situation which is not uncommon in the domestic life in Indian society.

The Dark Room is an authentic picture of a traditional Hindu housewife. Her silent suffering and temporary rebellion ending in abject surrender is in keeping with the Hindu culture dominating the Indian society. Savitri, a middle class housewife finds her husband Ramani infatuated with Shantabai, his new office assistant, and leaves him in a fit of desperation only to realise the bitter truth that a traditional Hindu wife of her class is totally helpless, cut off from home and children. Savitri ultimately pockets her pride and returns home broken, defeated and sullenly acquiescent to her still unrepentant husband. Narayan's observations in this context are worth quoting. He says: "I was somehow obsessed with a philosophy of Woman as opposed to Man, her constant oppressor. Man assigned her a secondary place and kept her there with such subtlety and cunning that she herself began to lose all notion of her independence, individuality, stature, and strength. A wife in an orthodox, milieu of Indian society was an ideal victim of such circumstances. My novel dealt with her, with this philosophy broadly in the backgrounds."[1] True to his observations, Narayan's Savitri of *The Dark Room* appears to be a truthful portrayal which by and large, reveals the condition of the wife in the Hindu family.

Savitri's predicament is primarily because of the fact that she lacks the moral courage to assert herself owing to the religious taboos which have a far-reaching effect on the women-folk of the Hindu society. When Savitri tried in vain to fuss over Babu who suddenly fell ill, and put him to bed, Ramani sternly asked her to mind her own business and leave the training of a grown-up boy to him. Savitri realised how impotent she was. She thought, "She had not the slightest power to do anything at home, and that after fifteen years of married life. Babu did look very ill and she was powerless to keep him in bed."[2]

Janamma, another woman character in the novel is also the victim of the religious toboos, who advised Savitri to know beforehand the man's impetuous character and behave accordingly. She says: "Men are impetuous. One moment they will be all temper and the next all kindness. Men have to bear many worries and burdens, and you must overlook it if they are sometimes unreasonable.... After all they are better trainers of children than we can be".[3]

Janamma went on in this strain for an hour more recounting instances of the patience of wives with a view to make Savitri come out of the 'dark room' where she was sulking after her showdown with Ramani over the beating he gave to Babu. She quoted her own grandmother who slaved cheerfully for her husband who had concubines at home, her aunt who was beaten everyday by her husband and had never uttered a word of protest for fifty years; another friend of her mother's who was prepared to jump into a well if her husband so directed and so on, till Savitri gradually began to feel very foolish at the thought of her own resentment. The instances are enough to sum up the picture of a Hindu housewife and her secondary role in the society realistically presented in the novel.

Total submission, even when the husband neglects his wife is an idea ingrained in the women themselves. It is through the characterization of Janamma, we come to know how women submitted themselves to men in the Hindu culture. "As for me", Janamma says: "I have never opposed my husband or argued with him at any time in my life. I might have occasionally suggested an alternative, but nothing more. What he does is right. It is a wife's duty to feel so".[4]

It is Manu and the later moralists who have made the woman what she is today, weak and utterly helpless. That a woman should have no freedom, is so deeply embedded in the minds of both Ramani and Savitri, that Ramani could bluntly tell her that she has no right whatsoever over the children. Savitri could not question him. The Savitri of ancient legend is a paragon of virtues and courage who confronts even Death to save her husband Satyavan and is finally victorious in the encounter. But Narayan's Savitri is certainly no tragic figure; she appears to be only a weak whimpering, timid, spineless and vacillating character. Her plight fails to evoke even pathos, for she is shown to be a bundle of changing moods and conflicting responses. Savitri's pathetic utterances showed how miserable she was in her married life. "I don't possess anything in this world. What possession can a woman call her own except her body? Everything else that she has is her father's, her husband's, or her son's".[5]

For all her weakness and helplessness Savitri's half-hearted attempt to assert herself as a human being is much appreciating. She is at last stirred to revolt at her husband's infidelity and passionate attachment with one Shantabai, his office assistant. At first she tries to persuade him to leave the woman and she would forgive and forget. But when she finds, nothing is of any use, she musters enough courage to warn her husband. "I'm a human being," she said, through her heavy breathing, "You men will never grant that. For you we are playthings when you feel like hugging, and slaves at other times. Don't think that you can fondle us when you like and kick us when you choose."[6]

Though the spark of revolt does not last for a long time, the awakening in her mind is a clear indication of the individuality and the rights and liberties, women of the Hindu society have been relentlessly struggling for. It is anybody's guess that the bang of her brave speeches would end in pitiful whimper when Savitri finds herself alone in the ill-lit secluded temple. She grew homesick. A nostalgia for children, house and accustomed comforts seized her. Lying here on the rough floor beside the hot flickering lamp, her mind racked with fears. She could not help contrasting the comforts, security and unloneliness of her home. And she returns in the end as a spiritual cripple. She has to face the shame and suffering mutely as a price for the emotional need of a home and children. This has roots in native realities.

Savitri's self-evaluation towards the end of the novel speaks volumes about the survile role the woman is condemned to play in the house. "What despicable creations of God are we that we can't exist without a support. I am like a bamboo pole which can not stand without a wall to support... This is defeat. I accept it. I am no good for this fight I am a bamboo pole".[7]

It requires an intellectually strong mind to put aside all these emotional factors and to come out of the Sita-Sati-Savitri image and the tradition of submission. Shantabai is one such woman character Narayan portrayed in *The Dark Room.* She is a bold, self-possessed and educated woman who has left her husband because he ill-treated her. But Narayan appears to be in no mood to project a serious contrast between the traditional and suffering Saviti and the new woman Shantabai. There seems to be a half-hearted attempt to present Shantabai as a romantic figure. "In this world Khayyam is the only person who would have understood the secret of my soul," says Shantabai, "No one tries to understand me, this is the tragedy of my life."[8] On the whole, Shantabai is shown to be a pathetic figure despite her education. While narrating her autobiography she remarks: "It is all non-sense to say that women's salvation lies in education. It doesn't improve their lot a bit."[9]

Shantabai of *The Dark Room,* is an early incarnation of Shanti of *Mr. Sampath* and Rosie of *The Guide.* The majority of women are like Savitri in *The Dark Room,* suffering, tolerating injustice helplessly, with their brains washed by traditional taboos or unable economically and still more emotionally to lead an independent life.

It is through the character of Ramani, Narayan reveals the established views of the society towards women:

> Of course, he granted, there was some sense in the women's movements : Let them by all means read English novels, play tennis, have their All India conference and go to the pictures occasionally; but that should not blind them to their primary duties of being wives and mothers! They mustn't attempt to ape the Western women, all of whom, according to Ramani's belief, lived in a chaos and promiscuity and divorce. He held that India owed its spiritual eminence to the fact that the people here realised that a woman's primary duty (also a divine privilege) was being a wife and a mother. And what woman retained the right of being called a wife who disobeyed her husband? Didn't all the ancient epics and scriptures enjoin upon woman the strictest identification with her husband? He remembered all the heroines of the epics whose one dominant quality was a blind, stubborn following of their husbands, like the shadow following the substance.[10]

It is for the far-reaching effect of the ancient Hindu epics and the scriptures that the men-folk are very unlikely to change their outlook, and the women-folk will continue to suffer. However in the present-day society, the plight of women has considerably changed possibly because of the western influence and rapid industrialisation of the country. Several organisations have been coming forward to take up their cause and are fighting against the atrocities and humiliating treatment being given to them.

In keeping with the changing times Ramani has taken Shantabai on the staff of the Engladia Insurance Company as the chief woman agent. The sole purpose of taking Shantabai on the staff was to spread the business of the company. There was whispering among the staff working under him to accommodate her in the office. However, they got used to her presence. "It was all nonsense to keep men and women separate in water-tight compartments; women were as good as men and must be treated accordingly."[11]

However, Ramani seems to be a bundle of contradictions, a mean, hypocrite and callous by nature. He is utterly self-centred and self-indulgent who makes his whole family dance to his tune. On one hand Ramani flirts with a woman probationer, Shantabai, giving an air that women have every right to be treated at par with man. On the other hand, his dictatorial face at home is more than enough to sum up that he is an upholder of the ancient Manu-Smriti to keep the women-folk under strict surveillance. Savitri, the traditional orthodox Hindu woman as she is, bears it all out of fear that in Yama's world the cauldron must be ready for her sin of talking back to a husband and disobeying him.

One part, Savitri feels, is dead, then in another part a faint stirring of personal life begins, and in yet another part, the Indian habits or gifts for acceptance as strong in the middle class as in the peasants, still prevails. When one afternoon she is lying on the carpet in her hall half asleep, she hears a voice crying in the street. Mari who saves her from drowning is passing up the dusty street with his tool-bag slung over his shoulder, a couple of dilapidated umbrellas under his arm and his dark face shining with sweat.

> "Locks repaired, sirs..." came from the next street. The poor fellow's face shone with sweat; perhaps he had been tramping the streets in the hot sun, foodless; perhaps he had not earned a pie yet in the town. How this man and Ponni had begged her to take the coconut and plantain.... "Very unjust to let him go, but what can I do?", she reflected. She called Ranga and told him, "Call that lock repairer who was crying in the street just now. He must be in the next street."
>
> "Yes, Madam."
>
> As Ranga was about to step out she changed her mind: "Let him go, don't call him." She thought: "Why should I call him here? What have I ?"
>
> "Locks repaired, sirs; umbrellas repaired!" came from four or five streets off.
>
> She sat by the window, haunted by his shining, hungry face long after he was gone, and by his "Locks repaired...long after his cry had faded out in the distance."[12]

One agrees with Meena Shirwadkar when she observes: "The Savitri who returns is a spiritual cripple. She has not even the courage or confidence to call Mari, the burglar who had saved her, and repay him, for now she thinks she is a non-entity."[13]

In fact, it is the women who have comparatively more faith in fate and destiny rather than their male counterparts. Besides, they are steeped in superstition and blind belief. In a fit of desperation Savitri left her home and children in the dead of night and stood in the waters to commit suicide. She prayed to her gods on the hill to protect the children. But the meek and traditional wife in her did not allow her to take the drastic step. She was also reminded of the sin of disobeying her husband. Savitri was seized with fear, and she at once changed her decision, she said, "...no, no, I can't die. I must go back home. I won't, I won't."[14]

Like Swami in *Swami and Friends,* Chandran in *The Bachelor of Arts,* Balu in *The Vendor of Sweets,* Savitri in *The Dark Room* is also constrained to return home, to her children, to a life of routine. M.C. Bhatnagar is right when he says: "Narayan's characters...remain captive of their circumstances even though they make a faint and feeble attempt at self-determination."[15]

Ramani's callous behaviour strikes some fire in Savitri and she is transformed into Ibsen's Nora, asserting elementary rights as a woman. But she lacks even the moral courage of Gouri (Mulk Raj Anand's *The Old Woman and the Cow*) who deserts her husband and joins the nursing profession under the inspiration of Dr. Mahindra. Narayan's Savitri could not shake off her traditional role of a Hindu housewife. Virtue for them lies in the perfection with which they acquaint themselves in the role allotted to them in life. To quote K.C. Bhatnagar again, "There may or may not be Karma, the idea of deserving a higher birth, as a reward for good or bad deeds is to my thinking, a myth promoted to keep men and women work for the slave drivers.... They will not easily give up their servility."[16]

Narayan is superbly successful in presenting Savitri as to his ideas. He says in his interview with S. Krishnan : "In *The Dark Room* I was concerned with showing the utter dependence of woman on man in our society. I supposed I have moved along with the lines."[17]

Ponni, a low caste woman is the only woman character who stands out prominently with the status and individuality of her own. Ponni who is both contrasted and linked with Savitri, stands upto her husband, who cannot be intimidated, leave alone oppressed by the male world. Ponni, in fact, is the only one in this novel who genuinely attempts to help Savitri to find the life of independence she wants, at the same time respecting and guarding the privacy she needs. She is outspoken and straightforward when she tells the priest : "You can see her, and take her in good faith and on our word, and if you find anything wrong with her later, you can dismiss her. There are some questions which hurt one; you mustn't ask them."[18] Narayan gives Ponni extra dimension of sympathy and this sharpens and throws into relief the inevitable loneliness to which Savitri returns when she goes home to Malgudi.

The priest depicted in the novel is always seen grumbling and scolding the village folk saying, 'you fellows now-a-days don't bring offerings to the God'. However the priest has a good time when Savitri enters the service of the temple god. Strange are the ways of the religious folk who flock the temple the moment they see Savitri working there to earn her living. Rumour had gone abroad that a mysterious woman was engaged in the temple, and this brought in more visitors than usual. "Everybody looked about, stared at Savitri, nudged at each other, went round the corridor, prostrated before the image and gave the old man the offerings. So many people kept staring at her that Savitri slipped out and shut herself in the shanty."[19]

The priest was very pleased, "People are once again becoming godly."[20] The story of *The Dark Room* is suggestive of natural sorrows and pains suffered by a tongueless creature who can only dream of freedom and die heart-stiffled in her den. Savitri's is a split personality:

> This cleft in Savitri's personality is at the root of the novel the spirit of which is expressed through the image of *The Dark Room* which follows her whenever she goes. This darkness is an externalisation of her mental condition created by the stuffy oppressiveness which women of the orthodox middle class are destined to endure. Her rebellion, though naturally arising from her own soul, exemplifies the modern awakening as also the return to the freedom of the natural, if not primitive, life led by Mari and Ponni. Her rebellion is complex, a product of both of the East and the West having its roots in both primitivism and modernity.[21]

Narayan depicted the breakdown of feudal society and expressed the changed ideas concerning the family as a unit and the conflict between the old and the new. S.C. Sanyal is right when he says: "In *The Dark Room* the conflict between Ramani and Savitri...is a clash of principle and ideology."[22]

The entrance of modern evil in the guise of glamorous Shantabai in the domestic world of Ramani and Savitri causes storms. He is slipped away into the arms of Shantabai. His callous behaviour is made the cause of a major quarrel and the reconciliation that foreshadows the defeat of Savitri in the end. And Savitri accepts the defeat because our society has not yet been ready to recognise the elementary rights of womanhood. However, Savitri's utterances echo the revolutionary voice of the rising womankind.

Notes and References

1. Quoted by William Walsh, *R.K. Narayan : A Critical Appreciation* (New Delhi : Allied Publishers Pvt. Ltd., 1983), p. 22.
2. R.K. Narayan, *The Dark Room* (Delhi : Orient Paperbacks, 1978), p. 8.
3. *Ibid.*, p. 42.
4. *Ibid.*
5. *Ibid.*, p. 75
6. *Ibid.*, p. 73
7. *Ibid.*, pp. 123-124
8. *Ibid.*, p. 99
9. *Ibid.*, p. 46
10. *Ibid.*, pp. 92-93
11. *Ibid.*, p. 136
12. *Ibid.*
13. Meena Shirwadkar : *Image of Women in the Indo-Anglian Novel* (New Delhi : Sterling Publishers Pvt. Ltd., 1979), p. 54.
14. R.K. Narayan, *The Dark Room*, p. 80.
15. *Ibid.*, p. 93.
16. Dr. K.C. Bhatnagar, *Realism in Major Indo-English Fiction* (Bareilly : Prakash Book Depot, 1980), p. 80.
17. *A Day with R.K. Narayan* : 'Span' (Vol. XVI, No. 4th April, 1975), p. 40.
18. R.K. Narayan, *The dark Room*, pp. 114-115.
19. *Ibid.*, p. 122.
20. *Ibid.*
21. O.P. Mathur : *West Wind Blows Through Malgudi* : Dr. Atma Ram's *Perspectives on R.K. Narayan* (Ghaziabad : Vimal Prakashan, 1931), p. 29.
22. S.C. Sanyal, *Indianness in major Indo-English Novels* (Bareilly, Prakash Publication, 1984), p. 83.

IV. The English Teacher

The English Teacher (1945) published under the title "Grateful to Life and Death' in the U.S.A. is logical sequence to Narayan's earlier novel, *The Bachelor of Arts.* Written in reminiscent mood, Narayan records the growth of the artist in him through Krishna the chief protagonist in *The English Teacher.* The novel is highly supernatural. The experiments in psychic communication with Susila, his dead wife with the help of a medium, introduce a whimsical or fantastical element into the story that has so long been very much truthful to life. Automatic writings and attempts at psychic contact with the dead are not altogether uncommon: and the soil of India doubtless breeds every type of idealist and eccentric, waif and vagabond. The novel which starts as an interesting account of domestic felicity, thus gets bogged down in the so-called spiritual things, and philosophic discussions, which have in them, no grain of truth at all. Even the writer's own psychic contact with the spirit of his dead wife that has occasioned the novel, is but a hallucination on his part. The profound realization that dawns upon the protagonist, the end as the unmitigated loneliness, is the only truth of life that makes him survive the death of his beloved wife.

Narayan's recording in his Memoir *My Days* of the event of his wife's death deserves attention here :

> More than any other book, *The English Teacher* is autobiographical in content, very little part of it being fiction. The English Teacher of the novel, Krishna is a fictional character in the fictional city of Malgudi; but he goes through the same experience I had gone through, and he calls his wife Susila, and the child is Leela instead of Hema. The toll that typhoid took and all the desolation that followed, with a child to look after, and the psychic adjustments, are based on my own experience.... The dedication of the book to the memory of my wife should to some extent give the reader a clue that the book may not be all fiction.[1]

The English Teacher was occasioned by the sudden death of the writer's wife Rajam in 1939. She caught typhoid in May and died in the first week of June 1939. The novelist was shocked, overwhelmed with impenetrable despair. He lost all interest in life and found no meaning in existence. However, he was encouraged by his friends, Graham Greene, and Dr. Paul Brunton who prophetically observes: "You will write a book which is within you, all ready now, and it is bound to come out sooner or later, when you give yourself a chance to write."[2] Narayan did take the chance of writing the novel based on the psychic contact with the spirit of his dead wife, which he himself experienced in his life.

The novel is divided into two parts, the first half being an interesting account of Krishna's domestic felicity till the untimely death of his beloved wife. Krishna is shown as a Lecturer in English at Albert Mission College. The second half of the novel is devoted to the psychic communion of the protagonist with the spirit of his dead wife. And it is this part of the novel which requires greater attention.

Irrational belief of the Indians in their previous birth has been realistically presented in the novel. When Krishna goes out in search of a suitable house, he comes across an old house owner who fondles a foolish belief: "I revere college teachers, our Gurus. Meritorious deeds in previous births make them gurus in this life...."[3] There is however, no comment on this from *The English Teacher* who, too, perhaps believes in such absurdities which have far-reaching effects on the mind of the young ones, who should have otherwise been scientific in their attitudes.

Steeped in superstitions they believe that children are born to them by going to gods and goddesses. At the behest of some greedy Brahmin pundits they are prepared to do what they are asked to. And even after that, in case they fail to have any issue, they just link it to the deeds in their past life. While returning to their house Krishna and his wife, Susila happens to come across a small newly built temple. Asking about it, an old lady sitting on a gunny sack at the temple gate selling offerings, says to Susila: "Srinivas — the greatest god; you need not visit Tirupati Hills to see him, if you visit him here — he grants all your boons and blesses all your efforts..." she further adds, "You are both so young and bright, He will bless you with numerous children and may they all be sons."[4] An educated Susila simply laughs and enters the temple. She comes out feeling quiet and happy.

In Susila we see depth and strength of a girl of a simple traditional upbringing and habit of mind whose exquisite manners and deference to her husband, go with conviciton and self-respect. She also possesses that serenity of psyche which seems so powerfully a part of the mature Indian sensibility, achieving a point of equilibrium between the unavoidable accommodations with, and the necessary responses to the 'rhythm of life'. This period of grace and maturing is brought to a brutal conclusion when Susila catches typhoid after being accidentally locked in the fouled lavatory of a prospective new house. The onset and progress of the disease, first mis-diagnosed as malaria, then the collapse and coma and death of Susila and a grim account of an Indian funeral, are vividly presented with clinical coolness. Narayan writes in his Memoir *My Days*: "Within a hundred days of her arrival, Rajam (his wife) had departed from this world. She caught typhoid in early May and collapsed in the first week of June 1939. Looking back it seems as if she had a premonition of her end, and had wanted to stay back with her parents and sister. I have described this part of my experience of her sickness and death in *The English Teacher* so fully that I do not, and perhaps cannot go over it again."[5]

Susila suffers from typhoid. She simply could not touch her food, the thought of that unclean closet, in the new house, all the time haunting her "that closet, and those, oh, oh", she shuddered, "flies and other things come before me and I can't eat. And that fly which sat here."[6] Susila pointed at her lips and finished the rest of the sentence with a shiver.

Susila's mother saw her and at once jumped to the conclusion that an Evil Eye had fallen on her daughter and that at the new house a malignant spirit had attacked her: the foolish belief not uncommon in India. She visited a nearby temple and prayed to the God for her daughter's recovery. She regularly brought sacred ash and vermilion and smeared it on her daughter's forehead. Finding that Susila's fever did not come down, she called in one exorcist, a fearful man with his forehead ablaze with sacred ash and thick rosary around his neck and matted hair. Krishna of course, was furious and asked him to go away taking him to be a beggar. But he lacked the necessary courage to argue with his mother-in-law. Moreover there was a secret fear lurking in his mind as to how it would be viewed by the 'Swamiji'. Krishna confessed: "I watched it all from the doorway in fury, but I had to be silent because I couldn't argue with my mother-in-law.... I felt ashamed and wished I could spirit away this mystic."[7] It is all the more shocking to see that even the doctor was seen encouraging the exorcist though he might have no other purpose but to please the elders. Mark the comment: "Ah, no; don't be-little these people", said the doctor, "there is a lot in him too, we don't know. When we understand it fully I am sure we doctors will be able to give more complete cures."[8]

It is this type of attitude of such so called educated people that these foolish irrational beliefs have continued to plague the Indian society. It is absurd to believe that there are spirits and that they can be summoned to answer questions. It is all due to the hypnotic influence of such cults that some Kattiiadiyes and religious priests achieve occasional successes on the suspectible minds of the patients through poojas or prayers. And ignorant persons attribute such cures to the gods, and demons invoked by the exorcists. As a result of indoctrination and brainwash from childhood, inevitable in the society we live in, that, not only the illiterate but also the educated men like the doctor fall an easy prey to the exorcists.

The second half of the novel is wholly devoted to the psychic communion of Krishna with the spirit of his dead wife. In his interview with Ved Mehta, Narayan said that "all that he has set down in the second half of *The English Teacher* had actually happened to him and that he would frequently visit a lawyer in Madras who claimed to communicate with the dead through so called automatic writing."[9]

The psychic contact which the writer himself experienced after the death of his wife, has been presented in the novel through Krishna the chief protagonist of the novel. In order to know about his psychic contact, we will have to take in to consideration the state of mind of Krishna after he has lost his wife. Krishna himself says: "I am an imbecile, incapable of doing anything or answering any questions. I'm incapable of doing anything except what our priest orders me to do....there are no more surprises and shocks in life, so that I watch the flames without agitation. For me the greatest reality is this and nothing else...nothing else will worry or interest me in life hereafter."[10]

His mind kept buzzing with thoughts and memories of his dead wife. In the darkness he often felt an echo of her voice or speech or sometimes her moaning and delirious talk in sick bed. It is all due to derangement of his 'body chemistry'. Dr. Abraham Kovoor says: "Talking like a possessed person, often in a changed voice and fabricated language — this in psychology is known as glossolalia, ecstatic trance during poojas...are nothing but the effects of auto or hetero hypnosis on the subject's suggestive mind." He further adds, "Utterances of persons in deep meditation or trance, are nothing but the hallucinations of deranged minds, and should not be regarded as divine revelations or occult messages.[11] Krishna and his friend through the medium of which he got messages come in this category and Dr. Kovoor labelled such persons as fit subjects for the psychiatrist's coach.

Dr. Abraham Kovoor in his book *Begone Godmen*, has quoted similar case of Mr. X who claimed to have received message from the spirit. Once Mr. X was called in and made to lapse into trance. "Yes, now I can see my wife clearly there! There she is standing, looking at me," shouted Mr. X pointing to a life size portrait of The Very Rev. Kovoor

Eipe Thomma Kattanar, Vicar General of St. Thomas Syrian Church of Malabar, hanging on that wall. On asking 'can you see that photo hanging on that wall?' Mr. X answered, "there is no wall there. I can just see the blue sky with my wife standing among the clouds."[12]

Mr. X was obsessed with the thoughts of his dead wife. His constant readings about spiritualism and spirit materialisation have helped to confirm his belief in the existence of spirits and the possibility of holding conversation with them.

Exactly same is the case with Krishna and his friend through the medium of which he gets the occult messages. As already seen, Krishna is very much obsessed with the thought of his dead wife. Even without her presence, he could see her in her sick bed. This is nothing but the hallucination on his part. As with Krishna's friend, it can be said that the so called occult messages that he claims to have received from the spirit are but the utterances of a person in ecstatic trance, and should not be regarded as divine revelations. Mark his utterances allegedly coming from the spirits. "There is hardly any personality on earth who does not obstruct our effort. But we're glad we've found you."[13] He thought himself as the only person on earth fit (chosen by the spirits) to receive the message. Only a man of deranged mind can speak out such utterances. And he is, without any obstacle, passed on as a Godman. It is the Hindu culture which is mainly responsible for the mushroom growth of such Godmen.

Secondly, we noticed that Krishna's friend produced a sheet after sheet covered with scriblings (hardly clear or legible). Krishna said, "not a word of it could be deciphered. It looked like the work of a very young child with paper and pencil."[14] It was clear that no one did make out anything except the writer himself. And it was all nothing but the figment of his own imagination scribled under an ecstatic trance. Sometimes he scribled each things which had absolutely no connection whatsoever. However, he was able to convince the distressed Krishna saying: "She promises to do better next time...there are some difficulties both in expressing and picking out of memory the exact items".[15] Even Krishna confessed: "Except one or two references, the rest was all too wild...I grumbled and went home in a most unhappy state of mind".[16]

Krishna's friend was very cunning and intelligent in the sense he took a week's time for his next sitting during the period of which he had every chance to collect the required information for his so called divine communications. And all that Krishna's friend said during seances, allegedly coming from his wife's spirit was mere projection of his own ideas conditioned by his absurd and irrational beliefs and supernatural things. The idea that the departed souls maintain their earthly bodies is in complete harmony with Krishna's foolish ideas regarding the rustle of her dress, food, language and form act, pertaining to the spirits. Dr. Abraham Kovoor rightly asks : "Are these bodies reconstituted from the separate elements after the decomposition of the corpses?"[17]

Narayan's writings in this connection appeared to be contradictory. On one occasion the spirit of his dead wife is reported to have been saying: "I'm without the encumbrance of the physical body and everything is finer and quicker than on earth".[18] On another occasion the same spirit is reported to have said, "But by and by, you will hear my bangles clanking and feast your eyes on my dress and form". It further adds: "I think I look the same person as on earth. Only free from all ailments, ills and cares."[19] And Krishna saw her sitting by his side : mere phantasy of his dead wife and nothing else.

More interesting and typical of the novelist's genius are the eccentric headmaster and his stupid and ill-natured wife. Since both of them are at poles apart from each other in preference and attitudes, they live very unhappily in a terrible domestic condition. The wife of the headmaster is illiterate and lacks good manners. She is always quarrelsome and vociferously blames her husband in the presence of Krishna for taking no interest in his family. This tense family atmosphere naturally has bad effect on their children who become unruly, wayward and wild. To the headmaster, his wife is absolutely in-corrigible, and quite often she has proved herself to be so: "...I'm not going to be another woman than myself even if the King is here. What did I do to him?"[20]

Disgusted with his quarrelsome wife, the headmaster finds peace in a children's school. That she realises her helpless position without him after she receives the false message of his death, makes her all the more miserable, for the headmaster is so fed up with her that instead of pardoning her and living with her, he enters the Sanyas Ashram and lives permanently at his school.

The headmaster was not interested in the life after death. He declared that it was all a matter of personal faith and conviction. He said, "My knowledge of past, present and future, strictly pertains to this life. Beyond that I have nothing to say, because I believe I shall once again be resolved into the five elements of which I'm composed...."[21]

And yet the same headmaster could not help believing in astrological predictions. He had an unwavering faith in his astrologer whom he called a great hermit who predicted: "This person's earthly duties over, he will pass over on this day, surrounded by his wife and children at his last moment."[22]

That the predictions did not come true and the headmaster was happy. We find a remarkable change in his life. He ceased to be a householder and adopted the primary school as his residential place. When Krishna saw him the very next morning, he could not help muttering to himself 'ghost' for he heard him to have reported it as his last day according to the astrological predictions. As he was brought up in such cultural surroundings right from his childhood, it was but natural that he shuddered at the deceptive sights of ghosts and demons. Dr. Abraham Kovoor remarks: "Due to the fear artificially created by brain-washing from childhood most persons will not have the courage to go near and verify the truth about these apparitions. All those who have conducted investigation courageously and scientifically, have come to know that such apparitions are either due to optical illusions, or mental hallucinations."[23]

Narayan has touched upon some of the present day ills of the society. The education system came under severe criticism. One may recall here examples like Shakespeare's Macbeth, Coleridge's Christabel wherein the supernatural is portrayed in its sinister aspect, while Narayan's aim is to show the opposite. All the same, the poets like Milton have under similar situations, achieved remarkable success with the sheer magic of poetic faculty which Narayan is certainly lacking. M.K. Naik rightly observes: "As an able realist, he can certainly paint a neat, accurate faithful picture of what he sees; but he certainly lacks the poetic vision, and the creative power to hint at subtler emanations which alone can make the supernatural an uncanny experience to the reader."[24]

Some pointed out that the second half of *The English Teacher* is neither pure autobiography nor a scientific treatise on spiritualism but a work of fiction and must be judged as such. And through the agency of the amiable, homely medium Narayan succeeds in persuading the reader to accept Krishna's efforts to regain touch with his wife by sober-conversational prose, though it is much in the form of "in-consequential prattling, 'communications' coated with warbling Tagore-like mysticism, to be cloudily and clumsily irrational."[25] This coherent and beguiling universe that is Malgudi, has the charm and authenticity of an Indian colouring with a substantial and common human nature.

Notes and References

1. R.K. Narayan, *My Days* (Mysore : Indian Thought Publication, 1979), pp. 134-135.
2. *Ibid.*, p. 136.
3. R.K. Narayan, *The English Teacher* (Mysore : Indian Thought Publication, 1981), p. 25.
4. *Ibid.*, p. 69.
5. R.K. Narayan, *My Days*, p. 134.
6. R.K. Narayan, *The English Teacher*, p. 74
7. *Ibid.*, p. 93.
8. *Ibid.*
9. Quoted by Dr. R.K. Badal, *R.K. Narayan : A Study* (Bareilly : Prakash Book Depot, 1976), p. 38.
10. R.K. Narayan, *The English Teacher*, pp. 106-107.
11. Dr. Abraham Kovoor, *Begone Godmen* (Bombay : Jaico Press Pvt. Ltd., 1977), p. 53.
12. *Ibid.*, pp. 95-96.
13. R.K. Narayan, *The English Teacher*, p. 126.
14. *Ibid.*, p. 128.
15. *Ibid.*, p. 142.
16. *Ibid.*, pp. 142-143.
17. Dr. Abraham Kovoor, *Begone Godmen*, p. 98.
18. R.K. Narayan, *The English Teacher*, p. 149.
19. *Ibid.*, p. 150.
20. *Ibid.*, p. 164.
21. *Ibid.*, p. 187.
22. *Ibid.*, p. 186.
23. Dr. Abraham Kovoor, *Begone Godmen*, p. 50.
24. M.K. Naik, *The Ironic Vision* (New Delhi : Sterling Publishers Pvt. Ltd., 1983), p. 29.
25. William Walsh, *R.K. Narayan : A Critical Appreciation* (New Delhi: Allied Publishers Pvt. Ltd., 1983), p. 58.

V. Mr. Sampath

Mr. Sampath first published in 1949 by Eyre and Spottiswoode, London, delves deeper into the complexities of human relationships and circumstances. The two most important motifs — money and sex — supply the novelist with his basic raw material. However, the theme that is uppermost in Narayan's mind is no other than the restoration of the old order and the social values upheld by our ancestors. In *Mr. Sampath* Narayan presents some of the important events of his life through the character of Shrinivas, an editor of *The Banner,* a journal with a two-fold task: "On the one hand, attacking ruthlessly pigheadedness wherever found, and on the other prodding humanity into pursuing an ever-receding perfection."[1]

Shrinivas was sincere to *The Banner* till he came to think that everything in the world is pre-ordained, and that it is a futile and presumptuous occupation to analyse, criticise and attempt to set things right anywhere: "things being neither particularly wrong nor right, but just balancing themselves."[2] This line of thinking has perhaps made Shrinivas, as in case of Narayan himself, a detached observer of the social evils that have plagued the Indian society: the thinking which is entirely in keeping with Hindu view of life Narayan has upheld throughout his life, presenting all the while, a realistic portrayal of the people around him, and their social surroundings.

Shrinivas, one of the chief characters in the novel, begins as a pragmatic young man working as the editor of '*The Banner*'. But it is a pity that such a young person who has had high ideas of setting the world right within twelve pages of his journal '*The Banner*', should have developed a fatalistic attitude in the end and be a helpless on-looker of the social evils. A regular feature entitled 'Open Window' of *The Banner* Shrinivas devotes for the abolition of slums and congestion. "It described the tenements, the pigsties constructed for human dwellings in the four corners of the town by rapacious landlords..., it constituted itself an enemy of a great many institutions and conditions."[3] It is with this lofty purpose that Shrinivas launches '*The Banner*' with the whole-hearted support by the printer of Malgudi, Mr. Sampath. The editor himself writes: "Banner has nothing special to note about any war, past or future. It is only concerned with the war that is always going on — between man's inside and outside. Till the forces are equalised, the struggle will always go on."[4]

It is ironic that the editor whose aim is to instruct the world, becomes a puppet in the hands of his printer — a breezy, energetic, and aggressive man who not only decides the type to be used (he makes the first dummy copy look like a hand-bill of a wrestling tournament), but also devises the layout, fixes the subscription, and enrol subscribers; arranges for the supply of paper, completes all the legal formalities required, and ultimately tries to take a hand in the editorial also.

Shrinivas who has only a few days earlier, been used to sitting down comfortably in his room with a copy of the Upanishada in his hand, now finds the hectic pace set by his editorial labours quite an ordeal. All his plans to turn out a copy in a phased manner every day of the week go awry and he finds himself "doing everything every day, and all things on Friday, the printer shouting from the bottom of the staircase for copy every five minutes...."[5] He works under a continuous nightmare of not being able to meet his printer's demands.

On top of everything comes the brush with the R.M.S. office which complains that the posting of the Journal in a mass at the last clearing time is causing great moment of inconvenience to it, and suggests that the dispatch be distributed throughout the day or if possible throughout the week. Shrinivas's reply is a masterpiece of irony: "If we acted up to your suggestion it would result in something like the following: at 12, Midday we should be posting the fourth page, at 1 p.m. the sixth page, at 5 p.m. ninth and tenth, 7 p.m. eleventh, and 8 p.m. twelfth page. Since our readers would doubtless have a great objection to receiving the journal piece-meal, we are forced to post the journal in its entirety at 8 p.m.".[6]

Shrinivas made it his mission to attack the conditions in the town, which were terribly deplorable. And he was pleased to have found that Malgudi Muncipality thought it better to revise an old plan, which they had shelved years ago, of subsidising the development of a new town on the eastern outskirts of Malgudi. The District Board and the Municipality had launched a feverish scheme of road development and tank building, and three or four cotton mills had suddenly sprung into existence. Narayan comments: "Overnight, as it were, Malgudi passed from a semi-agricultural town to a semi-industrial town, with a sudden influx of population of all sorts. The labour gangs, brought in from other districts, spread themselves out in the open spaces. Babies sleeping in hammocks made of old pieces of cloth, looped over three branches, women cooking food on the road side, men sleeping on pavements — these became a common sight in all parts of Malgudi."[7]

For all its outward change from semi-agricultural to semi-industrial town, Malgudi failed to shake off the traditional outlook. The strange activities that followed Ravi's mental derangement in the house of Shrinivas, showed how people were irrational and wild in the treatment of Ravi's mental ailment. Intense infatuation with the young and beautiful Shanti acting as Parvati, made Ravi, in a fit of madness, rush to free his dreamgirl from the passionate embrace of Sampath, playing Shiv in a shooting scene of *The Burning of Kama.* A Sunrise Pictures venture, being jointly produced by Sampath and his friends. It was a total ruin, and Ravi was sent to the police lockup. Without a moment's hesitation it was declared that Ravi was possessed by the ghost, and elaborate preparations followed for his treatment. A wild looking man with huge beads around his neck, clad in red silk, his forehead dubbed with vermilion was brought in to officiate at the function. In front of Ravi were set out trays of suffron and flowers, huge twigs of margosa leaves and a camphor flare. The whole air chocked with insense burning in a holder. Shrinivas comments in utter despair: "The whole thing is too silly for words."[8]

Shrinivas recollects the tribal worship done before the camera at the studio on the inauguration day. Now he finds himself totally incapacited to check the activities which have continued unhindered, the exorcist enjoying the full support from his wife. His wife whispers to Shrinivas: "He (exorcist) knows all about the ghost that haunts this house that people talk about. He says it has got into Ravi. He will drive it out, and we can live here with a free mind afterward".[9] She feels herself a part of the affair and seems to feel specially gratified at being the hostess of this exotic function.

> Ravi sat oblivious of his surroundings; a few margosa leaves were scattered on him. The chants and rhythmic beats went on and produced a kind of hypnosis in every one assembled there, and Shrinivas saw Ravi gradually shaking his head and swaying. He found the atmosphere oppressive and unbearable — the gong and the drumbeats, the pungent, piercing smell of the incense, its smoke hanging in the air, and the camphor flare illumination.[10]

It was with this background specially created for the occasion, the exorcist undertook his activities for driving the ghost out of Ravi. "The exorcist picked up his cans and thwacked it sharply over Ravi's back and asked at the same time: 'Now will you go or not?' Ravi smarted a little under the blow, rolled his eyes, and the thwacking was renewed with vigour. The question was addressed to the evil spirit possessing him. Ravi winced under the repeated blows."[11]

Shrinivas felt an impulse to cry out 'stop it. It is absurd and cruel.' But he found himself incapable of any effort. The whole episode was set aside saying: "Madness or sanity, suffering or happiness seemed all the same.... It didn't make the slightest difference in the long run — in the rush of eternity nothing mattered. It was no more important or remembered than an attack of malaria in the lifetime of a centenarian. Whether one was mad or sane or right or wrong didn't make the slightest difference: it was like bothering about a leaf floating on a rushing torrent whether it was floating on its right side or wrong side."[12]

He marvelled at the invisible forces that maintained the subtle balance, and he found it so perfect that it seemed to be unnecessary for anybody to do anything. And the very purpose with which Shrinivas launched *The Banner* was abandoned half way. Hereafter Shrinivas was a mute observer of the social evils. A fatalistic attitude that everything in this world is pre-ordained and that he has nothing in this world to set it right anywhere, completely gripped his mind. Mark the comment, "Just the required number of wrong doers as there are people who deserved wrong deeds, just as many policemen to bring them to their senses, if possible, and just as many wrong doers again to keep the police employed, and so on and on in an infinite concentric circle."[13]

Shrinivas thought it a revolutionary discovery in the realm of human existence — solutions to many of the problems that had been teasing his mind for years. The attitude of Shrinivas who acted to a certain extent as the mouth piece of R.K. Narayan, has done irreparable loss to the Indian society. The cunning few specially of the high caste, systematically divided the Indian society into four castes, and ruled over the so called lower caste people treating them worse than dogs till they have lost their very identity. They worked at the mercy of the so called Brahmins who successfully convinced them to accept the lot as if it were 'God given.'

P.S. Sundaram in his article, *The Ambivalence of R.K. Narayan,* rightly points out: "...Where so much requires to be done urgently and those who should be doing them merely sit back and philosophise. Shrinivas is by profession a journalist who would like to wield his paper *The Banner* less as a flag than as a broom to sweep the many cobwebs that have taken possession of every nook and corner of our land". P.S. Sundaram further asks, "Is it for him to talk of the futility of action, of reform?"[14]

It is hardly surprising that Shrinivas lapsed back to his old self with the cutltural heritage weighing on his mind more than ever. A small image of Natraj which his grand-mother had given him, was one of the possessions he had valued most for years. It seemed to be a refuge from the oppression of time. It had never left Shrinivas since he received it on his eighth birthday from his grandmother. He often sat before it, contemplated its proportions, and addressed it thus: "Oh, God, you are trampling a demon under your foot, and you show us a rhythm, though you appear to be still. I grasp the symbol but vaguely. You hold a flare in your hand. May a ray of that light illumine my mind!"[15] Shrinivas never started his day without spending a few minutes before this image.

Shrinivas even left to its fate the story that he wrote for a film, the story of one Ram Gopal, the hero who had devoted his life to the abolition of the caste system and evils of society. The story was rejected on the ground that only Russians or Americans would be able to tackle it. And hence, it was unanimously decided that the mythological story of *The Burning of Kama* would be most suitable for the Indian public. Shrinivas, of course, a product of the same cultural atmosphere, readily accepted to write the script afresh.

> He now seemed to be camping in Kailas, the ice-capped home of lord Shiva and his followers. Shrinivas could almost feel the coolness of the place and its iridescent surroundings. He saw, as in a vision, before his eyes Shiva, that mendicant looking god, his frame ash-smeared, his loin girt with tiger hide, his trident in his hand; he was an austere god; he was the god of destruction. His dance was in the burial ground, his swaying footsteps produced a deluge. As Shrinivas described it, his mind often went back to the little image of Natraj that he had in a niche at home, before which his wife lit a small oil lamp everyday.[16]

William Walsh rightly observes: "The relating of the story to Indian myth which is usually managed with subdued tact and skill, is done here with very much more explicitness. There is some warrant for this, perhaps, in that the story Shrinivas is working on is itself one of the Indian myths."[17]

The untouchability that is being practised in the villages and town, is a social stigma on the Indian society. Born in a Brahmin orthodox family, Shrinivas's wife refuses to touch the food brought from a hotel for fear of being polluted. It is the result of, "rigorous up-bringing, fear of pollution of touch by another caste, orthodox idiocies — all the rigorous compartmenting of human beings."[18] R.K. Narayan has done nothing wrong in depicting the incidence in the novel. For, S.G. Sanyal rightly points out, "Some beliefs which are common places of Indian thought and which most closely affect the novelist in his interpretation of human character and human action are Varnashram Dharma or a man's role and duties according to his place in a scheme of castes." The writer further adds, "Not all Hindus would hold these beliefs in their scriptural form to the same extent; nor would they apply them to all situations, yet they are constantly referred to and they are taken for granted in many Hindu institutions and rituals."[19]

The ancient epics like *The Ramayan* and *The Mahabharat* are held in great reverence by the majority of Indian masses.

They have such a large spell that they always prefer for themes epic stories to any theme on modernity. R.K. Narayan depicts this trend. We have the example of *A Sunrise Pictures,* the owners of which, have a dilemma, whether to produce a film of topical interest about modernity according to the script written by Shrinivas, with the main character Mr. Ram Gopal, devoting his whole life for the social reform, or produce a film on mythological story. The preference however, is given to the mythological theme of *The Burning of Kama* taking into consideration the general mood of the cinema goers, for commercial purpose.

Oblivious of the mythological theme for the film, the District judge, who is to preside the inaugural function, makes a beginning of his speech with a strong appeal to the public to throw overboard all the mythological and ancient subjects. His advice to the owners of the cinema and the public in general is thought provoking. He continues: "The film must not only tell a story but must also convey a message to the ignorant masses. There are problems of cultivation and soil — all these you can tackle: there is nothing that you cannot include, if only you have the mind to be of service to your fellow men...you have been too long concerned with demons and gods and their prowesses. I think we had better take a vow to boycott Indian films till they take up modern themes."[20]

Hypocrites like the old landlord who has owned several houses in the city but stayed in a small room, his friend has given him free of rent, are realistically portrayed in the novel. He is a rapacious fellow, and though a propertied man, lives on alms and calls himself a Sanyasi. In the characterization of the old landlord, Narayan presents a class of people who are bent on extracting huge amount of money exploiting the gullible masses. It is these people who, for their selfish ends, perpetuate the social evils like the untouchability and caste system. In fact, the old landlord has a water tap at his house, but he always uses the public water tap for bathing purpose, causing much inconvenience to the poor low caste people who are forbidden to go near him. And nobody has courage to question his using the tap, for he belongs to the so called Brahmin caste.

Sampath, another important character in the novel, is a vociferous, effusive man, of flamboyant sentiments, large gestures, practical ability and distinctively Machavellian gifts. He dominates the novel ever since he appears on the scene. It is Mr. Sampath who is largely instrumental in the publication of *The Banner,* when others of the town are reluctant to publish it for one reason or another.

Sampath owns a *Truth Printing Works* with some set principles which he has laid down for others to follow. He never allows any person to look through the curtain dividing him from his staff. Natraj in *The Man Eater of Malgudi* also seems to have set the same principles in his press. Shrinivas never could pluck up enough courage to peer into that sanctum and see how many people might be slaving at the task of turning out *The Banner.* Shrinivas hears the printer declare with considerable emphasis: "That is the one point on which I'm always very strict — the best of my friends and relations, have not seen inside there. For instance, you have never seen my machine room, Sir, and how much I appreciate your respecting my principles: I've pointed out your example to hundreds of my customers."[21] This has kept Shrinivas away from that room more than ever. "He remembers that at Chidambaram temple there was a grand secret, beyond the semi-dark holy of holies, beyond the twinkling lights of the inner shrine. He has always wondered what it might be; but those who attempted to probe it too deliberately, lost their sight, if not their lives. There was a symbolism in it.... And Shrinivas saw no reason why he should grudge the printer his mysterious existences and mazes beyond the purple curtain".[22]

There is nothing wrong when Mr. Sampath in collaboration with his friends, and Mr. Shrinivas as script writer ventures to go in for *A Sunrise Pictures.* Elaborate preparations are made for the inauguration of the shooting of *The Burning of Kama.* A committee of astrologers have been consulted for the auspicious period. And when the District judge, who is to be the chief guest, does not turn up at the appointed time, Mr. Sampath himself comes forward to inaugurate the function lest the auspicious period may slip out of their hands.

But Mr. Sampath made a fool of himself, and we found him a ruined man in the end. Everything went smoothly but for Ravi who saw his dreamgirl in Shanti (acting as Parvati in *The Burning of Kama*) and in a fit of madness in the most unexpected manner, rushed to free her from the passionate embrace of Sampath playing 'Shio' in the picture. He knocked 'Shio' aside with such violence that he fell amidst his foliage in Kailas in a most ungodly manner, Parvati was seen struggling in the arms of Ravi who was trying to kiss on her lips, and carry her off. Ravi, however, was overpowered and sent to the police lockup. But the whole venture came to an abrupt halt. In fact, both Sampath and Shrinivas knew beforehand that Ravi was abnormal in his behaviour ever since he lost his job in the bank. At this critical juncture with so many family members depending on him, it was very kind of Shrinivas, and Sampath as well, to allow him to work at Sunrise Pictures. However, Sampath a shrewd man as he was, lost no time to request Shrinivas to sufficiently inform Ravi and keep him under check, for he would peep his head whenever he got a chance to have the glimpse of Shanti. But Shrinivas failed on his part to warn Ravi of his activities and allowed the events to take their own course. And the result was a total ruin of the Sunrise Pictures. Mark Shrinivas's comment on Ravi's deranged mind. "Half the madness was his own doing, his lack of self-knowledge, his treachery to his own instincts as an artist, which had made him a battle ground."[23]

Secondly, it is Sampath himself who is partly to be blamed for the ruin. K.C. Bhatnagar rightly points out, "Sampath makes a fool of himself with Shanti (neglecting his wife at home); and Shanti, being fed up with this sort of clandestine love walks out on him from the railway waiting room, taking a train to Madras, leaving a note which is more of a threat than an explanation: "If I find you pursuing me, I will shave off my head.... I am after all, a widow." The writer further adds, "thus Parvati, whom Indian women invoke for inviolability of their marriage turns out to be a widow in Narayan's Malgudi circus!"[24]

Thus, Mr. Sampath portrayed in the beginning as an ambitious, hard working, and energetic printer, ended a ruined man. Had Shrinivas seriously taken it on himself to warn Ravi beforehand, perhaps the mishap would have been averted. But he chose himself to be a detached observer and allowed the events to take their own course, little minding that it would bring about a total ruin to Mr. Sampath who had given him a name and fame as the editor. Shrinivas had betrayed the printer, and lost the readers' interest in him for his fatalistic outlook.

In the novel, man's struggle in the universe does not work in the manner he wishes rather in accordance with the dictates of a mysterious providence. Shrinivas, the editor of *The Banner* gets invovled ino the film venture as a script writer, but has to return to his own profession in the end. Here there has been a reversal of the original myth. Instead of love God Kama being burnt by the fire from Shiva's third eye, we have Sampath roasted alive on the fire of love; so also Ravi who dares the fire and gets his fingers burnt.

Here we also find vividly portrayed a contrast between the simple Indian life of Shrinivas and the ostentatious, glamorous life of the film. William Walsh aptly writes: "A comparable distinction exists between the simple Indian family life of Shrinivas, with his deferential but by no means servile wife and his indulged child, lived in bare but clean surroundings, and expressive of a long standing tradition as well as modest personal happiness, and the ostentatious establishment, the imported manners, and chaotic sexual freedom of the film studios; a theme repeated in the contrast between Sampath's own home life and his infatuation with the girl he was making a star of."[25]

All the major characters in the novel are drawn with great restraint. They have not been allowed to have their upper hand, rather they seem to move within the accepted social norms. Mr. Sampath that energetic and ambitious printer of Malgudi is shown a ruined man in the end. Shanti, the heroine in *The Burning of Kama* runs away from the shooting scene leaving Sampath to his fate lamenting and repenting for the mess he has made of himself. Ravi, the young artist, is almost mad after Shanti, a dreamgirl of his heart. It is Ravi who is largely responsible for the ruin of the film company so laboriously built by Sampath and his friends. There is only Shrinivas, with his detached way of life, who survives the shocks, and continues as before minding nothing. And Narayan seems to approve of the line of approach Shrinivas upholds in his life. He is most of the time a silent, passive and detached observer of the comic drama that unfolds itself before his eyes. Even at the age of thirty seven when he left his native town for Malgudi to start *The Banner* with philosophical idealism of a crusader, he was mentally a recluse, absorbed in the study of the Upanishadas after a prolonged bout with life.

The sudden closure of *The Truth Printing Works* throws him into the zany filmdom. Thereafter, he loses much of his identity, all the time working under the shadow of Sampath who dominates the novel. Narayan here gets the chance to portray and expose the glamour world of cinema. Somu, the ex-president of the District Board, now a film producer. Sohan Lal, a rich capitalist and film financer; De Mello of Hollywood, the brain behind the studio Organization, and then Sampath and Shrinivas — all these figures complete a realistic portrait of the filmworld. Shanti, the heroin of the film, who gets enchanted and disgusted with life, reminds us of Shantabai of *The Dark Room* who upsets the homely life of the traditional Savitri. Both Sampath and Ramani have more or less the same approach towards life, as for as their free sex life is concerned.

Here, as elsewhere, whether it is the launching of film company or starting of life's career as in case of the lawyer in *The Painter of Signs,* the 'holy' men have an important role to play. With their forehead stamped with ash and vermilion and their backs covered with hand spun long wraps, they sit before the portraits reading some 'sacred' texts. In front of them are kept trays loaded with coconut camphor and offerings for the gods. Then they approach the camera to stick a string of jasmine and a dot of sandal paste on it. Seeing their recklessness in dealing with the camera, De Mello could not help commenting: "In this country, Sir, one doesn't know when religious suspectibility is likely to be hurt. A mere sneeze will take you to the stake sometimes, better be on the safe side."[26] De Mello looks intimidated by these religious observances.

Narayan's purpose in depicting the episode is certainly a comic one; but he just touches the right vein. It speaks volumes and presents the reality largely in vogue in the society, especially amongst religious fanatics; a slight slip here and there and the trigger is let of killing hundreds of innocent people in communal holocaust. In his introduction to *Gods, Demons and Others,* Narayan refers to the inexhaustible vitality of our classical mythology which is as rich and variegated as the Greek mythology. There is no doubt about it. And often the myth is brought in to galvanise reality, to point a moral. But here there seems to be no desire on his part to modernise the myths so as to fit them into the contemporary scene. Narayan seems to be pleased in presenting the myths as he finds them in Hindu scriptures.

Notes and References

1. R.K. Narayan, *Mr. Sampath* (Delhi : Hind Pocket Books, 1979), p. 4.
2. *Ibid.*, p. 76.
3. *Ibid.*, p. 4.
4. *Ibid.*, p. 5.
5. *Ibid.*, p. 26.
6. *Ibid.*, p. 31.
7. *Ibid.*, pp. 27-28.

8. *Ibid.*, p. 257.
9. *Ibid.*
10. *Ibid.*, p. 258.
11. *Ibid.*, p. 261.
12. *Ibid.*
13. *Ibid.*, p. 76.
14. P.S. Sundaram, *The Ambivalence of R.K. Narayan.* From *Explorations in Modern Indo English Fiction*, edit. R.K. Dhavan (New Delhi : Bahri Publications, 1982), p. 145.
15. R.K. Narayan, *Mr. Sampath*, p. 19.
16. *Ibid.*, p. 126.
17. William Walsh, *R.K. Narayan : A Critical Appreciation* (New Delhi : Allied Publishers Pvt. Ltd., 1983), p. 67.
16. R.K. Narayan, *Mr. Sampath*, p. 40.
19. S.C. Sanyal, *Indianness in Major Indo English Novel* (Bareilly : Prakash Book Depot, 1984), p. 20.
20. R.K. Narayan, *Mr. Sampath*, p. 166.
21. *Ibid.*, p. 55.
22. *Ibid.*, p. 55.
23. *Ibid.*, p. 260.
24. Dr. K.C. Bhatnagar, *Realism in Major Indo English Fiction* (Bareilly: Prakash Book Depot, 1980), pp. 184-185.
25. William Walsh, *R.K. Narayan : A Critical Appreciation*, pp. 63-64.
26. R.K. Narayan, *Mr. Sampath*, p. 164.

VI. The Financial Expert

The Financial Expert, first published in 1952 by Metheun, London, turned out to be a major literary event of the year. Unlike *Mr. Sampath*, this novel has a concentration and compactness of form that lends it tremendous dramatic power. It is pre-eminently the story of one man Margayya aspiring to reach the summit of Mount Everest like a fanatical mountaineer. Rechard Church rightly commented: "*The Financial Expert* is likely to survive as one of the most original pieces of fiction published this year."[1]

In Margayya, the chief protagonist of *The Financial Expert*, Narayan presents a financial wizard bent on reaching to the top of his profession; that he becomes a pauper in the end is but an outcome of his own deeds. Margayya has been portrayed as an astute businessman of Malgudi now changed into a semi-agricultural, semi-industrial town wherein the castes seem to have disappeared from the social scene; and in place of the feeling of inferiority that had haunted Margayya's ancestors for about three generations for their originally belonging to the caste of corpse bearers, now comes the sense of supriority which Margayya possesses with a longing to have his son's marriage alliance with the daughter of a rich tea-estate owner of the Mempi Hills. The individual who undergoes a great ordeal for forty days to acquire wealth by propitiating the goddess Laxmi, believes at the same time that man is not the victim of circumstances or fate, but that man is a creature who can make his own present or future, provided he works hard and remains watchful. Margayya appears to be modern in outlook, but never dares to overlook the religious roots. The juxtaposition of the age old conventions and the modern characters provides much of the comedy. Graham Greene rightly comments on Margayya : "Margayya — the sad ambitious, absurd financial expert is perhaps the most engaging of all Mr. Narayan's characters. In his ambition for his boy, his huge dreams, his un-intended villainies, and his small vanities, his domestic tenderness, he has the hidden poetry and the unrecognised pathos we so often find in Tchechov's characters who on the last page vanish into life."[2]

Margayya makes a modest beginning of his business under a banyan tree. "His tinbox, a grey, discoloured, knobby affair, which was small enough to be carried under his arm contained practically his entire equipment : a bottle of ink, a pen and a blotter, a small register whose pages carried an assortment of names and figures, and above all — the most important items — loan application forms of the co-operative Bank."[3]

People under stress come to Margayya because he is so accommodating and unfussy about formalities in advancing cash which he does very easily and promptly. Margayya strikes a humanitarian concern for his brethren. "I want to do so much for you fellows, do you known why?... It is because I want you all to get over your money worries and improve your lives. You must adopt all civilized ways. That's why I am trying to help you to get money from that bastard office."[4] However, this is only one side of his face. The other one is far more vicious. He charges interest in so subtle a way and compounds it so deftly that any one who has signed one of his bonds is more or less finished. Margayya blends cunning with kind and raps the knuckles of his customers. William Walsh observes: "*The Financial Expert* is an exact account of village usury and city deceit and a controlled probing into the motives of money making."[5]

In fact, it was the insult and the threat by the secretary of the Co-operative Bank that has caused a turmoil and weighed heavily on the sensitive mind of Margayya. He at once drew the conclusion that the world treated him with contempt because he had no money. He reflected, "I look like a wayside barber with this little miserable box under my arm. People probably expect me to open the lid and take out soup and a brush. No wonder the Secretary feels he can treat me as he likes. If I looked like him, would he have dared to snatch the papers from my box? I can't look like him. I am destined to look like a wayside barber, and that is my fate."[6] Margayya was thoroughly vexed with himself and the lot he fared for centuries together. Now it appears he has come out of it, and resolves to look like the secretary of the Co-operative Bank so that people in the society may not treat him with contempt.

The stinging blow to his ego has set Margayya on his great financial adventure; and his almost mystic feeling for money is inseparably mixed with his craving for respectability, prestige, and the approval of his fellowmen. He had a strong social inferiority complex because his ancestors were once lowly corpse bearers and the family had to struggle for two or three generations to wash off this stigma. Margayya, therefore, considers the acquisition of wealth as a pre-requisite for an individuality, status and honour in society: a totally wrong view as far as Indian caste-ridden society is concerned. For, however, learned and propertied a person he may be, he is still viewed as low caste and looked down upon by the members of the higher castes. An example of Dr. Babasaheb

Ambedkar will serve the purpose. Even after his yeoman's service to the nation as an Architect of Indian Constitution, he was humiliated, looked down upon, only because he belonged to lower stratum of the society.

However, Margayya comes to realise that "Money alone is important in this world. Everything else will come to us naturally if we have money in our purse".[7] The sense of inferiority that engulfs his mind prompts him to reflect on his weak financial position and the style of living. He says to his wife: 'You see, if we are treated with contempt by people it is our fault. Our style of trying dhoti and our style of dressing it is all so silly! No wonder".[8] He talks like a man who has just arrived from a far-off land. He speaks with such detachment and superiority, his wife is somewhat taken aback.

Born in Hindu cultural surrounding, it is hardly surprising that Margayya's thoughts turned to gods for help. He could not overcome the irrational outlook of resorting to the forty day ordeal of Laxmi Puja; his cultural heritage almost pressed him to undergo the rites to become wealthy as suggested by the old priest. Though he began the rites on a doubtful note, he made all out efforts to acquire a red lotus and the milk of a smoke grey cow. Margayya was lost to the outside world for forty days during the Laxmi Puja. Each day he sat in a small room repeating: "Oh, goddess who affordest shelter to all the fugitive worlds. Thy feet, by themselves, are proficient in affording immunity from fear and bestowing boons."[9]

Wearing a red silk dhoti and smearing his forehead and body with sacred ash, he has to repeat it a thousand times each day sitting before the image of the goddess. Each day it took him eight hours of repetition to complete the thousand and then he reverentially put the black paste on his forehead, lit the camphor, called in his wife and child and sprinkled the holy water on them. Narayan writes : "His jaws ached, his tongue had become dry,...he felt faint with hunger, since he had to fast completely while praying."[10]

Even in present day society the tribals are seen so deep in their traditional customs and superstitions that they sacrifice human beings at the altar of gods and goddesses with a feeling to appease them and make them shower their boons.

There is no clear evidence to prove that Margayya's getting wealth is the direct result of the ritual he has undergone. It is a sheer co-incidence that he comes across one Dr. Pal who offers him a book on 'Bed life' which has earned him thousands of rupees. M.K. Naik rightly says : "The result of the ritual is also couched in deliberate ambiguity, for though Margayya's luck does turn after it, there is no clear evidence to prove that it is the direct result of the Laxmi worship, and it could as well as be just a co-incidence. The entire episode has thus a distinct touch of fantasy about it, but it does not strain the reader's 'willing suspension of disbelief' excessively."[11]

Indian society with its irrational attitude and superstition is a reality Narayan presents in *The Financial Expert.* At the behest of his elder brother, Margayya has to make offerings to the God, though reluctantly, for a son to be born. He remembers how he has clutched a brightly polished pot and followed by his suffron clad wife, has gone from door to door begging for alms. He has carried the alms and the sovereign equal the weight of the child to the Tirupati Hills and deposited them all in the treasure box in the shrine. For he has prayed for him and promised the gods his weight in silver rupee if he should be born. The trend of such attitude however, is largely on the decline, though gullible villagers are still not completely immune from it.

The belief in ghosts and demons is widely rampant amongst the villagers. It is said that the Registrar of Co-opeative societies died while serving on a rural indebtness sub-committee. After his death it was discovered that he had left all his savings for the construction of the Bank. People believed : "He now watched, from within a teak frame suspended on the central landing, all the comings and goings, and he was said to be responsible for occasional poltergeist phenomena, the rattling of paperweights, flying ledgers, and sounds like the brisk opening of folios, the banging of fists on a table, and so on evidenced by successive night watchmen. This could be easily understood, for the ghost of the Registrar had many reasons to feel sad and frustrated."[12]

Margayya never spared a dig at the custom of tallying horoscopes as a preliminary to marriage. When he called in a pundit to match his son's horoscope, he gave him sufficient hint that the horoscopes be matched according to his own wishes. But, when he found that the pundit failed to match favourably, the horoscope of his son with that of the daughter of a rich tea-estate owner, he just handed him one rupee note and unceremoniously saw him off. Margayya now "no longer believed that man was a victim of circumstances or fate but that man was a creature who could make his own present and future, provided he worked hard and remained watchful."[13] Later we learn that Dr. Pal helped Margayya find a different astrologer who rearranged the stars of Balu to suit the circumstances. And he paid him Rs. seventy five towards his fee as was suggested by Dr. Pal. Margayya was of a firm opinion that he was going to have no nonsense from the planets, and that he consulted the astrologer only as a formality, but he did not forget to add, "of course goddess Laxmi or another will have to be propitiated from time to time."[14] It becomes that Margayya could not uproot himself from the religious taboos. Though he did not believe in astrology, he was afraid to ignore the priest's suggestion. He felt crushed under all the metaphysical explanation. He bowed his head in humility. The priest continued, "The Shastras lay down such and such rituals for such and such ends. Between a man who performs them and one who doesn't, the chances are greater for the former. That's all I can say. The results are...you may have results or you may not...or you may have results and wish that you had failed."[15]

Margayya himself was largely responsible for his ruin in the end, though Dr. Pal's contribution to the rise and fall of Margayya's financial empire could not be overlooked. The feeling of inferiority complex experienced by him when rebuked by the bank servant for hanging around its doors, burnished his ambition and provoked in reaction a new aggressive self-confidence. His contact with Dr. Pal was a sheer co-incidence which immensely helped him to establish his financial edifice largely based on credit. Where he went wrong, was putting away bags of currency notes in the hastily cleared rooms of his house instead of starting productive enterprises with them which would have yielded him a higher rate of interest than what he has promised his creditors. Secondly, he was so obsessed with money that he has lost his food and sleep, and neglected his family and son so much so that his affluence, his bank balance buoyed him up and made to bear the loss of his son when he ran away from home. He now forgot his own self. The Margayya of the former days when he used to help the poor peasants in acquiring loans from the bank, was gone, we have now the Margayya, eccentric, overambitious and completely obsessed with money. Had he been in constant touch with his son and not been much worried about Dr. Pal's free contact with him, the end would have been different. On a sudden impulse Margayya assaulted Dr. Pal so savagely that the latter had no choice but to report the matter against him. And in no time the entire financial empire crashed like a pack of cards. The creditors who deposited their amount in Margayya's bank, come rushing to him to take back their money. He reflected later, "What would have become of him if he had started back home after speaking to his daughter-in-law a little earlier and missed Dr. Pal's Austin that night, or if he had remained in the shadows and had allowed Pal to go off after dropping Balu, when he might preferably have tackled with more circumspection and diplomacy: he might even have shared his property with him as he demanded: that would have saved him at least the rest of it — and prevented the doctor from doing what he did."[16]

In the end Margayya advises his son Balu: "Have an early meal tommorrow, and go to the Banyan tree in front of the Co-operative Bank.... Go there, that is all I can say: and anything may happen there-after.... If you are not going, I am going on with it, as soon as I am able to leave this bed."[17] It clearly shows that inspite of his traumatic experience, Margayya remains unchanged. He is still hopeful that the next turn of the wheel of fortune will again restore his dream. This only underscores the fundamental irony of human nature, viz., that one learns little from experience.

The novel offers interesting glimpses of Indian social life, impaired by the demoralizing effect of materialistic civilization. Hoarding, black marketing and curruption in every walk of life are rampant in the society. The rice merchant hoarding rice in a secret godown, and the contractor building a small hut and getting enormous bills passed easily by bribing the Garrison Engineer are the familiar sights in the present-day society, and then there are drug stockists, actors, politicians etc. Narayan comments: "...all these people had lot of money — the town was racking with it. Only a part of it came out in income-tax returns, and the balance remained hidden in bundled up currency notes in dark boxes."[18] Not only that, people have sold out their souls and do not hesitate to make money out of collections for the disposal of an unclaimed dead body. Narayan writes: "They even haggled with the grave digger and were left with as much money at the end of it all that they drank and made merry for three or four days and gave up temporarily their normal jobs."[19]

The portrayal of Mrs. Margayya is a typical homely Indian housewife whose field of activity is strictly restricted within the four walls of her house. She is very docile and maintains silence in the face of provocation. She never contradicts her husband for she knows that the recent affluence has made Margayya emphatic in all matters whether he is right or wrong. The secondary place Indian woman occupies in the society is a reality even today.

Dr. Pal, like Vasu in *The Man Eater of Malgudi* is a dominating figure. It is he who is largely instrumental in the rise and fall of Margayya's financial edifice. His Ms. *Bed Life* later changed to Domestic Harmony, has fetched Margayya sufficiently large amount of money. It is again with his co-operation Margayya launches a noble scheme for attracting hidden money from the hoarders and black marketeers. Dr. Pal is a very strong characters, self-possessive and determined. He never yields to fate or circumstances. William Walsh comments: "...certain characters have a kind of personality which is both hard and rigid in outline, in which there is, as it were a massively bony structure which does not yield to the environment, which thrusts strongly into it. The conduct of such a character has about it a certain peremptory authority, which we observe in Marco, Vasu and in Dr. Pal. They lack that sensitive accommodation to the interlocutor which the Indian sensibility regards as an essential in human relationship."[20]

The society Narayan presents in the novel, is largely superstitious and full of blind beliefs. They have absolute faith in what the priest prescribes for them to do. Moreover, they are so gullible that they go by the so-called sacred shastras which they believe to have emanated from God himself, little knowing that the scriptures were written by men with their selfish ends. The reasoning faculty is hardly used in drawing reasonable inference at the time of crisis that occurs in their life, with the result that if anything happens, they simply attribute it to gods and goddesses, and leave no stone unturned to appease them at the behest of the priests who are always bent on extracting huge amount from the gullible folk. In case any person like Margayya comes forward to question, the priest has well-prepared, ready-made stories from the so-called sacred scripts to tell and convince him. The story of Markandaya told to Margayya by the priest about the efficacy of Puja has convinced him to undertake forty-day ordeal to acquire wealth. Markandaya, the boy devotee of God Shiv, was destined to die the moment he completed his sixteenth year. He says: "When the moment came, the emissaries of Yama (the God of Death), arrived in order to bind and carry off his life, but he was performing the Puja — and the dark emissaries could not approach him at all! Markandaya remained sixteen to all eternity, and thus defeated death. That particular Puja had that efficacy — and it's that very Puja I am performing on behalf of the child, who is much better for it. 'Will the child live?' asked Margayya, his interest completely roused. 'How can I say?' it's our duty to perform a Puja; the result cannot be our concern. It's Karma."[21] It is this philosophy of Karma that has done irreparable loss to the Indian society.

Margayya is an interesting but sad figure with mixed up philosophy of life; sensitive at heart, he has gone all the way to the top of his profession by dint of his courage and determination only to collapse in the end by sheer negligence on his part to utilize the accumulated wealth in some productive enterprises. Modern in outlook, Margayya has come out openly to oppose the age old customs like tallying of horoscopes, with his material obsession. The ordeal of Laxmi Puja for acquiring wealth is but an outcome of the far-reaching effect of the Hindu culture with its irrational and superstitious approach the Indian masses are reluctant to forget even at the cost of their downfall.

Notes and References

1. Quoted by Shio K. Girla, *R.K. Narayan : His World His Art.* (Meerut: Saru Publishing House, 1984), p. 34.
2. Graham Greene, Introduction to *The Financial Expert,* p. viii.
3. R.K. Narayan, *The Financial Expert* (Mysore Thought Publication, 1981), p. 2.
4. *Ibid.*, p. 20.
5. William Walsh, *R.K. Narayan : A Critical Appreciation* (New Delhi : Allied Publishers Pvt. Ltd., 1983), p. 72.
6. R.K. Narayan, *The Financial Expert,* p. 15.
7. *Ibid.*, p. 17.
8. *Ibid.*, p. 19.
9. *Ibid.* p. 55
10. *Ibid.*, p. 56.
11. M.K. Naik, *The Ironic Vision* (New Delhi : Sterling Publisher Pvt. Ltd., 1983), p. 51.
12. R.K. Narayan, *The Financial Expert,* p. 1.
13. *Ibid.*, p. 152.
14. *Ibid.*
15. *Ibid.*, 45.
16. *Ibid.*, pp. 173-174.
17. *Ibid.*, p. 178.
18. *Ibid.*, p. 158.
19. *Ibid.*, p. 22.
20. William Walsh, *R.K. Narayan : A Critical Appreciation,* pp. 77-78.
21. R.K. Narayan, *The Financial Expert,* p. 26.

VII. *Waiting for the Mahatma*

Waiting for the Mahatma, first published in 1955 by Metheun, London, appears to be a political novel. For it seems to be very much concerned with characters engaged in contemporary political life. However, Narayan is seen ieast interested in the political happenings in the country; and the Gandhian ethics and the values upheld by him seem to pervade the novel. Reference to major political events during India's freedom struggle and the Great Partition thereafter, have no doubt, surfaced, with average Malgudians like Shriram and others stirred to activities on Gandhi's visit. Narayan's chief concern seems to be with how the adolescent Shriram reacts to the events with Bharati rather than Gandhi, serving as guiding spirit around, to shape and mould his mind to maturity.

Narayan is not concerned with the impact Mahatma Gandhi makes on the millions in India, but rather with one individual very ordinary, mentally and morally, with no pretence to any idealism who reacts to this great man. Shriram, the chief character in the novel, has not understood what the whole non-violent non-cooperation movement is about. His is the path of blind obedience. Led by Bharati to join the Gandhian movement, he is easily taken in by Jagdish, a terrorist. Having no ideas of his own, he is carried away by circumstances. When Gandhi visits Malgudi and speaks about untouchability and caste system; he becomes reflective for the first time, and realises that there must be a great deal in what he says. He recalls how Granny bullies that rugged scavenger who comes to sweep the backyard and would not let him approach nearer than ten yards. Having been brought up in the same household and cultural atmosphere, Shriram does not question her attitude to the scavenger. On the contrary, he appears to have taken devilish pleasure in joining the baiting and finding fault with the scavenger's work.

However, Shriram is uneasily conscious of the pointlessness of his life, closetted as it is by layers of customs and female devotion. He is awakened out of his discontended trance or his 'age-long somnolence' as Narayan puts it, by the beautiful young Bharati collecting for Gandhi's Harijan fund. "Your contribution? She asked, shaking a little tin collection box. Shriram's throat went dry and no sound came. He had never been spoken to by any girl before."[1] Shriram fumbles in his jibba side pocket for loose change and brings out an eight anna silver coin and drops it into the slot. The girl smiles at him in return and disappears into the market like a bird gliding on wings. She turns out to be a protege of the Mahatma. In temperament she is almost a projection of the saint himself; and Mahatma Gandhi who appears only intermittingly, by means of this girl is indirectly present throughout the novel.

Shriram has no will of his own and loses much of his identity when he comes under the enchanting spell of the domineering Bharati. "He would not hesitate to fall at the feet of any villain if Bharati desired him to do so. Anything to please her and earn her approval. His whole being acquired a meaning only when he was doing something in relation to Bharati."[2] At the instance of Bharati, Shriram becomes an agent, a radio operator, a protester, whose orbit of operation lies in the mountain villages. He also appears busy pasting notices decrying the war efforts, distributing nationalist literature and demanding that the British clear out.

In absence of Bharati, he comes under the revolutionary photographer, Jagdish by name, who declares himself as the follower of Subhash Chandra Bose. At his behest, Shriram sets fire to the records in a dozen law courts; he derails a couple of trains; he paralyses the work in schools, explodes a bomb outside the agricultural research station. He does these things with a sort of misty responsibility having no fear of the police whom he sees as a remote theoretical body quite detached from him.

A stupid, weak, ignorant young man like Shriram can hardly make himself the dedicated disciple of the Mahatma. It is only in relation with Bharati, an adopted daughter of Gandhi that Shriram's identity comes to light, nor could he take up any challenge against the established customs of the society. There are some exceptional moments in his life when he gears up his strength to go against the priest. Firstly, Shriram declines the suggestion of the priest for shaving off his moustache and the top of his head on Granny's death. Secondly, he has shown admirable courage in pushing the priest out of the way. When he has found that Granny's big toe on the left foot has been seen moving, he cries, "You want us to burn Granny alive, do you? Get out of our way, priest."[3] He kicks away the pile of fuel, lifts Granny's body out of the funeral pyre and places it on the ground. He sprinkles water on her face. The priest stands aside with a doleful expression.

But the submissive attitude, an outcome of cultural atmosphere in which he is brought up, overwhelms him, and he can do nothing but remain a passive onlooker when people okey the priest's verdict, that the old lady should not be taken into the town. The priest's comment is noteworthy:

"The whole town will be wiped out by fire or plague. It is very inauspicious. Do anything you like, but she can't come back into the town."[4] Shriram and all others who throng the old lady are helpless at the stand taken by the priest. Being steeped in superstition, they lack the courage to question the attitude of the priest. Moreover, he is held in high esteem by the public. Challenging the priest, supposed to be the custodian of ths social values, and therefore revered, enrage the whole society. It requires great humanitarians like Mahatma Fule and Babasaheb Ambedkar to fight against the much respected priesthood of the Hindu society and bring about a cultural renaissance in the country.

The old Granny is a realistic portrayal of the custodian of old social values. She bullies and ill-treats the scavenger who comes to sweep the backyard of the house. She does not allow the scavenger to come nearer than ten yards thinking that he would pollute her. Her reaction to the Mahatma's preaching is shocking. "For her the Mahatma was one who preached dangerously who tried to bring untouchables into the temples."[5] She never questions the priest. And in deference to the priest's decision she allows herself to be carried to one of the small abandoned buildings on the riverbank. As enshrined in the holy scripts, she goes away to Benaras. The Fund office manager presents a graphic picture to Shriram who is in jail then : "She is with a number of others, who spend their last years there...waiting to die, ...and look forward to the final fire and the final ablution in the sacred Ganges."[6]

The priest makes it a point to see that the ignorant, uneducated village folk should remain superstitious and God fearing, the base on which the entire priesthood in a sense depends. This has been a selfish motive for all these years, on the part of the priest to exploit to his advantage, the gullible masses of the society. If at all, anybody comes forward with a rational approach, he is very tactfully handled and easily outwitted. On Kanni's objection to the priest for demanding more coins at the time of rituals, the priest softens him saying: "our olders have decreed that the Dear Departed should have two silver coins on his or her chest from the hand of the nearest and the dearest. It is said to smooth out the passage of the soul into further regions. I am only repeating what the shastras say...."[7]

The Shastras, supposed to be God given, have been a powerful weapon in the hands of the priests who are bent upon crushing the ignorant village folk under the weight of social customs and traditions. They have, in a sense, looted and driven the gullible masses to their miserable lot. The priest continues : "Don't think I am after money: I only do things in order to satisfy a great soul known to me for several decades now."[8] "And what happens to the coins? asked the Fund office manager. The priest pretended to ignore the question, but Kanni said, 'It goes the way of other coins that is, into a priest's money-box.'."[9] But the priest is cunning and shrewd. He has twisted the matter, giving it a philosophical meaning that has silenced both Kanni and the Fund Office Manager.

On Gandhi's visit to Malgudi, Mr. Natesh, the Municipal Council chairman, makes elaborate preparations to receive the Mahatma in his building, renovating it afresh..., spending two lacs of rupees; his lawns and garden alone casting twenty five thousand rupees. Mr. Natesh enjoys the privilege of receiving Mahatma Gandhi, no doubt. But it has come as a thunderbolt on the Municipal Council chairman when Mahatma Gandhi prefers to stay in a hut of a city sweeper, instead of in a palatial building specially prepared for him. Immediately beyond Nalappa's Grove are the sweepers' huts, "Just hovels, put together with rags, tinsheets, and shreds of coconut matting, all crowded in anyhow, with scratchy fowls cackling about and children growing in the street dust."[10] One fails to understand Mahatma Gandhi's logic in preferring one of these huts located on the riverbanks. Does Mahatma Gandhi want ot show that he is one amongst them? For, we should not overlook the comment by a Malgudian who says: "let us not forget that Mahatmaji takes up his residence at Birla House at Delhi and Calcutta...."[11] Is it that he pities them, that he has all sympathy for what they are doing? Or is it because Mahatma Gandhi likes their profession very much, and that he wants them to be perfect in their traditional jobs? Whatever is the Mahatma's logic behind this exercise of body and mind, one thing is certain that he wants to pat them for the commendable work they have been doing of cleaning the city of its dirt. Nevertheless, he has preached brotherhood, that the high caste people should think them as their fellow brethren and that they should not practise untouchability towards these low caste people. "Reformers looked on with wrath and horror, but did little also, since as an untouchable class they lived outside the town limits, beyond Nallapa's Grove, whereby nobody went, and they used only a part of the river on its downward course."[12]

The Hindu caste system has kept a large part of the population segregated from the mainstream of life. The sweepers' colony located on the banks of the river, away from Malgudi, is evidently the outcome of this unnatural caste system supposed to be created by God. It is a pity that Mahatma Gandhi who has preached brotherhood, and fought for abolition of untouchability, should defend the system of Chaturvarna. Mahatma

Gandhi was never seen advising the untouchables to give up their traditional jobs. He had not taken upon himself the task of eradicating the "Varna Vyevastha' as he did whole-heartedly help bring the country on the road to political independence. Shiv M. Pandeya writes : Narayan presents "Gandhi as primarily interested in liberating the spirit of India; the rest of the levels of his action follow as an inevitable corollary of his basic interest."[13]

Gandhi's too much emphasis on God has made the ignorant village folk fatalistic; and they believe that everything on the earth is pre-ordained and that it is the Almighty to see that justice prevails in the society. On Shriram's request to kindly guide him, Mahatma Gandhi answers: "Well, young friend, if God wills it, you will do great things, trust in Him, and you will be all right."[14] While touring the famine-stricken villages Gandhi comforts the suffering people by talking to them about God. All these years the low caste people looked to God for salvation but the untouchability that has stuck to them by caste is still being practised. That they are being treated worse than animals, is the fact nobody can deny.

Narayan touches upon the problem of orphans, Gandhi has taken up in his life. Bharati refuses to marry Shriram unless she gets sanction from the Mahatma. In the end, Gandhi okeys their marriage but with an additional responsibility that Bharati be mother and father to thirty children, which she gladly takes upon herself and accepts the motherhood of the orphans. This is a challenging role Bharati plays much against the social traditions prevalent in the society.

She remains a true disciple of Mahatma Gandhi. She has an absolute faith in him and does not budge an inch from the ideals shown by him. It is but natural for Bharati to move along the guidelines as and when instructed. For, her father died when she was born in 1920. After her mother's death she is practically adopted by the local Sewak Sangh, and she has not known any other since, except her Godfather, Mahatma Gandhi who has named her Bharati. She describes her line of action to Shriram: "I do whatever I am asked to do by the Sewak Sangh, sometimes they ask me to go and teach people spinning and tell them about Mahatmaji's ideas. Sometimes they send me to villages and poor quarters. I meet them and talk to them and do a few things. I attend to Mahatmaji's needs."[15] Despite repeated requests and persuasions from Shriram to marry him, Bharati remains steady and firm in her decision and relents only when the Mahatma gives his approval in the end. This resolute, young and beautiful

Bharati who has been a domineering figure all alone, should feel drawn to the weak and timid Shriram, remains a puzzle.

Mr. Natesh, the Municipal Council Chairman is portraited as an orthodox hypocrite, actively busy with the preparations to receive the Mahatma. He spends about two lacs to renovate his building and hangs on the walls the photographs of almost all the national leaders to show that he too is a true patriot moving along the line shown by great leaders like the Mahatma. Before him, Natesh appears helpless and tongue-tied. But he is red with anger when Mahatma Gandhi beckons an urchin of a sweeper and has him hoisted on his diwan. He cried in his heart of hearts, "Oh lord, all the world's gutters are on this boy, and he is to leave a permanent stain on that Kashmir counterpane."[16]

Mahatma Gandhi appears in person addressing the Malgudians. Somehow he does not click with the people in Malgudi. Gandhi does not seem to inspire Shriram either, except as a means to secure Bharati for his bride. He remains almost untouched by the atrocities in Calcutta and Noakhali except in so far as they affect Bharati. In fact, Narayan's chief concern in *Waiting for the Mahatma* seems not to highlight the inhuman and cruel events during the Great Partition but only to pinpoint the attention of the readers on the course of the life and love of the couple. After Gandhi's assassination, the novel ends with the supposed union of Shriram and Bharati.

Narayan does not seem to project a 'Gandhi image' nor does he try to involve us in any historio-political events however significant they are to the people in general. The hero here, is Shriram, a poor middle class family young man suddenly come to wealth, regretting his ingratitude to his self-sacrificing Granny, a conservative religious lady. Though the progress of events is viewed through the consciousness of Shriram, the apathy of the Malgudians to doctrines of non-violence and satyagraha is also made clear in no uncertain terms. The priests are looked upon with great reverence and the public by and large remain passive, looking crippled and tongue-tied before these so-called custodians of social values, however selfish they are, filling their own coffers. The sense of awakening amongst Malgudians that we observe, is a welcome sign. But Narayan sees to it that the old order prevails, bringing everything to normalcy. And this he has done remarkably well with a sense of humour that pervaded even the most tragic situations in life.

Notes and References

1. R.K. Narayan, *Waiting for the Mahatma* (Mysore : Indian Thought Publications, 1981), p. 13.
2. *Ibid.*, p. 109.
3. *Ibid.*, p. 123.
4. *Ibid.*, p. 124.
5. *Ibid.*, p. 41.
6. *Ibid.*, p. 138.
7. *Ibid.*, p. 121.
8. *Ibid.*, p. 122.
9. *Ibid.*, p. 121.
10. *Ibid.*, p. 23.
11. *Ibid.*, p. 26.
12. *Ibid.*, p. 24.
13. Shiv M. Pandeya, *Studies in Modern Fiction* (New Delhi : Vikas Publishing House Pvt. Ltd., 1983), p. 195.
14. R.K. Narayan, *Waiting for the Mahatma*, p. 51.
15. *Ibid.*, p. 39.
16. *Ibid.*, p. 31.

VIII. The Guide

The Guide published in 1958, is one of the most popular novels, which has been successfully filmed, and fetched for its writer, the Sahitya Academy Award, in 1960. *The Guide* is not a social chronicle as such. However, the problem of the gullible masses steeped in superstition, the problems of mal-adjustment in marriage, of guilt and sin are some of the social evils, Narayan touches upon in the novel.

The drought in Mysore is the source on which the novel is based. Narayan writes, "A severe drought had dried up all the rivers and tanks; Krishnaraja Sagar, an enormous reservoir feeding channels that irrigated thousands of acres, had also become dry, and its bed, a hundred and fifty feet deep, was now exposed to the sky with fissures and cracks, revealing an ancient submerged temple.... As a desperate measure, the Municipal Council organized a prayer for rains. A group of Brahmins stood knee-deep in water (procured at great cost) on the dry bed of Kaveri, fasted, prayed, and chanted certain mantras continuously for eleven days. On the twelfth day it rained, and brought relief to the country side."[1] *The Guide* is the story of a man whose apparently whimsical nature of interfering in the affairs of others lands him in an awkward situation. It is the spicy tale of a people who take an ex-prisoner for a saint. It is a farce on a Swami whose mind hovers on Bondas while preaching the Bhagwad Geeta. The novel ends with the fake Swami sacrificing his life at the altar of Rain god.

The chief characters in the novel Raju, Rosie, and Marco are but the products of Hindu culture coming down to us for generations. And though, they are seen discarding the age old traditions, the half-hearted attempts on their part could only make them a laughing stock in society. Raju flouts the suggestion of his mother that he should marry Lalitha, a girl from the village. He does not consider it, possibly for the reason that this kind of proposal is useless and outdated, and he wants to marry the girl of his heart. Later, we find him emotionally involved in the illegitimate love affair with the wife of Marco: an act certainly not in keeping with the Indian values. He also gives up the business of his father and becomes a tourist guide, a new profession wonderfully suited to his nature. "It was in his nature to get involved in other people's interests and activities. Otherwise, Raju often reflected, I should have grown like a thousand other normal persons, without worries in life."[2] This is a remarkable change seen in the attitude of Raju who adopts a new profession of his liking thereby discarding the traditional views of the society.

Marco is portrayed as cultured, and broadminded in the sense that he accepts Rosie, a dancing class girl as his wife. But he pays only lip service to a casteless, conventionless society that is slowly, very slowly taking shape before him. The woman's point of view has been totally consigned to oblivion by Marco. A woman is not gadget by any chance is evidently revealed in the character of Rosie who is replete with desires and spirits. And hence, there are bickerings in the married life of Rosie and Marco. Som Dev rightly remarks : "If Rosie is driven to the arms of a stranger, it is partly not her fault.... Had he considered the basic needs of the woman whom he takes for a wife, perhaps their union would not have sundered in this manner. He has offered insult to the womanhood, and in turn the womanhood in Rosie raises its hood to leave 'fang-marks' on him."[3] What Marco really wants is a wife like the servant Joseph who is in his opinion, a wonderful man. Secondly, for all his outward appearance, he looks down upon dancing, and misunderstands the art as something below his rank and position. "Old prejudices die-hard, and Marco for all his erudition looked upon dancing as just street acrobatics, and he killed Rosie's instincts for life and love of art by denying her both of them."[4]

Rosie belongs to a family dedicated to the temple as dancers, and yet she obtains an M.A. in Economics. Not only that, she discards the convention and enters in matrimonial agreement with Marco. But to her utter shock, she discovers that he is more interested in the sculptured figures on walls and stones in the caves, than in his wife who is the living embodiment of these images. Dead and decaying things have attracted him, but not things that live and move and swing their heads. Her position in his company is no better than that of an animal. For Rosie "followed him, day after day, like a dog-waiting on his grace."[5] In the company of Raju too, she fares no better. She feels like one of those parrots in a cage taken around village fairs : the position of a Hindu housewife realistically presented by Narayan. In utter helplessness she gives vent to her feelings: "it is far better to end one's life on his (Marco's) doorstep."[6]

The submissive attitude in Narayan's major characters is but the outcome of a tremendous impact of the Hindu culture and its traditions on their mind; their will power lies crippled under the weight. They do not control events but let the events control them. They appear as helpless creatures, torn by desires and tossed this way and that by the caprice of fortune.

After his release from the jail Raju finds shelter in a shrine where he is taken for a saint by Velan and others. When the drought hits the countryside, he is forced to undertake fast unto death much against his will. "It occurred to him that the best course for him would be to run away from the whole thing". But he feared that "any one might spot him within half an hour.... They might drag him back to the spot and punish him for fooling them.... He thought suddenly that if they would at least leave him alone at night, he could make some arrangement and survive the ordeal. The ordeal then would be only standing knee-deep in water (if they could find it), muttering the litany for eight hours."[7] He surrenders himself completely to the circumstances. And Raju dies a ruined man, not because he wanted to die, but circumstances so conspire that the only alternative before him is to become an unwilling martyr.

The only character that appears rational and unyielding to circumstances is Marco who devotes his life to the study of cave paintings. He seeks Raju's help while doing so, which he accepts readily, guiding him to the caves. It is quite possible that Marco is aware of Rosie's love affairs with Raju who forgets his food and everything for her company. However, Marco appears quite undisturbed, fully absorbed in his studies. Nor does he rebukes Rosie for what she is doing. This appears to be a calculated step on his part. The time he completes his study at Malgudi, he makes a clean breast of everything and disowns Rosie saying: "You are here because I'm not a ruffian. But you are not my wife. You are a woman who will go to bed with any one that flatters your antics."[8] Even Rosie, suppressing her guilt-conscience all along, confesses it later: "Any other husband would have throttled me then and there. He tolerated my company for nearly a month, even after knowing what I had done."[9]

Marco is like an oasis in the desert of Malgudi. This is but natural, for he hails from the metropolitan city of India. He is different from the locals and yokels of Malgudi. But he too is eccentric in the sense, he remains wedded to the study of paintings inside the caves forgetting Rosie's basic needs altogether. This has resulted in family disorder culminating in Marco's parting away from Rosie. Marco and Rosie, though artists in their individual spheres, are not happy in marriage. Lack of understanding is the major cause for them to be miserable in life. Further, fidelity which is the mainstay of husband and wife is missing from the wedlock of the two.

The kind of helplessness and the miserable lot in which the characters are placed, make them believe that everything on the earth is pre-ordained and that no amount of human efforts can ease the situation, Raju convinces the gullible masses with — "what must happen, must happen; no power on earth or in heaven can change its course, just as no one can change the course of that river."[10] As a matter of fact, what happens in the life of Raju, Rosie or Marco, is the result of their own deeds. It is their inherent weakness or fault or the misdeed that has brought about the catastrophe in the characters. Raju becomes a prisoner not because of some divine agency, the utter vagary of providence, but as a logical result of deviation from moral duty. Raju violates the social behest and commits adultery while getting involved with the wife of Marco. But the nemesis falls on him not because he is immoral from the sexual point of view, but because he is immoral from the point of view of avarice. Som Dev rightly remarks: "At first he grabs the wife of another person, and then he grabs the money. The first unsettles him socially, and the second sees him clapped into prison."[11] What Raju does in the novel, is the part of his own will and not that of the providence. Fate stands within the confines of his own doing and will.

Then again, Raju is caught in the coils of his own self-deception. He is aware that he could not make a living out of hard work. When he finds that food is coming to him unasked, he adjusts himself to the inner sanctum of the Shrine and begins to play the saint, the role Velan has given him. "He had not trained himself to make a living out of hard work. Food was coming to him unasked now. If he went away somewhere else certainly nobody was going to take the trouble to bring him food in return for just waiting for it."[12] Accidentally, Raju gets himself invovled, through the misunderstanding of an idiot boy, in undertaking a total fast as an act of intercession to the gods for rain when there is a drought. Raju has to play the saint. He could not help himself, though he wanted to cry to those that thronged round him, "Get out, all of you, and leave me alone. I am not the man to save you. No power on earth can save you if you are doomed."[13]

Every ordinary action that he performs is deemed as an action signifying deep mystical connotation. Every word that he utters is revered as a word of wisdom. Sometimes Raju feels guilty at his own duplicity. At others he tries to debunk himself a little. Again there are moments when he floats without calculation into some spiritual realms where everything he utters is profound and important, and he is startled at the wisdom welling from the depth of his being. Raju's nature is but the product of several influence — the drought, the plight of the people, the context of tradition and religion which force him into his predicament.

Raju is essentially an oriental, his conscious personality shaped and formulated by values, judgements, prides and prejudices of a typical South

Indian Hindu society. In spite of its impact right from his childhood, Raju exhibits the individualistic drive and initiative to throw aside the despairing burden of these values and follow the dictates of his deeper urge.

Raju invites obvious comparison with Kalo, the protagonist in Bhabani Bhattacharya's *He Who Rides a Tiger*. Both Raju and Kalo deceive society and are carried away by their deception until a point comes when it is difficult to undo the enormous lies. However, while Kalo throws away the mask and goes back where he began, Raju dies a ruined man at the altar of his own deception. Meenakshi Mukharjee rightly observes: "In Bhattacharya's book Kalo's deception is a deliberate act of revenge against society. Raju in *The Guide*, on the other hand, drifts into the role of a sadhu willy-nilly, and once he finds himself cast in the role of an ascetic he attempts to perform the act with gusto, partly for the sake of self-preservation, partly because it suits his personality, wonderfully."[14]

The crocodile, an archetypal symbol of hypocrisy, provides a fitting parallel of the fake saint in Raju. We are told that it infests the river which flows by the side of Raju's sanctuary, but no one in the village has actually seen it, though they all know it is there. It is a myth which like Raju's sainthood, becomes a reality only in death; for it is seen for the first time when the drought which is to kill Raju, also kills it. In its death, it enriches the villagers who find quite a treasure in its belly as Raju's death brings into limelight the fame (perhaps rains too) to the village.

The society as presented by Narayan in the novel is traditional and superstitious. The people are illiterate and poor. And they are always on the look out for some divine help to solve their problems. As a result, even the ex-convict Raju is mistaken for a holy man. He has been pulled into so-called holiness by the gullible country folk including Velan. The situation is taken full advantage of by hypocrite Raju. It is a frontal attack made against the fake pretenders, made much of, by the ignorant masses like Velan. "Narayan grabs the Indian mind fully with all its superstitious comprehension or life, gullibility, an appreciation of pseudo-scientific things and that simplicity which is the warp and woof of our life."[15]

Whenever there is a drought, people pray and fast and it rains(?). Even after a candid confession by Raju of his illegitimate love affair with Rosie and his subsequent conviction for forgery, society compels him to undertake a total fast to the bitter end. Raju said "Velan, it's raining in the hills. I can feel it coming up under my feet, up my legs — He sagged down."[16] The end is obscure. It is curious that the irrefutable logic of the situation should evade a sensitive writer like Narayan. But the vagueness and obscurity are not the result of the failure of the artist in Narayan.

The temples and worshippers present a strange sight in India. Particularly in the place of pilgrimage, we notice a typical atmosphere. Here is the holyman called Raju, ex-convict finding asylum in the pillared hall of the Mangla village. Men and women throng round the place in the spirit of the holy worship. They do all this for the fake and hypocrite Raju, wasting their time, energy, everything. He is looked upon with profound awe; they touch the water at his feet and sprinkle it over their heads. Above all, the pen of wandering journalist spreads the miracle, and even the government machinery is brought in full swing. The present-day society is no better. There are many such hypocrite saints exploiting the gullible masses of rural India, making pray to their passion, innocent women who come to have their 'holy darshan'. There is no way out unless the leaders of masses come forward with a rational approach and coax and convince the gullible masses to give up their traditional outlook.

One cannot help quoting Raju here for his plausible solution to the problems when Velan approaches him for the first time. He quotes the Buddha, citing the example of a grief-stricken woman. A woman once went wailing to the great Buddha clasping her dead baby to her bosom. The Buddha said, "Go into every home in this city and find one where death is unknown; if you find such a place, fetch me a handful of mustard from there, and then I'll teach you how to conquer death".[17] Toeing the same line, Raju convinces Velan to accept the fact that there is no person without problems in his life. Such rational approach will certainly help the masses to get rid of superstitions and blind beliefs in their lives.

Rosie is portrayed as the representative of a new class of women who have the opportunity to be released from the conventional confinement to join colleges and universities. Rosie acquires a Master's degree in Economics : no mean achievement in relation to her place in a scheme of castes in Hindu society. On the one hand, her education has enhanced in her, the awareness of her own individuality. On the other, it pits her against the society which still has certain well-defined attitudes towards women. Moreover, the class to which she belongs is looked down upon as a low community which does not deserve equal status with the higher caste. Despite the hurdles, she has established her own individuality. Her inner being, it appears, is not prepared to go on playing the traditional role of a suppressed Indian wife for the rest of her life.

Rosie is an artist par excellence. She has an aesthetic sense and wishes to nurture it. She is of course, grateful to Raju who has made her a national celebrity as the greatest dancer of Bharat Natyam. Rosie now has become Nalini. But, the same Raju remains responsible for the abrupt end of her career. He has made Rosie's dancing art a commercial venture tainted with the vices of cheap popularity. The loud fanfare with which it storms, defeats the very purpose on which Rosie is so keen. And yet Rosie shows a remarkable consideration for Raju and we feel, he scarcely deserves it. She slogs day in and day out, parts with her diamonds, and give dance performances enough to raise funds to satisfy an expensive lawyer to save him from jail. And Raju, instead of feeling grateful, grows jealous of her self-reliance. Raju later admits : "Neither Marco nor I had any place in her life, which had its own sustaining vitality and which she herself had underestimated all along."[18]

Rosie has had a bitter experience in the house of Raju whose mother, an old orthodox woman, refuses to accept her on the ground that she belongs to a different caste. His uncle's insulting questions make her lower her head in shame and disgust "Are you of our caste? No. Our class? No. Do we know you? No. Do you belong to this house? No. In that case, why are you here? After all, you are a dancing girl, we do not admit them in our families."[19] Rosie survives the shocks and shows to the world that she too has an individual status and aspirations in life, which she tries to accomplish all her life. However, her guilty conscience makes her restless and in the end we see her painful longing to die at the threshold of her husband's house.

Velan, another important character, discoverer of Raju's (non-existent) sainthood and his self-appointed first devotee, is a prisoner of his own credulity, so much so that even when Raju talks to him all night, making a clean breast of everything, he refuses to accept that the saint is a charlatan; and Velan's self-chosen bondage to his own role as a devotee ensures the perpetuation of Raju's bondage of enforced sainthood. This is for a lack of education and superstitious attitudes which make the pseudo saints exploit them to their fullest advantage.

The society by and large is God-fearing and deeply religious. They have absolute faith in 'Almighty' and pray Him day and night for their salvation. Not only that, every care is taken to see that their children and grandchildren should also imitate them in their worship to God. Raju narrates his routine at the daybreak, when his father wakes him up at the shattering cry by an eccentric cockerel: "I washed myself at the well, smeared holy ash on my forehead, stood before the framed pictures of Gods hanging high up on the wall, and recited all kinds of sacred verse in a loud, ringing tone."[20]

The country folks with all their attending poverty, innocence and gullibility are well represented by Velan and others of Mangla. They depend on rains for their crops and for everything. When the drought hits the countryside, they quarrel at the waterhole for priorities, with fear, desperation, and lamentation in their voices. In utter helplessness, they turn to Swami. Raju merely raises his hand and stares as if to say. "Be peaceful; everything will be all right; I will fix it with the Gods."[21] The reference to God here and there confirms the prevailing religious outlook in the Hindu culture. The mere utterance of God is enough to transform their life. For, whatever happens, they believe, it is for the Almighty to save us. 'How can we ever help it,' is the mentality of the people. And Velan and others find the holy Swami as the proper person to undertake the fast for rains. They compel him to fast unto death. The rains do not come. It is only the optical illusion of the dying Raju when he says, 'It's raining in the hills'.

The civility that Raju and Velan display to each other and which exists in everybody is an essential ingredient of the tradition that has come down to us. The society, says William Walsh, in *Critical Appreciation*, "appears, for all its hierarchical stiffness, to prize the mobility of relationships higher than the status of the solitary individual. It also tells us something about the attitude of the author himself, who sees beneath the details of poverty and hypocrisy, the residual, enduring significance of his subjects as human beings."[22]

The orthodox Indian sentiment denies the spectacle of sex play which the modern novelists with all seriousness display realistically in the novels. Narayan remains contented with the psychological changes in Rosie, for she in the end, gets drawn to her husband, to the chagrin of the lover. Sex has been treated with cursory description. He restricts himself, to the situation of the lovers engaged in the act but there is a suspicion of morals creeping in stealthily. Perhaps to his mind it results in social debacle. Narayan at once accepts the external facts of life pertaining to the reaction of sex in the novel rather than putting deeper shades of emotion caused by it.

Narayan has taken a radical view of the subject of marriage. Because of lack of understanding and a lot of bickerings in the married life of Rosie, she gets drawn to Raju for emotional gratification. However,

Narayan sees to it that relations between Raju and Rosie get strained and that Marco, Rosie's husband, appears triumphant in seeing the seducer (Raju) of his wife being clapped into prison.

Narayan has a dig at the social as well as political life of the country. The rich, though immoral in their private life, become influential in the society, and their show of social service gets undue importance as we find in case of Raju himself. His own remarks are enough to sum up the social scene. Raju says, "Well, the prohibition law was not for a man of my influence. I had managed to get a medical certificate to say that I needed alcohol for my welfare". He further continues, "Through my intimacy with all sorts of people, I know what was going on behind scenes in the government, at the market, at Delhi, on the racecourse, and who was going to be who in the coming week, I could get a train reservation at a moment's notice, relieve a man summoned to jury work, re-instate a dismissed official, — all of which seemed to me important social services, an influence worth buying at the current market price."[23] The rules and government laws enacted from time to time are meant only for the have-nots; the rich remain entirely untouched: a reality presented by Narayan in the novel.

There is a clash of caste, class interest and persistence of time honoured customs and the old values on the one hand, and the awakening of modern, social and moral structure on the other. Crumbling of traditions and changing social values form the background of the novel. Narayan exposes the absurd self-deception and ritual deceitfulness among a people who credulously dream of things that are not there. Their vain attempts to hide themselves from the simple prosaic realities are almost farcical. Here is a strange transformation of the protagonist from a tourist guide into a jailbird, then a fake sadhu into a famous martyr.

The characters are seen adapting to the new ideas. The old ones do not relish the new-fangled views of the sprouting generation. The novelist seems to be an upholder of the old values. The present-day permissiveness does not appeal to his temperament.

Notes and References

1. R.K. Narayan, *My Days : A Memoir* (Mysore : Indian Thought Publications, 1974), p.167.
2. R.K. Narayan, *The Guide* (Mysore : Indian Thought Publications, 1958), p. 9.
3. Som Dev, *The Guide : A Critical Appreciation* (Bareilly : Prakash Book Depot, 1982), p.115.

4. *Literary Criterion*, Vol. IV, 1961.
5. R.K. Narayan, *The Guide*, p. 151.
6. *Ibid.*, p. 220.
7. *Ibid.*, p. 111.
8. *Ibid.*, p. 152.
9. *Ibid.*, p. 201.
10. *Ibid.*, p. 22.
11. Som Dev, *The Guide : A Critical Appreciation*, p. 159.
12. R.K. Narayan, *The Guide*, p. 33.
13. *Ibid.*, p. 235.
14. Quoted by Dr. Varshney, *R.K. Narayan, And his The Guide* (Bareilly : Student Store, 1979), p.72.
15. Som Dev, *The Guide : A Critical Appreciation*, p. 66.
16. R.K. Narayan, *The Guide*, p. 247.
17. *Ibid.*, p. 14-15.
18. *Ibid.*, p. 223.
19. *Ibid.*, p. 169.
20. *Ibid.*, p. 11.
21. *Ibid.*, p. 94.
22. William Walsh, *R.K. Narayan : A Critical Appreciation* (New Delhi : Allied Publishers Pvt. Ltd., 1983), p. 117.
23. R.K. Narayan, *The Guide*, p. 196.

IX. The Man Eater of Malgudi

The Man Eater of Malgudi, one of the mature novels of Narayan's creative genius, first published in 1961 by The Viking Press, New York, is the outstanding work of fiction based on a mythological story of Bhasmasur. It is at once a recreation of the old Hindu myth and a thoughtful presentation of two diametrically opposed attitudes to life, the inadequacies of both being ironically exposed.

Narayan's use of Bhasmasur myth in the novel was a piece of conscious efforts. As he told an audience at Columbia University 1972, "At some point in one's writing career, one takes a fresh look at the so-called myths and legends and finds a new meaning in them. After writing a number of novels and short stories based on the society around me, some years ago suddenly I came across a theme which struck me as an excellent piece of mythology in modern dress. It was published under the title, *The Man Enter of Malgudi*.... I based this story on a well known mythological episode, the story of Mohini and Bhasmasur."[1] Based on the mythological story of Bhasmasur, *The Man Eater of Malgudi* presents a taxidermist of inimical spirit with the characteristics of rakshas. The silent and peaceful life of Malgudi gets disturbed with his coming to occupy the upper attic of Natraj, the chief protagonist of the novel. In the person of Vasu, the taxidermist, is embodied a ferocious spirit who carries within himself a tiny seed of destruction, and is found dead in the end. However, the chief task of Vasu is to expose absurd pretensions of Natraj and his bohemian circle, making the book a comic allegory of India with its conflicting traditions of epic violence. The story implies a fatalistic outlook of the Indians praying for an emergence of some Saviour in their distress, or any miracle to occur to cure the ills of the Indian society. Narayan here shows himself as an exponent of Hindu culture with its philosophy enshrined in the so-called sacred shastras which the Hindus held so dear to their heart.

We come across numerous changes in Malgudi. But the Malgudians have miserably failed to change themselves with the passage of time. They stick to their age old customs and traditions and the approach they adopt even today is one of a fatalist little knowing that it is mainly the human efforts that matter. Natraj, the chief protagonist of *The Man Eater of Malgudi* is portrayed as a cowardly, submissive and good for nothing fellow. He sits in his press all the time surrounded by the monosyllabic poet, and Mr. Sen the journalist — who simply waste their time. Vasu enters the quiet scene of Malgudi and Natraj gets totally upset, for he has never seen in his life a person so savage and wild by nature. He looks totally helpless before him. He has no courage to contradict or oppose the statements of Vasu. The submissive and fatalistic attitude he has developed under his orthodox parents never encourage him to face the challenges of life. No wonder, that a person of this mentality leaves everything to the divine power, hopefully praying for help. It is in this context that Ramesh Shrivastav's remark claims due attention. He rightly points out : "like the growth of an adolescent to a young, educated modern man, Malgudi — "the microcosm of traditional Indian society" changes from 1930 "to the modern times but without losing its basic character."[2] While Japan triumphantly raises its head upward even after a complete ruin of its two big industrial centres — Hiroshima and Nagasaki — in World War II, Indians still consult their astrologers or palmists for good or bad events in their life. And whatever they achieve they attribute it to gods and goddesses which they daily worship for hours together. Natraj proudly says, "I hung up a framed picture of goddess Laxmi poised on her lotus holding aloft the bounties of earth in her four hands, and through her grace I did not do too badly."[3]

Natraj cuts a sorry figure before Vasu. He is overwhelmed by the spirit and indomitable courage of the taxidermist. Afraid of him, Natraj says : "I was longing for a word with Vasu. I stood like a child at the treadle, hoping he would look at me and nod that all would be well again. He was a terrible specimen of human being no doubt, but I wanted to be on talking terms with him."[4]

He is a demonaic creature who possesses enormous strength, strange powers, and genius but recognised no sort of restraints of man or God. Sastri, an orthodox minded Sanskrit semi-scholar consoles Natraj by quoting examples from *The Ramayan* to prove that "every rakshas gets swollen with his ego. He thinks he is invincible, beyond every law. But sooner or later something or other will destroy him."[5] Unable to arrive at any concrete solution to check Vasu's attempts to kill the temple elephant, Natraj looses his mental balance, and in a fit of temper, gives a piercing loud cry for help that has attracted a huge crowd including the Municipal Committee Chairman who has stopped his Inaugural Address on the eve of Radha-Krishna marriage festival.

Natraj believes God Krishna is really an incarnation of Vishnu who has saved Gajendra, he would again come to the rescue of the same animal. The sight of the God, the sound of music, the rhythm of cymbals and scent of Jasmine and incense induces in him a temporary indifference to everything and softens his uneasy heart. Natraj remembers "The elephant of mythology who stepped into a lake and had his leg caught in the jaws of a mighty crocodile; and the elephant triumpeted helplessly, struggled and in the end desperately called on Vishnu, who immediately appeared and gave him the strength to come ashore out of the jaws of the crocodile."[6]

He acts like one possessed. It is with this belief in mind perhaps Natraj lets out a terrific cry which drowns the noise of children, music everything. "Oh, Vishnu ! I howled, save our elephant and save all the innocent men and women who are going to pull the chariot. You must come to our rescue now."[7]

God appears specifically very attentive to the problems of the so-called high caste people. Natraj makes a fervent plea for help, and lo, Vishnu listens to him. The same night when Vasu is to kill the temple elephant, he stamps himself to death. But one is at loss to understand why God should turn a deaf ear to the sufferings of the underdogs at the inhuman and cruel hands of the Brahmins. For, He has never come to their rescue even in the worst days of their life. Where was He when they cried aloft for help against social injustice, tortures, merciless killings, rapes and what not? Nobody listened to them, not even gods, and that too, for centuries together. But the Brahmins systematically convinced them all that it was because of their past sins, that they have miserable plight in this life. They had to remain contented and wait for good days. What a sheer waste of time and energy, being totally inactive thus. But the miseries and sufferings the underdogs faced in their life we never come across in the novels of R.K. Narayan. "How one wishes," writes Ramesh Shrivastav, "that Narayan, too, like Mark Twain, had sweetened the bitterest truths of life, coated with laughter the pangs and sufferings of a subjugated and dumb race...."[8]

Narayan sets aside all the social issues which have plagued the country and takes up a mythological story of Bhasmasur: a totally irrelevant one in the present make up of the society, when one notices a tremendous upsurge in the field. Narayan's refusal to see life beyond its ambiguous trappings leads him to a somewhat misplaced and distorted world view. In *The Man Eater of Malgudi*, it is evident that Narayan takes the plunge and is not afraid of being called a teller of fables and fairy tales. And so all Natraj does is to go to the temple on the fateful day and let out a terrific cry. William Walsh rightly says :

> The truth is that the Hindu myths and religious parables, like D.H. Lawrence's congregational hymns, are important not as theological scaffolding to the fiction but in being part of a whole economy of feeling itself sunk deep into the constitution of the novelist. These things are present and influential not as dogma or metaphysics but as a part of a mode of perception.... They flow in and out of writer's thought and touch. The religious sense of Indian myth is part of Narayan's grip of reality, of his particular view of human life and his individual way of placing and ordering human feeling and experience. What one can say about Narayan without qualification is that he embodies the pure spirit of Hinduism.[9]

The demons in ancient Hindu mythology are seen actually skilled in learned and scientific pursuit and capable of the hardest penance with which they secure valuable boons from the gods. Sukracharya, the guru of the assuras was a learned scholar who could bring the dead to life with his skill in *Sanjivani Vidhya*; Ravana was well-versed in the Vedas; and Mayasur, who designed the wonderful assembly hall for the pandavas, was an accomplished architect. This description of the rakshas fits Vasu perfectly in all respects. His very appearance is rakshas like. A large man about six feet tall, he has, 'a bull neck', a 'tanned face', a 'hammer fist', and large powerful eyes under thick eyebrows, "a large forehead and a shock of unkempt hair, like a black halo."[10] His clothes, loud and gaudy, ('red check bush shirt and field grey trousers') are all of a piece with his appearance; so is his vehicle, a jeep which he drives at break neck speed. Natraj aptly describes him as "the prince of darkness."[11]

The portrayal of Vasu is based on the mythical Bhasmasur. He acquired a special boon that everything he touched should be scorched, while nothing could ever destroy him. Humanity suffered a lot. Then we notice God Vishnu himself incarnating as a dancer of great beauty, named Mohini with whom Bhasmasur became infatuated. She promised to yield to him only if he imitated all the gestures and movements of her own dancing. And the moment Mohini placed her palms on her head, the demon followed the same gesture and was reduced to ashes. Drawn on these lines, whatever purpose Vasu serves in the novel, his views on the celebrations and Hindu festivals are thought provoking. It is a sheer waste of national income spending lacs and crores of rupees just on the celebrations like Radha Krishna Marriage in the whole of India, while a large section of the Indian population go without food and shelter. Vasu says: "If I had any authority, I'd prohibit celebrations of this kind as a waste of national energy."[12] At the Kumbha Mela, thousands and thousands gather; less than the original number go back home — cholera, or small spox, or they just got trampled. Vasu asks Natraj, "How many temple chariots have run over the onlookers at every festival gathering? Have you ever paused to think why it's arranged thus?"[13] Of course, no one will appreciate his wild plan for killing the temple elephant for whatever reasons.

Vasu thinks himself as all powerful and invincible. And as Shastri hinted earlier, his ego gets swollen with the feeling as in the case of mythical Bhasmasur or Mahisha, the asura — who meditated and acquired a boon of immortality and invincibility. His conduct with Natraj is very rough. In fact, he should have been grateful to him for allowing him to stay in his upper attic rent free. On the contrary he brings in all kinds of dead animals and sets the whole neighbourhood against the innocent Natraj. Not only that, he entertains all sorts of girls of the town. Sometimes a slim girl goes by, sometimes a fair one, sometimes an in-between type, sometimes a fuzzy haired woman. Above all, he sets the House Rent controller against Natraj. He has filed a complaint against him as a landlord.

Like the mythical Bhasmasur, Vasu, drawn on the same lines, is found dead in the upper attic of Natraj. As Rangi, the temple dancer narrates later, Vasu hates mosquitoes. She sees him flourish his arms like a mad man, fighting them off as they buzz about his ears to suck his blood. The next moment she hears a sharp noise like a thunder clap. He evidently traps a couple of mosquitoes by bringing the flat of his palm with all his might. It is also the end of Vasu. Shastri's approach is traditional. He says: "Every demon appears in the world with a special boon of indestructibility. Yet the universe has survived all the rakshasas that were ever born. Every demon carries within him, unknown to himself, a tiny seed of self-destruction, and goes up in thin air at the most unexpected moment. Otherwise what is to happen to humanity."[14]

Vasu's chief task in the novel seems to be to expose the absurd pretensions of Natraj and his friends who are seen indulging in meaningless day dreaming. They remain utterly ineffective in checking Vasu's nefarious activities. All the time, they are seen preoccupied with the arrangement of Radha-Krishna Marriage celebrations. It is a noble task for them to arrange the function successfully, of course, they could succeed possibly because there was the end of Vasu that very night. But so long as Vasu was alive, he mocked at Natraj and his friends and the values they adopted in their life. No one had the courage to contradict or oppose Vasu, in any matter. Natraj himself confessed, "He might do anything bellow at me, or laugh scornfully, or rattle my bones. I felt dwarfed and tongue-tied before him."[15] Gods and demons that are seen in Hindu myths and Puranas, make the people crippled and forget the reality around them. They simply roam in the realms of imaginary stories when one requires a scientific approach for his all-round progress.

In the society as revealed in *The Man Eater of Malgudi,* we come across corruption in every walk of life; the bus conductor is seen pocketing a lot of cash collected from passengers. He turns to Muthu and confides: "Sooner or later I want to give up this endless ticket punching and drive a baby taxi — I know a man who earns a net income of fifty rupees a day with just one baby vehicle. I have saved enough to buy a car now."[16] Narayan humourously comments : "He was a compassionate conductor who filled his pockets with the wayside fare, never issuing a ticket. 'At this rate he could buy a Rolls Royce rather than a Morris Minor'."[17]

Dowry system appears to be coming down to us from generations. It is the parents who are bent on perpetuating the social evil which has caused a number of deaths of young and beautiful brides. The adjournment lawyer in the novel reveals the reality when he says : "It's only after a marriage that one discovers how vicious one's new relatives can be. How many things they demand and keep demanding! " 'Oh', God," he further adds "...he must be given a present because it is the sixth month after the wedding, because it's the month of Adi, because it is Dipawali, because it is this and that; every time you think of the great man, you must part with a hundred rupees in cash or clothes! It is all an old, silly custom; our women are responsible."[18] And the old silly custom continues to eat into the vitals of Indian society even today.

The breaking up of the joint family system is but natural when there are more than two families sharing the same roof, unless there is some cementing force behind it like Natraj's grandmother. All the four brothers of Natraj's father with their wives and children numbering fifteen, had lived under the same roof for many years. It was his father's old mother who had kept them together, acting as a cohesive element among members of the family. But when his grandmother died the unity of the family also was gone. They began to quarrel on trivial matters. And the result was,

> everything that could be divided into five was cut up into equal parts and given one to each, such things as could not be split up were given to those who clamoured the loudest. A rotten easy chair on which my grandfather used to lie in the courtyard, watching the sky, was

> claimed by my second uncle whose wife had started all the furore over the property. She also claimed a pair of rosewood branches which shone with a natural polish,..... My father's third brother, as a compensation for letting these items go, claimed a wooden almirah as his own and a 'leg' harmonium operated by a pedal....[19]

The class of temple dancers as a whole is looked down upon with contempt. But it is the high caste people in the society, who nurture the profession for selfish ends. One should not at all be surprised when Rangi, a temple dancer exposes the reality. She says, "Sir, I am only a public woman, following what is my dharma, I may be a sinner to you but I do nothing worse than what some of the so-called family women are doing...."[20] And the so-called Dharma as they call it and lure the innocent, poor low caste girl to the profession of 'Devdasi' is the most henious crime which is unashamedly extolled by the so-called custodians of the Hindu culture. Is there any Hindu temple where a Brahmin girl or a high caste woman for that matter works as a dev-dasi or temple dancer. The logic behind is that the poor low caste girl to be wedded to the God in the temple under beautiful name called devdasi should satisfy the carnal desires of the priestly class as and when the later demand. They are to surrender to them completely for they were laid to believe that they are Bhu-Gods.

Then there is Sastri, the sagacious and worldly wise assistant to Natraj, with his silver spectacles and inexhaustible fund of mythical lore. It is Sastri who on the clues supplied by Rangi, the temple dancer, unfolds the mystery of Vasu's death, which he has all along felt, would come sooner or later. In fact, the situation after Vasu's death in mysterious circumstances baffles everybody, and everyone starts suspecting every one else of being the murderer. Sen suspects Muthu, the tea shop owner, for he is a rustic and the rustices are habitually vindicative; Muthu suspects the police inspector whose wrist has been broken in a brush with Vasu. The poet suspects Sen because a long iron belt is found in his house and he looks embarrassed when questioned about its presence. They are all Natraj's constant companions throughout the novel; but now they are all unanimous in suspecting Natraj, who obviously has the strongest motive of all. It is ironic that Natraj who initially shudders at the idea of being considered a murderer, starts believing that, may be, he has really done the deed. Natraj's abnormal timidity is only an extreme manifestation of what is actually a typical Malgudi middle class trait. It throws light on Natraj's roots in the kind of culture in which he is born and brought up.

The excessive altruism is perhaps the result of an extreme congenital timidity and weakness in Natraj. As he ruefully admits: "The trouble with me was that I was not able to say 'no' to any one and that got me into complications with every one."[21] Every one bullied him right from the dare devil Vasu down to his own assistant Sastri who did not care whether he had time for food or not — he was tyrant when it came to printing lables; but there was no way of protesting.

The interplay between Vasu and Natraj indicates a larger theme namely the contrast between two diametrically opposed attitudes to life, each shown to be disastrous in its own way. It is a contrast between the demoniacal, self-centred egotism of Vasu and the ineffectual, self-effacing altruism of Natraj, between the temerity of Vasu and the timidity of Natraj. Natraj's altruism is as extreme as 'Vasu's egotism.

The Man Eater of Malgudi shows that men are helpless in eradicating the social evils which they themselves are responsible, for Natraj and his friends have been presented as total failure in their efforts to check Vasu's nefarious activities. A greater emphasis is laid on the Divine role. It is a pity that R.K. Narayan should prefer a puranic approach, that man has to pray and wait for Divine help to clear the society of its evils, "The Bhagavad Gita presents this in a striking manner with the assertion that whenever the world is threatened by disorder, then Krishna appears to restore order to human affairs."[22] The approach upheld in the novel is one of a fatalist, giving free licence to the high caste cunning for exploiting the have-nots in the society, who are made to believe that it is because of their past sins that they are so miserable in their present plight; and there is nothing in their hands to do or undo what is there in store for them.

Notes and References

1. R.K. Narayan, *Gods, Demons and Modern Times* (The Literary Criterion, X, 3. Winter, 1972), pp. 47-48.
2. Ramesh Shrivastav, *What is so Great in R.K. Narayan*? From *Perspectives on R.K. Narayan* edited by Dr. Atma Ram (Ghaziabad: Vimal Prakashan, 1981), p. 201.
3. R.K. Narayan, *The Man Eater of Malgudi* (Mysore : Indian Thought Publication, 1980), p. 1.
4. *Ibid.*, p. 94.
5. *Ibid.*, p. 96.
6. *Ibid.*, pp. 182-183.
7. *Ibid.*, p. 183.
8. Ramesh Shrivastav, *What is so Great in R.K. Narayan*? From *Perspectives on R.K. Narayan*, p. 207.

9. William Walsh, *R.K. Narayan : A Critical Appreciation* (New Delhi: Allied Publishers Pvt. Ltd., 1983), p. 166.
10. R.K. Narayan, *The Man Eater of Malgudi*, pp. 12-13.
11. *Ibid.*, p. 216.
12. *Ibid.*, p. 172.
13. *Ibid.*, p. 198.
14. *Ibid.*, p. 243.
15. *Ibid.*, p. 67.
16. *Ibid.*, p. 50.
17. *Ibid.*, p. 55
18. *Ibid.*, p. 76
19. *Ibid.*, pp. 6-7.
20. *Ibid.*, p. 158.
21. R.K. Narayan, *The Man Eater of Malgudi*, p. 209.
22. Quoted by Ainslie T. Embree, *The Hindu Tradition*. From *Readings in Oriental Thought*, edited by William Theodore De Bary (New York : Modern Library Book, 1966), p. 129.

X. The Vendor of Sweets

In *The Vendor of Sweets* Narayan presents an eccentric widower of sixty with his high-minded Gandhian philosophy which he appears to have been following to suit his own purpose. Largely, he seems to be a fake disciple of Gandhi, totally distressed and disgusted with his son. Circumstances so conspire that he has to leave the house. It shows Jagan's inability, to achieve the possible compromise with the world. G.S. Amur rightly says, "His act is an act of despair; he runs away in tears."[1] The clash between Jagan and his son is a clash between the age-old traditions and the modern occidental civilization. And the solution Jagan arrives at in the end after much pain, humiliation, and self-searching is but running away from the realities of life.

Jagan is portrayed as a fanatic observer of all the externals of Gandhism. He spins and produces yarn for his own clothes, scrupulously observes dietary restrictions, (twenty drops of honey in hot water...is the natural way of taking in all the sugar we need). Jagan himself says: "I don't drink more than four ounces of water a day, and that must be boiled at night and cooled in mud jug open to the sky."[2] He uses only those sandals which are made of hide of a cow that has died a natural death. As Jagan sits in his sweet mart reading the Gita, he has one ear perpetually cocked at the frying noises in the kitchen, and one ear permanently glued to the front stall where customers and beggars crowd.

Jagan's hypocrisy is so deeply ingrained that it has become a second nature with him. He keeps double account books and treats parts of sale produce as 'free cash' a sort of immaculate conception, self-generated, arising out of itself and entitled to survive without reference to any tax, thus amassing a huge wealth. And unashamedly he declares: "If Gandhi had said somewhere, 'Pay your sales tax uncomplainingly,' he would have followed his advice, but Gandhi had made no reference to the sales tax anywhere to Jagan's knowledge."[3] He rationalizes the recycling of stale stuff by saying philosophically, "after all, everything, consists of flour, sugar and flavour."[4] Prof. Tara Malhotra has drawn a realistic picture of Jagan. She writes :

> Jagan is a bundle of contradictions, a professed Gandhian whose high-minded Gandhian principles are soon found to be a smoke-screen. As a result, he is ever playing a hide and seek game with his conscience as freely as he hoodwinks almost everyone he meets producing plenty of fun.... An inveterate enemy of sugar in personal

> life, one wonders how this Gandhian disciple could; without compuction, continue to live on the profits of selling sugared sweets to all and sundry. His frequent protestations that his sweet vending is meant solely to serve the country, particularly the children and the poor, is as hollow as a drum. He could not pass his B.A. from sheer incapacity, he is never tired of declaring unashamedly that it was his love for his country which made him give up college and throw himself headlong into struggle for political emancipation — under the leadership of Mahatma Gandhi. Penetrating beneath these boasts we discover that his noisy altruism is a mask worn to hide a selfish nature.[5]

The dialogue between Jagan and the cousin will make the point very clear.

"You have perfected the art of living on nothing," said the cousin.

Encouraged, Jagan added, 'I have given up rice too. I cook a little stone-ground wheat and take it with honey and greens.'

'And yet' said the cousin, 'I cannot understand why you go on working and earning, taking all this trouble.' He waved his hands in the direction of the sweets displayed on trays at the window, but stopped short of asking why Jagan should expect others to eat sweets and keep him flourishing.[6]

Jagan came of an orthodox Brahmin family with all the pujas and the gods; a menstruating woman had to isolate herself as the emanations from her person were supposed to create a sort of magnetic defilement, and for three days she was fed in a far off corner of the house, and was unable to move freely. She was being treated almost as untouchable. His brother was an orthodox man who managed the headquarters of a religious order, established ten centuries ago with a million followers. And yet Jagan plucked up enough courage to join the Gandhian movement. His brother did not approve of Jagan's outlook. His sister wrote that he (Jagan) had lost all sense of caste, dining and rubbing shoulders with untouchables. going to jail and getting up to all kinds of shameful things. His loyalty to Gandhi made him rebel against many of the caste laws. He found it difficult to enter into the spirit of most of the rites and religious celebrations. To him, sanctity of the age old usages and customs had made the reform in the family or in the society impossible. They stuck to their old ways and never allowed the young ones to develop their individuality. Looking at the bathroom, which remained very much what it had been in the days of his father, Jagan remarked, "everything in this home had the sanctity of usage, which was the reason why no improvement was possible."[7]

Though a Gandhian disciple, Jagan failed to make a compromise with the world. His Gandhian planks alienated his brother and sister. Besides, there were no persons whom he could address as friends. This had made Jagan confine himself to his sweetmeat shop, and the house shared by Mali and Grace not married, and yet living there as husband and wife; he was terribly shocked, the result being a complete dislocation of his relations with Mali. The only solace to him in his life was the cousin, a practical man of the town-helping Jagan in his difficulties.

Jagan's duplicity had upset Mali altogether. When he declared that he was a poor man and quoted Gandhi to have advocated poverty and not riches, Mali reacted with a vicious smile, "And yet you earn your thousand rupees a day."[8] Jagan tried in vain to convince his son to adopt to the traditional ways of his ancestors. Mali snapped it saying, "Oh, these are not the days of your ancestors. Today we have to compete with advanced countries not only in economics and industry, but also in culture."[9] Jagan's staying in the house had become unbearable to him. Demand from his son for fifty thousand dollars seemed to him totally unreasonable. He was aware that pressure was being subtly exercised on him to make him part with his cash. And he declared that he was going to meet the situation by ignoring the whole business; a sort of non-violent non co-operation.

But Jagan found his domestic life irksome. The expectant stars of Grace when she opened the door and the significant side-glances of Mali got on his nerves. If he heard them open the front door, he retreated far into the backyard of the house or sometimes even locked himself in the bathing shack. But the state of being alone like a burglar in his very house, had made Jagan decide once for all to leave the house. While leaving the house he did not fail to take the cheque book with him. Kirpal Singh points out: "within the context of the novel, the cheque book has played a central role, and since Jagan takes it along with him at the very end, we wonder how sincere his conversion to a 'new life' is."[10] How at all could one take seriously the so-called renunciation of hypocrite and a charlatan, who was clearly incapable of a real change of heart for the simple reason that his heart had already been corrupted beyond redemption? If old Jagan's Gandhism was only skin deep (as it unmistakably appeared to be) his renunciation could not be authentic either. It was more or less running away from the realities of life.

Modern occidental civilization represented by Mali had been brought in sharp contrast with the traditional Hindu culture. And Jagan found himself chocked up in the modern atmosphere. In running away from the realities, Jagan accepted, "a kind of death actually, although he'd breathe, watch, and occasionally keep in touch, but the withdrawal would not be different from death."[11]

The social surrounding and the family in which Jagan was born and brought up, was deeply orthodox and steeped in superstition and blind belief. It was only after the offerings to the God on Badri Hills that Mali was born to Jagan. He had been married to Ambika for almost ten years now; he had failed repeatedly in the Intermediate and was now failing in the B.A. class and still there was no sign of a child in the house. It was but natural under such circumstances, that Jagan's father, an old orthodox man as he was, took Jagan and his wife to the temple of Badri Hills, which was known as Santana Krishna, (a visit to it, they believed, was the only remedy for barrenness in women), and made offering to the God. And as if in fulfilment of the coconut seller's prophecy, Mali was born; the very minute he was delivered, he was weighed on a scale pan, and an equivalent weight in gold, silver and corn was made up to be delivered to the God on Badri Hills, according to the solemn vow made during their visit.

The kind of blind belief which made Jagan and his wife go to Badri Hills is still in vogue amongst the gullible Indians. It is being fully exploited and taken full advantage of by the Brahmin Pandits and the trustees of the temple. Lacs of rupees (black and unauthorised) are being poured in the form of presents and offering to the God, the poor and the rich alike finding their daughters become victims to the inordinate desires of the so-called agents of the God. Where does all the money that come in the form of presents and offerings in cash, go? surely not to the God, but to the luxury of the Brahmin Pandit.

Narayan had a dig at the dowry system, another social evil prevalent in the society. Before Jagan's marriage was celebrated, the bride's parents had to give in five thousand rupees in cash, and some presents in gold and silver vessels which Jagan was totally opposed to for fear of losing his would-be-wife, in case they refused. And when the bride's father failed to present a gold belt, Jagan's mother was heard taunting: "one doesn't ask for extraordinary things; they are not for us, we are not destined to enjoy the spectacle of a gold waist band, like hundreds of others, but one wants at least a sensible..."[12], to which Ambika snapped: "Why are you so obsessed with the gold belt? What has it to do with salt or sugar? Have you never seen a gold belt in all your life?"[13]

The dowry system is still being practised in the society on a large scale. It has now affected almost all the communities of the Indian society. And unless some concrete steps are taken to eradicate the social evil, the situation may slip out of hands. The worst sufferers are the illiterate poor persons. For, the situation is being fully exploited by the cunning foxes of the flesh business, who dupe them very cleverly first by marrying their daughters, and then selling them to the owners of brothels.

The cousin introduced in the novel is an excellent comic creation, the irony of whose parasitical existence is brought out quite admirably. He seems to be the cousin of the whole of Malgudi; and in that capacity he has entry into the houses of judges, businessmen, advocates etc. It seems that he does chores for a great number of families in the city of Malgudi. A great lover of sweets, he is a self-appointed sweet taster extraordinary to Jagan. Flattery is his accredited business in life. However, he is of immense help to Jagan in his difficulties. He serves as a mediator to Jagan whenever he wants to contact with his son Mali, for, there is a complete dislocation of his relations. It is only through this cousin of the town that Jagan, somehow, is in touch with Mali.

Mali, on the other hand, has no interest in him. He is a college drop out lured away by the West. Rifting the house loft of his father's hidden saving, Mali goes to the United States, and returns a few years later with new fangled ideas and contempt for Indian ways. He embarks on a grandiose scheme for marketing a story writing machine with the help of Grace, a half American-half Korean girl. Mali's Westernism appears to be as skin deep as Jagan's Gandhism and takes very superficial forms like eating beef and tinned food, drinking and putting on a suit. This is set in complete contrast with the ways and manners of Hindu society of which Jagan is the product. Mali's girl friend, Grace is post-graduate in Domestic Economy from Michigan University. In the company of Mali, she makes every effort to become a good Hindu wife bending down and decorating the threshold with white flowers on Friday. Jagan has great liking for her, though he knows to his utter shock, that Mali and Grace are not married.

As for Chinna Dorai's role in the life of Jagan, Narayan is in two minds. On the one hand he makes Jagan view him with suspicion when Chinna Dorai tells him, "My master supported me for years." Jagan retorted inwordly, "How could he not, as you were his only son by a passing concubine?"[14] and yet a little later his impact on Jagan is shown to be extraordinary. Jagan suddenly realises.... Am I on the verge of a new Janma? Chinna Dorai can hardly be expected as a credible agent for

Jagan's conversion in his last days, which, we find, is unconvincing for other reasons too in relation to Hindu ethics of renunciation.

In Jagan, the chief character in the novel, Narayan has created a person close to his own image. Like Narayan, Jagan has also lost his wife at an early stage. And more important, Jagan and Narayan were both sixty years old at the time the novel was written. Besides, Jagan was of the same caste to which Narayan himself belonged. One may recall here that almost all the chief characters Narayan has drawn in his novels, like Swami, Chandran, Ramani, Krishnan, Shrinivas and now Jagan come from orthodox Brahmin families of which Narayan himself is a member. He simply does not venture to come out of his caste circle to portray the lower caste people. And how could he? the lower caste people never came within his purview. And if at all they did come into his view, he has never gone deep into their lives. He has never thought to give them any substantial role to play in his Malgudi circus. Whatever chief characters we come across in his Malgudi, they all belong to the upper caste. But they all have been grouped together to belong to the lower middle class, owing to their weaker financial position in which Narayan himself is placed. His is a narrow circle realistically portrayed in a satirical tone.

That the old social values have been fast changing is revealed by Narayan through the characterization of Mali. And Jagan, that Gandhian disciple has been made totally incapable to compromise with the world, the end being Jagan's retreat from the realities, which is nothing but a kind of death to him. Jagan's renunciation of the world is of a piece with the Indian tradition. But he is also pushed into it by his personal circumstances: "Jagan felt so heartily in agreement that he wanted to explain why he needed an escape — his wife's death, his son's growth and strange development, how his ancient home behind the Lawley statue was beginning to resemble hell on earth...."[15] Owing to mutual misunderstanding and inability to cope up with the changing values one finds amongst the members of the family, the existence of Hindu joint family seems to be at stake.

Notes and References

1. Quoted by G.S. Amur, *R.K. Narayan in his own Culture: An Approach to The Vendor of Sweets*. From *Explorations in Modern Indo-English Fiction*, edited by R.K. Dhavan (New Delhi : Bahri Publications Pvt. Ltd., 1982), p. 128.
2. R.K. Narayan, *The Vendor of Sweets* (Mysore : Indian Thought Publications, 1967), p. 109.

3. *Ibid.*, p. 117.
4. *Ibid.*, p. 19.
5. Tara Malhotra, *Old Places, Old Faces and Old Times : A Critical Study of R.K. Narayan's Latest Fiction.* (Banasthali Patrika No. 13, 1969), p. 53
6. R.K. Narayan, *The Vendor of Sweets*, pp. 16-17.
7. *Ibid.*, p. 25.
8. *Ibid.*, p. 95.
9. *Ibid.*, p. 84.
10. Kirpal Singh, *The Ordinary and the Average as Satiric Traps* : From *Explorations in Modern Indo-English Fiction*, edited by R.K. Dhavan, pp. 135-136.
11. R.K. Narayan, *The Vendor of Sweets*, p. 184.
12. *Ibid.*, p. 177.
13. *Ibid.*, p. 178.
14. *Ibid.*, p. 117.
15. *Ibid.*, p. 126.

XI. The Painter of Signs

The Painter of Signs presents a realistic picture of India in the post-Independence Era. It has caught the dilemma of Indian masses caught in between two worlds — one dead, and the other powerless to be born. The novel also highlights the change in human outlook with regards to some of the cherished ideals, established institutions and accepted values. Broadly speaking, the trend of the time is to be scientific and rational: the trend very well represented by Daisy and Raman who want to establish the Age of Reason.

The rise in population is a formidable problem. Birth rate needs a massive hit if the national calamity is to be averted. However, Narayan does not mean the novel to be a propaganda for family planning since it has been conceived and executed much before the family planning campaign has assumed a ridiculous dimension. But the problem he has dealt with in *The Painter of Signs* and the changes he has introduced in human outlook have undoubtedly represented a social change. However, along with these apparent and effective aspects of change or advancement it has very strong links with the past, the vestiges of which survive in the form of temple priest and the Sarayu river. Narayan's own attitude towards the change is representative of Hindu attitude - "unsure and ambivalent like the alternate denigration and idolization that the poor Sir Fredric Lawley received at the hands of the Malgudians."[1] It is but natural, therefore, that the "traditional values do often seem to prevail at the end...the triumph is superficial, uncertain and on a purely personal level."[2]

In the early eighties when the novel was written and even at present, many of the sadhus and miracle-mongers just cheat the gullible masses who, for their lack of scientific knowledge and rational approach to the problems fall an easy prey. It is not that only illiterate and the gullible, are the victims, even the literate and educated who have greater responsibility to mould the lives of their fellow brethren, are reluctant to challenge the so-called godmen. At the mention of the temple priest the teacher looks terribly afraid, and says, very much to the advantage of the priest: "he has all sorts of powers. Lives on nothing. Nourishes himself from air. It is not good to argue with him. He is a quarrelsome man and commands powers."[3]

That we have still been so deep in superstitions and irrational blind beliefs, explains for the fact that our saints and social reformers, scientists and engineers, and even the legislators of the country, have failed to adopt a rational approach to the problems they have encountered. Dr. Bhagvantam who was once a scientific adviser to the Government of India seemed a blind follower of Satya Sai Baba. How could he help the government when he, a scientist himself, believed in miracles? To the queries put by a staunch rationalist Dr. Abraham Kovoor, Dr. Bhagwantam had nothing to say but to keep mum and let his purse go fat. Rightly says a professor at the Indian Institute of Technology at Guindy: "the majority of youths who take to the study of science and technology do so not because they have any scientific attitude or aptitude, but just because such a course helps them to get lucrative jobs. The reason why some of the eminent scientists of India have given up their science, and become "devotees" of Godman of that country was because they have found that they can make more money by being in collusive devotion to such hoaxers than by continuing scientific pursuits."[4]

In such a traditional social set up Raman's approach to be rational and logical is a welcome trend which is lacking in majority of Narayan's characters. In fact, Raman belongs to a traditionally superior caste and to the middle class. He is however, determined to establish the Age of Reason, "I want a rational explanation for everything, he cries, otherwise my mind refuses to accept any statement. He is bursting with self-declaration, I'm a rationalist, and I don't do anything unless I see some logic in it."[5] When the lawyer continues to insist that the letters for his board must lean to the left because his astrologer believes that a left slant is auspicious for his ruling star, Saturn, Raman is very upset.

Raman has always preferred to be scientific and logical in everything. But the moment he meets Daisy, of the Family Planning Centre, he begins to behave and act like a romantic fool whose thoughts always dwell on his beloved. He invents excuses to meet her and extends his sittings with her to draw her attention. But in all his attempts to get familiar with Daisy he is discouraged by a calculated coldness in her outlook. The sense of non-recognition makes him analytical and he realises that he is sex-obsessed. "All that one can say for Raman", writes William Walsh, "is that this experience has helped him to achieve some measure of wry independence. No longer a child to be tended by his aunt, no more a lover and certainly not a husband, he does at least attain a degree of stability touched by disillusion."[6]

Malgudi has certainly moved with the times. It was the base for a hydro-electric project somewhere on the Mempi Hills, and jeeps and lorries passed through the Market Road all day. The city had a new Superintendent of police who was trying out new ideas. Policemen were posted every few yards."[7] However, despite all the planning and progress, it is painful to see people suill living in abysmal ignorance. Even long after independence the monster of illiteracy stands unvanquished, and social workers like Daisy have to make a strenuous effort to overcome it. Narayan visualises this inherent incongruity in the national life : material advancement on the one hand and wide rampant mental impoverishment on the other. For instance, the coming of a child in the family is still regarded as the gift of the Almighty. Barren women still seek the blessings of the goddess and pay visit to the old lonely priest in the cave temple to get rid of their sterility.

The temple priest has roaring business so long as the Hindu remain submissive and passive onlookers and have faith in all sorts of cheats and hypocrites. The persons like Raman show courage to question him, but he too gets discouraged and remains helpless before the collective force of the traditional Hindu society. The priest gets disturbed when Raman sarcastically asks him "And so the women who want to pray stay here?" The priest takes no time to make out what he has in his mind and immediately orders him to go out crying: "go away, man, you are a bad fellow with evil thoughts."[8] However, Narayan has no comments to offer when the priest declares : "Barren women come and pray here for three days, and conceive within thirty days."[9] The fact gets easily confirmed when we see Daisy, otherwise firm and resolute, getting a humiliating treatment at the hands of the priest who cheats the innocent women folk coming to him for their alleged barrenness. To top it all, the priest has been allowed to make derogatory remarks:" Be careful, you evil women, don't tamper with God's designs."[10]

Daisy is shown utterly helpless and very much restless before the priest who concocts fantastic stories and makes the gullible believe them: "The goddess came to me in a dream and commanded and I made it my mission in life. For a hundred miles around there is no temple like this. Barren women come and pray here for three days and conceive within thirty days."...Daisy, not having been prepared herself for such an onslaught blinks uncertainly; the priest goes on: "I know everything that goes on far a hundred miles around, though it's a hundred years since I stepped outside my temple. I know what goes on everywhere and in every one's mind."[11] He further hypnotises the gullible with cock and bull stories: "Oh soul, take that clumsy tiger body of yours off and don't come and trouble the people any more, and the tiger bolted away in shame. At another time I told the wild elephant who was ransacking the gardens and fields, "hey, Gaja! Get away, otherwise I will bring down on you the chastisement of Gajendra, the lord of all Elephants in the heaven."[12] And the foolish ignorant folk echo the same whenever they happen to go.

The general trend of the time is to be scientific and rational and the novel highlights this change in human outlook with regard to some of the cherished ideals of the past. The ideas of family obeisance and reverence to elders are being gradually shed for the sake of keeping one's individuality intact. Daisy refuses to pay obeisance to her would be in-laws; and Raman, too, agrees with her.

In fact Daisy attaches no sentiments to married life. She rebels against her parents and domestic orthodoxies. S.P. Bhardwaj rightly points out: "A girl's running away from the family, her bringing up and education at a missionary organisation, her acceptance of social work and her living, all by herself without male supervision and support, are some of those phenomena which would not be tolerated in an orthodox Hindu family; nor a girl of such a family would have ventured thus."[13]

Obviously she considers marriage as an impediment in her way to self-fulfilment. According to her, "there is nothing extraordinary for a man and a woman beginning to live under the same roof. A home in her view is only a retreat from sun and rain, and for sleeping, resting and depositing one's trunk. She approves of the relationship between a man and woman on equal footing, but not the imperatives, liabilities and interdependence customarily attached to Hindu marriage.

In fact, Daisy is a peculiarly modern young woman for whom the cult of independent individuality is the supreme value in life. Moreover, her dedication to work is her solemn and profound commitment to life. In this respect she is the replica of Bharati in *Waiting for the Mahatma*. When Raman asks her to move to his house, his aunt already having left for Kashi, she shows her helplessness. The call to duty proves mightier than the soft luscious accents of love. She moves away to carry on her social work and leaves Raman to suffer the bitter sweet pangs of separation and unfulfilled love. Of course, Daisy has her moments of weakness and enjoys herself with Raman when passion overpower her. But the moment she remembers that she has some mission to perform and educate people to be more cautious in child bearing, she instantaneously conceals her thoughts of a life of comfort and enjoyment; she represses her desire.

Narayan has plenty of opportunity to contrast Daisy's modernity and passionate pursuit of population control with the usual self-indulgent unhygienic ways of the villagers, to contrast, too, Daisy's rationality with their religion. This contrast is brought to sharp intensity in the encounter Daisy has with the old priest, in one village, who has a temple to the Goddess of plenty so that barren women could come, pray and conceive. The so-called sacred shastras too declare that the more the children in a home, the more blessed it becomes. For anyone to tamper with this design of the goddess seems to be evil to the priest and his followers. However, Daisy has indomitable courage. Her absolute conviction, untrammelled modern mindedness, steel will and practicality make her a superb missionary. She looks somewhat shaken before the priest but she does not budge an inch from her commitment to social work. She emphatically declares: "...five thousand men and women have to be taken care of immediately.... I cannot afford to have a personal life."[14] Raman is right when he says: "I don't know if she cares for any other god or religion, and I haven't asked. Her worship takes the form of service to the poor and the ignorant and helping them live a decent life. She cares not for wealth or luxury or titles. She can live with the poorest in their huts, eat their food, and sleep on the mud floor."[15]

Daisy remains an exceptionally modern and rational woman character in the whole of Malgudi. Asked during the interview by S. Krishnan how he come to give such an unorthodox cast of mind to his new heroine, so entirely different from Savitri, the heroine of *The Dark Room*. Narayan explained:

> " ...In *The Dark Room* I was concerned with showing the utter dependence of woman on man in our society. I suppose I have moved along with the times. This girl in my new novel is quite different. Not only is she not dependent on men, she actually has no use for them as an integral part of her life. To show her complete independence and ability to stand by herself I took care not to give her a name with any kind of emotional connotation. I am calling her simply Daisy. She is a very strong character. All the same, when you read the novel, you will find she is feminine also...."[16]

Narayan's new woman, however, remains as unconvincing as the traditional Hindu wife in *The Dark Room*, since Daisy's changing reactions which alternate between cold indifference and tender self-surrender are not always adequately motivated. This may be for the reason that Narayan is reluctant to arrive at a systematic philosophy of life. Though his plots follow a formula order-disorder-order again. We have in his novels evidence to show that life never takes a straight course, that whatever we may wish or strive for, the final result of our efforts is unpredictable. This has roots in the Hindu philosophy of life of which Narayan is undoubtedly a spokesman par excellence. K.R. Shrinivas Iynger rightly stated : "that there is no attempt on the part of Narayan to hazard a moral judgement on the conduct of his character."[17] This weakness of Narayan, is but the weakness of his conviction like a boy tethered by his own unfounded fears inhibiting him from risky ventures. This as well as constitutional, temperamental and social limitations account for his narrow range in characterization. Narayan depicts successfully only the middle class and fumbles when he moves out of his range.

In Daisy Narayan has viewed perhaps the model of woman who would be prospering after the women's lib-movement. He has certainly moved along with the times, and the change in his presentation of domestic life can be clearly seen when his two novels *The Dark Room* and *The Painter of Signs* are read side by side. However, despite the change and development for over forty years or more, Malgudi still remains substantially unchanged in its basic mores. It has retained its traditional middle class values intact. This becomes clear if one compares the two Grannies in the first and the last novels. Raman's Granny in *The Painter of Signs* must have been a young woman in the thirties, but her thought processes forty years later appear to be those which Swami's Granny would have readily understood. Her final decision to renounce the world and go to Benaras to die, has a context which has a relevance not to the seventies, but to a whole living ancient tradition. She is certainly more representative of Malgudi — this conservative town unused to modern life, then Daisy the new woman with her modern code of marriage and mores. The old orthodox world is still viewed with sympathy as in the case of Raman's aunt. Modernization and modernized characters are targets of irony in many of Narayan's major novels like *The Guide, The Man Eater of Malgudi, Mr. Sampath* and *The Vendor of Sweets*. However, in *The Painter of Signs,* one notices that modernity is slowly but surely seeping deeper and deeper. Narayan has effectively captured the movement of modern Indian History as it affects the lives of the common man in a conservative society shaping their mental make up and creating new tensions which are often at the root of his plots. But the theme has not been presented in terms of a vast social, economic or political conflict, nor in terms of a philosophical confrontation; its dimensions are ethical, so deep and unobstructive. "Narayan gives us the feel of life itself which is neither all white nor all black but the grey, twilight world of contemporary life, quivering hesitantly between tradition and modernity, East and West inextricably mixed up in the minds of individuals and creating what S.C. Harrex, in another context, calls the psychological and social tensions involved in the uneasy conjuctions of old ways and new evolving values."[18]

We have a variegated picture of life realistically presented in *The Painter of Signs*. Each of those that Raman meets in his search for work is both individual and representative, whether it is the excited economy consciously qualified lawyer with absolute faith in astrology, or the professor who addresses the public in a purple academic gown and sells the solution to every problem.... or the owner of the Bhandari stores who fears that the colour 'red' will upset his customers and stop them asking for credit,... or the sensuous bangle seller who concentrates on the wrists of his women customers, massaging them down to suit the circumstance of his bangles, ...or Gupta, the man incensed over government policies at every level, who gives Raman a great deal of work by starting a new business under a new name each year to confound the tax gatherers. Raman is one amongst them. "He felt abashed...picking his own talent in the general scramble of a money mad world! He wished he could do without it, but realised too, that it was like a desire for a dry spot while drifting along neckdeep in a cess-pool."[19]

How realistic is the portrayal of India's poverty drawn by Daisy by way of asking to Raman: "Don't you see how horrible it is with everything crowded, and an endless chain of queues for food, shelter, bus, medicine, and everything, with thousands of children, coming with nothing to eat, no clothes to wear, no roof, no civilized existence being possible on such a mass scale — each one of us has to do our bit in the corner of the country allotted to us."[20] It is possibly this horrible crowded scene in mind, Narayan seems to have decided to do a bit for the national cause in writing *The Painter of Signs*.

The novel is more a story of Daisy, the arch-priestess of population control, who is determined to reduce the birth rate, than that of Raman who is reduced merely to the painter of sign boards trailing behind Daisy committed to social work. Narayan does not certainly mean *The Painter of Signs* to be a propaganda for family planning, but he undoubtedly has some social purpose in introducing Daisy in its structure. Elsewhere it has been reported by Narayan himself that Daisy entered the novel unaware of him and dominated the whole of it. We cannot certainly deny the fact that Narayan has ridiculed Daisy's family planning campaign when one especially knows that she has been shocked and humiliated at the hands of the priest.

Narayan very consciously employs 'Santhanu Ganga' parallel in *The Painter of Signs* and juxtaposes antiquity and contemporaneity to demonstrate how the basic imperatives of the human condition remain the same, in spite of differences in time, place, milieu and even the plane of experience. But there is no serious attempt on his part to exploit the ancient thematic parallel, and all its possible implications. Daisy going out to pursue her social commitment, Raman seems to have lapsed back to his sign board painting as usual, after having been terribly upset over Daisy's refusal to marry him.

The novel contrasts the life of passion with the life of action. In the end Raman realises that true independence and real happiness lies in doing one's own job and in being practical rather than being romantic. He retreats to the most frequented place, the Boardless, "that solid, real world of sublime souls who minded their own business."[21] Raman's experience with Daisy, that woman of strong conviction and indomitable will, has made him self-analytical and brought him to a ripe conviction that, "the man woman relationship was not inevitable and that there were other more important things to do in life than marrying."[22] Narayan has certainly moved with the passage of time and caught the modern trend in depicting Daisy and her family planning campaign. But she has been made an eccentric in her attitude towards the institution of marriage, and the way she is treated at the hands of the priest, her family planning campaign too has been held upto mild ridicule.

Notes and References

1. O.P. Mathur, *The West Wind Blows Through Malgudi*. From *Perspectives on R.K. Narayan*. Edited by Dr. Atma Ram (Ghaziabad: Vimal Prakashan, 1981), p. 36. (Ref. R.K. Narayan, *Lawley Road and other stories*, New Delhi : Orient Paperbacks, 1982).
2. *Ibid.*
3. R.K. Narayan, *The Painter of Signs* (Great Britain, Penguin Books, 1982), p. 60.
4. Dr. Abraham Kovoor, *Begone Godmen*. (Bombay : Jaico Press Pvt. Ltd., 1977), p. 19.
5. R.K. Narayan, *The Painter of Signs*, p. 8.
6. William Walsh, *R.K. Narayan : A Critical Appreciation* (New Delhi: Allied Publishers Pvt. Ltd., 1983), p. 161.
7. R.K. Narayan, *The Painter of Signs*, pp. 13-14.
8. *Ibid.*, p. 63.
9. *Ibid.*, p. 57.
10. *Ibid.*, p. 58.
11. *Ibid.*, pp. 57-58.

12. *Ibid*., p. 62.
13. S.P. Bhardwaj, *The Painter of Signs : An Analysis*. From *Perspectives on R.K. Narayan*, p. 175.
14. R.K. Narayan, *The Painter of Signs*, p. 139.
15. *Ibid*., p. 120.
16. S. Krishnan, *A Day with R.K. Narayan*, 'Span', April, 1975, p. 42.
17. K.R. Shrinivas Iynger, *Indian Writing in English* (New Delhi : Asia Publishing House, 1962), p. 284.
18. S.C. Harrex, *The Fire and the Offerings* (Calcutta : Writers' Workshop, 1977), pp. 36-37.
19. R.K. Narayan, *The Painter of Signs*, pp. 14-15.
20. *Ibid*., p. 47.
21. *Ibid*., p. 143.
22. *Ibid*., p. 38.

XII. A Tiger for Malgudi

A Tiger for Malgudi, published in 1983 by William Heineman, is a 'haunting tale' about a tiger said to have possessed the soul of an enlightened human being. The novel establishes the fact that R.K. Narayan, committed as he is to Hindu way of life, consciously turns to legends and fables, which have given him a sustaining power all through his career as a novelist. He now takes up a tiger as the chief character. Narayan justifies the subject in his Introduction to the novel: "Why tiger? Why not a mouse?" asked a smart journalist who had come to inverview me, when I mentioned the subject of my novel. I could only reply, "so that the chief character may not be trampled upon or lost sight of in a hole."[1]

R.K. Narayan recalls the great event of Kumbha Mela which recurs every twelve years at the confluence of the three rivers, Ganga, Yamuna and Saraswati in Allahabad where he comes across a hermit with his companion a tiger. He does not hold the animal on a leash since he claims they were brothers in previous life.

Although Narayan has been highly acclaimed as the writer with a detached observation of life, he could not help modelling his novel on his views and mores in relation to his commitment to Hindu view of life. The Hindu philosophy of rebirth has kept on recurring in his novels, and more so in *A Tiger for Malgudi*.

The novel begins with "an aged tiger lying in its cage ruminating on its past, beginning with its cubhood and wild days in the jungle and later life in captivity as a circus star."[2] The hermit who appears to be the mouthpiece of the writer, is reported to have commented, "You probably in a previous life enjoyed putting your fellow beings behind bars. One has to face the reactions of every act, if not in the same life, at least in another life or a series of lives. There can be no escape from it."[3] While writing the novel, Narayan has in his mind the ethical base that... "deep within, the core of personality is the same in spite of differing appearance and categories, and with the right approach you could expect the same response from a tiger as from any normal human being."[4]

The major part of *A Tiger for Malgudi* is devoted to Grand Malgudi Circus with the star tiger as its sole attraction. It also displays Rita the captain's wife "in death defying trapeze acts, the chimp riding a motor cycle, the tusker carrying on its back the chimp dressed as a Maharaja with crown and all, a giraffe doing something or the other, and clowns tumbling."[5] The captain reserved the tiger's act for the night show. When the tiger was, wheeled in, the captain, dressed in satin breaches and a glittering vest, holding the whip in hand, appeared before the audience, bowed to the public deeply and introduced Raja performing an act which he termed as 'Four in one'; the usual running round inside the fence crossing hurdles and mazes, and labyrinths that appeared at appropriate places, and then rings of flames at some times, followed by the item of the goat and the milk. The tiger was very much accustomed to other animals and also human beings working in The Grand Malgudi Circus, obeying the commands of the captain "Whatever its disadvantage, circus life had accustomed me to understand commands...."[6] And his mind worked the same way even after he came under the charge of the hermit. It appears incredible that the hermit possessed strange powers, and that he exercised them on the tiger, and the tiger followed him meekly.

India is famous for Sadhus of every kind, many of them being fake in the garb of holy men. Narayan seems to believe in magical powers said to have been possessed by the yogis. He recalls the events : "one could become invisible, levitate, transmute metals, travel in space, control animals,...live on air, and so on and so forth."[7] All these come in the category of so-called miracles. In fact, there are no miracles but mysteries. 'All the so-called miracles' of God men, says Dr. Abraham Kovoor, "are mere juggling tricks performed before gullibles who have neither the courage nor the commonsense to investigate."[8]

The hermit portrayed in the novel *A Tiger for Malgudi* renounces his house, wife, children, his everything out of total frustration in his life. He has now nothing to do with his past or future. He says to his wife who has searched him out after all, "My past does not exist for me, nor a future. I live for the moment, and that awareness is enough for me."[9] However, it is interesting to hear his wife who says impassionately: "Don't deceive me or cheat me. Others may take you for a hermit, but I know you intimately. I have borne your vagaries patiently for a lifetime; your inordinate demands of food and my perpetual anxiety to see you satisfied, and my total surrender night or day when passion seized you and you displayed the indifference of a savage, never caring for my health or inclination, and with your crude jocularities even before the children, I shudder!"[10] The same character now claims brotherhood with the tiger.

The hermit has been reported to have left his house in the manner of Siddharth. But there is a sea of difference between the two. Siddharth never renounced his house out of frustration. In search of the truth of life, a way to make the entire mankind happy, he comes out with a profound philosophy of life 'Atta Dipo Bhava'. The hermit on the other hand, leaves his house in frustration and indulges in mere juggling of tricks. He is said to have tamed the wild beast who has disfigured the circus captain. Not only that, he speaks in the language of the tiger, or the tiger in human dialect, one is not sure. Narayan has read about him freely moving about with the hermit amidst that ocean of humanity gathered during the Kumbha Mela Festival. One does not believe it to be true. Even Narayan remarks: "Such a combination seemed incredible when I read reports of it and saw the photographs."[11] Such reports are not uncommon in Indian newspapers, and there is no iota of truth in them. For one, the reporters never seem to verify the truths themselves, they hear somebody telling them, and report the matter accordingly. Besides, they are not free from superstitions either, and they find nothing wrong in getting such absurd stories published in the newspaper. No wonder, Dr. Abraham Kovoor comes out with an open challenge. He declares : "nobody has and nobody ever had supernatural powers. They exist only in the pages of scriptures and sensation-mongering newspapers."[12]

One fails to understand as to why people should believe such absurd ancient saying: "Don't probe too far into the origin of a river or a saint! You will never reach the end."[13] It has encouraged every type of charlatan to exploit the gullible masses. Moreover, as it is found imbibed in their mind from the very childhood, no one has the courage to question the authority of the saint. Jayraj, the photographer represents the mood of the public when he says: "let us forget him and his tiger. Something uncanny about him...unsafe to talk about such men, who may be saints or sorcerers. Who knows what will happen?"[14] Fear plays an important role in the life of a Hindu. He is afraid of ghosts, demons and gods. The fear has made the Hindu mentally weak, and incapable of pursuing an independent line of thinking with courage and determination, since it has been artificially created by brain-washing from childhood. As a result, he simply does not have the courage to verify the truth. He accepts the things as they are, simply because same are written in the so-called holy shastras or because some saints or yogis have been reported to have said so.

Narayan presents a true mentality of the Hindus as revealed in *A Tiger for Malgudi*, through the master when he says : "A great power has determined the number of breaths for each individual, who can neither stop them nor prolong."[15] Narayan's mind is no exception. He belongs to the 20th century and has had the benefit of English education. During his college days he must certainly have come into contact with those inclined to dismiss many of our beliefs and superstitions. And he married a girl against all conventions and in the teeth of what the astrologers predicted. However, the Hindu philosophy that has moulded his mind overwhelmed him when he lost his beloved wife. P.S. Sundaram ironically remarks: "In the light of this terrible personal experience, who can blame him if he is firmly convinced that human effort counts for very little, and whatever happens is what has already been ordained?"[16] The personal tragedy has firmly gripped his mind; and Narayan could not free himself from age-old beliefs and superstitions. One cannot dismiss Kirpal Singh's contention when he says: Narayan's refusal to see life beyond its ambiguous trappings leads him to a somewhat misplaced and distorted world-view."[17]

Narayan seems to be fatalistic and conservative in outlook. He wants that the old moral order should remain intact in the changing circumstances. His belief in Hindu philosophy of Karma and Rebirth remains unchanged and he seems to have netted the novel accordingly.

In the novel Narayan touched upon the feudal character of government officials. Having lost several of their animals, villagers were convinced that they had some devil around them in the form of the tiger. They submitted a petition in writing to the collector for redressal of their grievance. Narayan comments :

> The deputation of villagers has to visit the collector almost once a week, spending time and money to no purpose. From within the jungle where their villages were situated, they had to trudge ten miles to the highway and wait endlessly for a chance lift in a passing bus or lorry. At the Collector's Office they could see, after much waiting, only the collector's clerk, who took their petition and then directed them to satisfy further official formalities. At the end of the day they returned to their villages, dreading lest the tiger should waylay them.[18]

Most of the regulations passed in government offices have no practical sense. A pathetic scene has been realistically presented in the novel. The tiger enters the school premises and the headmaster is locked inside. One Mr. Alphonse has been called in to shoot the tiger, but he is prevented from his shooting by the Chairman of the Local Chapter to Tiger Project, who asks Alphonse to submit the written proof of the tiger being a man-eater. Alphonse rebukes the chairman in no uncertain terms: "You and your government regulations...you have no practical sense...you'll see half the population destroyed in your zeal to protect the tiger: perhaps that's a ruse to keep down the population of our country!"[19]

Apart from the tiger of the Grand Malgudi Circus, the characters that figure in the novel, are the circus captain and his wife Rita. The captain was a backwood boy living and playing in the dust of Abu Lane. He was sent to Albert Mission School, but the fate willed it otherwise. Then, we find, Dhadhoji of Poona adopted him and trained him to clean the stables and then taught him to educate animals. Eventually, after the death of Dhadhoji, the captain becomes incharge of the Grand Malgudi Circus. As generally seen in family life, here too, there are bickerings in the married life of the captain. Rita appears quarrelsome and fed up with the same sort of activities that she has been performing in the circus. "I am not prepared to spare any of my girls or set fire to myself just to please your fancy. I'm not an orthodox wife preparing for Sati."[20] The captain makes a general comment: "Women are impossible, worse than twenty untamed jungle creatures on one's hand at a time...."[21]

As for the hermit, there are several versions about him. Narayan inserts an interesting passage here: "That hermit must have come from the Himalayas. I have heard that there are many extraordinary souls residing in the ice caves, capable of travelling any distance at will, and able to control anything by their yogic powers." "How could the yogi have known that there was a tiger in the headmaster's room, and why should he have wanted to protect it?"

"Probably they were family friends!" They laughed at the joke.

"It may be no laughing matter. I was at the school and could over-hear his conversation with tiger as if it were his younger brother."

"Don't be too sure, suppose that tiger makes a meal of his brother and turns now for more. We must be watchful...."[22]

Jayraj, the photographer, tried to recollect the face of the hermit right from his college days, cycling up the market road every morning to his college. He could not remember his name, but he felt sure that he lived in Ellamen Street in one of those solid houses built by an earlier generation. Then we have an echo of Jagan, the sweet vendor, who, in his young days, was arrested during the Independence Movement for climbing the collector's office roof and tearing down the Union Jack. He didn't pass his B.A. — too busy mixed up as he was, in every kind of demonstration in those days. Fed up with his life at home he left it altogether for good. However, that the hermit had vanished abandoning his wife and children, confused us further, for Jagan had no family when he renounced his home in utter disgust. And Jayraj, the photographer left the matter there, consoling us somehow that there was something uncanny about him. It was unsafe to talk about such man; let us forget him and his tiger.

'Separation' as being the law of life, is once again echoed through the pages of the novel. It is the master here, who seems to act as the mouthpiece through which Narayan presents his views. It is perhaps the only predominant truth of life that Narayan has in his view, on his own tragic experience in his life. He is left alone to face the challenges of life after his wife's death. And it is through the master himself that Narayan emphasises the truth: "No relationship, human or other, or association of any kind could last forever. Separation is the law of life right from the mother's womb. One has to accept it if one has to live in God's plans."[23]

Narayan, after much wandering in and around the Malgudi Circus, observing the ways and manners of human beings he is familiar with, comes to the conclusion that, "humans have monopolized the attention of fiction writers. Man in his smugness never imagines for a moment that other creatures may also possess ego, values, outlook, and the ability to communicate, though they may be incapable of audible speech."[24] He presents the tiger on the possible assumption that..."he has only the appearance of a tiger, but he is not one...inside he is no different from you and me."[25] And Narayan ends the novel, the hermit whispering to the tiger, "Both of us will shed our forms soon and perhaps we could meet again, who knows? So goodbye for the present"[26]; essentially life is same. It is outward appearance that is different. Narayan, is seen firmly rooted in the Hindu philosophy of life. The efforts at self-assertion or an awakening in them, though feeble and half-hearted make many of the younger generation, in view of the changing circumstances, come out of the traditional confinement as does even the tiger who frees himself from the bondage of circus life. As a whole, there is no such thing as wild animal. We call them so because they don't have, like human beings, social or moral restraints, and as such they roam freely in the jungle.

Notes and References

1. R.K. Narayan, *A Tiger for Malgudi* (New Delhi : Allied Publishers Private Limited, 1983), p. 8.
2. *Ibid.*, p. 8.
3. *Ibid.*, p. 48.
4. *Ibid.*, p. 10.
5. *Ibid.*, p. 71.
6. *Ibid.*, p. 147.

7. *Ibid.*, p. 9.
8. Dr. Abraham Kovoor, *Begone Godmen* (Bombay : Jaico Press Pvt. Ltd., 1977), p. 15.
9. R.K. Narayan, *A Tiger for Malgudi*, p. 171.
10. *Ibid.*, pp. 170-171.
11. *Ibid.*, p. 7.
12. Dr. Abraham Kovoor, *Begone Godmen*, p. VII.
13. R.K. Narayan, *A Tiger for Malgudi*, p. 154.
14. *Ibid.*
15. *Ibid.*, p. 142.
16. P.S. Sundaram, *Ambivalence of R.K. Narayan.* From *Explorations in Modern Indo-English Fiction* edited by Dr. R.K. Dhavan (New Delhi: Bahri Publications Pvt. Ltd., 1982), p. 153.
17. Kirpal Singh, *The Ordinary And the Average as Satiric Traps : The case of R.K. Narayan*, From *Explorations in Modern Indo-English Fiction*, p. 139.
18. R.K. Narayan, *A Tiger for Malgudi*, pp. 30-31.
19. *Ibid.*, p. 135.
20. *Ibid.*, p. 58.
21. *Ibid.*, p. 38.
22. *Ibid.*, p. 151.
23. *Ibid.*, p. 174.
24. *Ibid.*, pp. 7-8.
25. *Ibid.*, p. 146.
26. *Ibid.*, p. 176.

CHAPTER 2

NARAYAN'S CONCEPTION OF INDIVIDUAL

Narayan has been widely acclaimed as a detached observer of life. He never seriously involves himself in the activities of his characters. However, one cann't overlook his pre-occupation with the delineation of South Indian orthodox Hindus, the class and the caste to which they belong, and the persons Narayan is intimately familiar with. The range of characters portrayed in his novels is a narrow circle dubbed as Malgudi which has an imprint of a conservative Hindu society, vastly changing under the impact of modernization, and yet showing the perpetuation of old social values with a little or no interest in pushing the society on its onward march. However, the general trend in modern times is to be rational and scientific: the outlook represented by Raman and Daisy in Narayan's recent novel *The Painter of Signs*. But it is a pity that both Raman and Daisy have been considerably twisted, so as to have the colour of the mythological story of Santhanu. Characterized as eccentrics in their attitude, like most other characters, these two also have been held upto ridicule. On the whole, Narayan's characters with a few exceptions, have a fixed role to play with little scope for a fuller growth of their individuality. The role assigned to them seems to be pre-ordained, and they appear as helpless creatures torn by desires and tossed this way and that by the caprice of fortune. Heavily burdened with the weight of customs and traditions, and therefore totally frustrated with their life and the surroundings, most of his characters run away only to return home thoroughly chastened accepting defeat in life. They simply cannot withstand the collective force of the traditional society, and are forced to lead their life like "well dressed....life like clay models in a show case, moving along a predetermined mechanical track."[1]

Born in a conservative Hindu family, Narayan could not help portraying characters of the same class and caste of which he is a member. The Indian child of this class and caste, is introduced to the classical Indian tales, myths and Vedic poetry very early in life, in Narayan's case at his grandmother's knee, in a cosy corner of the house when the day's tasks are done and the lamps are lit. "Like the non-conformist hymns of Lawrence's childhood they become woven into man's consciousness giving an ultimate shape to his life."[2] It is so because from the very childhood our minds are trained to accept without surprise characters of godly or demonic proportions with actions and reactions set in limitless worlds and progressing through an incalculable time scale.

Under these social conditions it is but natural that we meet characters who are only too eager to follow the social values which they imbibe from their early childhood. To begin with, they start their day with prayers to God. Naturally, in times of difficulty their thoughts turn to gods or goddess, which they believe, would relieve them of their difficulties. When Swami (*Swami and Friends*), afraid of his parents left his home and roamed in wilderness, he was horrified to see "these half-distinct black shapes looming far ahead, which might be trees or devils or gate-posts of inferno."[3] He collapsed like an empty bag and wept bitterly. Utterly helpless Swami prayed to all the gods that he knew to take him out of that place. He promised them offerings : "two coconuts every Saturday to the elephant-faced Ganapathi; a vow to roll barebodied in dust, beg, and take the alms to the lord of Tirupathi."[4]

Similarly, when Natraj and his friends failed to check Vasu's nefarious activities, he and his friends had nothing left but to pray to Vishnu. And the elephant was miraculously saved when Vasu, while trapping a couple of mosquitoes, brought the flat of his palm with all his might on his forehead and died instantly.

Now, when one accetps any outside Agency to solve his problems, how irrational and superstitious he becomes in his attitude, is shown in *The Vendor of Sweets,* where Jagan and his wife have been taken to the God on Badri Hill for blessings for the birth of a child. "As if in fulfilment of the coconut seller's prophesy Mali was born. The very minute he was delivered (in the Village home of his mother) he was weighed on scale-pan, even before the midwife could clean him up properly, and an equivalent weight in gold, silver and corn was made up to be delivered to the God on Badri Hill, according to the solemn vow made during their visit."[5]

Margayya, (*The Financial Expert*) was shown as childless for twelve years and then he was made to pray to God, and his wife conceived giving birth to Balu. Margayya remembers, "how he carried the alms and the sovereigns equal to the weight of the child to the Tirupati Hills and deposited them all in the treasure box in the shrine."[6] The same Margayya was shown in his later years, carrying out a forty day ordeal of fasting and praying to Goddess Laxmi in order to propitiate her to acquire wealth.

We have another instance of superstition in *Waiting for the Mahatma.* Shriram's Granny declared dead by a doctor, was taken to the funeral pyre. All the required rituals for Granny's soul to rest in peace, have been performed by the priest. The funeral pyre was lit. The fire smouldered and crackled. But suddenly the big toe of the left foot of the lady was seen moving. Shriram immediately flung a pail of water on it and put it out. Now, with the fire out, they stood around and watched. The toe was wagging. Surely Granny was not dead. She was reviving little by little. When the doctor suggested that she should be taken back home, the priest interrupted: "How can you suggest such a thing? No one who has been carried here can ever step into the town bounds again...." He further adds: "The whole town will be wiped out by fire or plague. It is very inauspicious. Do anything you like, but she cann't come back into the town."[7] No one from the assembly had the courage to contradict the priest. It was shocking to find that the poor lady had to be taken to a small abandoned toll-gate station. After that she went off to Benaras to await her death, to the final fire and to the final ablution in the sacred Ganges.

The protagonist of a short story called *The Seventh House,* is the case of a foolish young man who is possessed with superstition and blind belief. This young and devoted husband whose wife lies on her death bed, suffering from a serious disease, is assured by an astrologer that if he is unfaithful to her, that could propitiate the evil planets and thus save her. The husband's timid attempts to visit a prostitute are frustrated by a well meaning horse carriage driver whom he engages to take him to his destination, and finally unable to explain his reasons to this cruel good samaritan, the husband pathetically resigns himself to his fate.

Caught in such cultural surroundings, many of Narayan's characters, particularly of the new generation find themseleves chocked up under the combined weight of irrational customs and traditions. They make attempts to rebel against the old social values, and try to assert their individuality. But they simply cann't face the collective force of the traditional orthodox society. And it is a pity that almost all his characters who make feeble attempts at self-determination, return to the former position accepting defeat in life. Happiness in submission seems to be the motto with them. They do not control the events, but the events control them. However, we see a marked change in their attitude as seen in Chandran's,

(*The Bachelor of Arts*) revolt against the orthodoxy of customs like the tallying of horoscopes as a necessary preliminary to marriage when he found that he could not marry the girl he loved.

Savitri, a middle class woman in *The Dark Room* finds herself burdened by the immense weight of the Indian past, by her caste, her religion and her role as wife and mother. And in a fit of determination, she revolts against her husband to assert her individuality. She bursts out: "I'm a human being," "....you men will never grant that. For you we are playthings when you feel like hugging, and slaves at other times. Don't think that you can fondle us when you like and kick us when you choose."[8]

Rosie's predicament in the prevalent social set up is a critical one. On the one hand, her education has enhanced in her the awareness of her individuality, and on the other it pits her against a society which is still very orthodox, a society which still has certain well-defined attitudes towards women. To top all this, she belongs to a class which has traditionally been looked down upon as a low community, which does not deserve equal status with the high caste. Against this social background and being a child deprived of the experience of a father we see Rosie as a highly ambitious woman. She wants to become a famous dancer, a dancer in a totally different sense and not like her mother who was a traditional dancer. She marries Marco through the agency of matrimonial advertisement. But in the course of time she leaves her husband and comes to live with Raju to fulfil her aspiration in life. Ram Dial rightly observes: "Her inner being, it appears, is not prepared to go on playing the traditional role of a suppressed Indian wife for the rest of her life.... Her education is responsible...."[9]

In Daisy (*The Painter of Signs*) Narayan has visualised perhaps the model of woman who would be prospering after the women's lib-Movement, for the betterment of woman-kind. The novel highlights the change in human outlook with regard to some of the cherished ideals, established institutions and accepted values. The ideals of family obeisance and reverence to elders in the family are gradually dropped for the sake of keeping one's own individuality intact. Daisy refuses to pay obeisance to her would-be-in-laws, and Raman too considers it odd to fall at anybody's feet.

Raman is determined to establish the Age of Reason in the world. "I want a rational explanation for everything, he cried," "...I'm a rationalist, and I don't do any thing unless I see some logic in it."[10]

Modernization and modernized characters are targets of irony in many of Narayan's major novels like *The Guide, The Man Eater of Malgudi, Mr. Sampath, The Vendor of Sweets*. But in *The Painter of Signs*, they are viewed with marked approval.

However, one thing that comes out unmistakably is that Narayan shies away from the world which by its portrayal might arouse controversy or antagonism, and in the processes he reveals his weakness as an author. Margayya's acquiring of wealth through Laxmi worship in *The Financial Expert*, and Raju's fast unto death for bringing of rains during drought in *The Guide* can be cited as good examples, in this regard. The strength of writers like Raja Rao and Mulk Raj Anand is the strength of their conviction and commitment. This hidden source of energy gives life and sustaining power to their creations. The weakness of Narayan is the weakness of his conviction.

It is perhaps for his lack of conviction that Narayan's characters too lack definite purpose in life. The protagonist in each novel is made to play his destined life role, during the course of which he or she, either matures in the process or rebels, or simply drifts, or again is chastised or even destroyed by a characterised inner weakness.

Chandran (*The Bachelor of Arts*) initially has enough courage to revolt against the irrational custom of tallying horoscopes. 'Why should we be cudgelled and nozzled by our elders?' Chandran asked indignantly. And yet he could not face the family orthodoxy and he has to leave his home taking up sanyas as an escape from the reality. However, Chandran returns home and marries another girl named Susila according to the wishes of his parents.

Savitri (*The Dark Room*) too, like Chandran, revolts against her husband after fifteen years of impotent life that she has led in her home. When it was too much for her to bear, she left her husband to commit suicide by drowning in the river. Somehow she was saved by the low caste Mari and Ponni who gave her shelter for a couple of days. Like Chandran, she too, ultimately pockets her pride and returns, broken, defeated and sullenly acquiescent, to her still unrepentant husband.

Krishna's is a typical Hindu case, talking with the spirit of his dead wife. Unable to bear the loss of his dear wife, Krishna finds a medium to speak with his dead wife as a temporary escape from the reality. However, the truth downs upon him in the end that unmitigated loneliness is the only truth of life. He resigns from his services as a Lecturer in the college, and accepts a low salaried job as a teacher, listening to the urge of his inner voice.

Shrinivas (*Mr. Sampath*) the editor of *The Banner* wanted to set the whole world right within the twelve pages of his weekly. He undertook to publish a regular feature entitled 'Open Window' "which stood for the abolition of slums and congestion. It described the tenements, the pigsties constructed for human dwellings in the four corners of the town by rapacious landlords."[11] But in the end we are really stunned to find a marked change in his outlook. His mind perceived a balance of power in human relationship. It seemed to him to be futile and presumptuous occupation to analyse, criticise and attempt to set things right anywhere.

Raju (*The Guide*) deceives himself playing a pseudo-saint thereby deceiving the gullible masses of Mangla. In fact, he has no morals to follow in his life. First he grabs the wife of Marco, and later grabs Rosie's jewellery by making forgery for which he is sentenced to jail for a term of three years. That this ex-convict Raju should be mistaken for a sadhu is typical of Hindu tradition. However, his confession to Velan: "I am no saint" reveals his helplessness and conscience of guilt. Raju is thus sacrificed in the end. The miracle that happens is not that the rains have come but that the bogus holy man changes into a dying god.

Margayya (*The Financial Expert*) who shows people the way out of financial difficulty, at once becomes rich almost by co-incidence. In fact, Margayya has made up his mind that he is going to have no nonsense from the planets. He no longer believes that man is a victim of circumstances or fate but that man is a creature who could make his own present and future provided he works hard and remains watchful. But Margayya fails to remain watchful as far as his financial edifice is concerned and a moment's indiscreation on his part in assaulting Dr. Pal, and his obsession to reach the top of his financial career have been enough to ruin him totally, making him a pauper in the end.

Jagan (*The Vendor of Sweets*) for from conquering the self, has become prosperous while attempting to follow the precepts of Gandhi, wearing Khaddar over softer clothes and practising ritual spinnning. Shun by his brother and sister for his Gandhian way of life, and yet himself being unable to swallow the modern ways, his attempts to change Mali's character prove futile. Utterly helpless now, and totally disgusted with the ways of his Americanized son, Jagan has no alternative but to go out in wilderness. But he does not forget to take the cheque book with him.

Natraj (*The Man Eater of Malgudi*) does not impress the reader so much as does Vasu, the taxidermist. His altruism is as extreme as Vasu's egotism. It makes him most unworldly and unbusiness-like in his own profession. Even after traumatic experience with Vasu, Natraj hardly learns anything from the incidents that have occurred in his life. His last remark: "Yes, Shastri, I am at your service," perhaps indicates that he is the same Natraj, Vasu or no Vasu, ready to be the cheerful victim of the next man-eater who might cross his path. He appears so helpless and frightened before Vasu, that he remains totally passive and waits for some god or goddess to take some 'Avatar' to check Vasu's nefarious activities, the attitude so perfectly in agreement with Hindu tradition.

Shriram (*Waiting for the Mahatma*) is uneasily conscious of the pointlessness of his life, closetted as it is, by layers of customs and female devotion. He is awakened out of his discontented trance by the beautiful young woman collecting for Gandhi. However, Shriram the weak, timid, empty headed drifter is hardly a lover. M.K. Naik observes: "Perhaps freudianism alone can explain why the intelligent, able and domineering Bharati (who evidently has an outside maternal complex) should at all feel drawn to this totally unheroic hero."[12]

Daisy's absolute conviction, untrammelled modern mindedness, still will and practicality make her a superb missionary for the cause of family planning to arrest population growth in the country. She pursues this aim with a religious intensity. And she would have been the most memorable woman in the modernized town of Malgudi had Narayan not twisted her character and mixed it with some old mythological story. In fact, Daisy (*Painter of Signs*) is a peculiarly modern young woman for whom the cult of independent individuality is the supreme value in life. But as Dr. K.C. Bhatnagar points out, "Narayan sees too much insecurity in the present-day cry for freedom. The relief from social and moral tensions for women lies in the good old ways of Malgudi."[13] Narayan does not seem to understand the rationale behind modernity in women.

Other characters that deserve mention here are Ramani of *The Dark Room*, Sampath of *Mr. Sampath*, Vasu the taxidermist (*The Man Eater of Malgudi*) and the hypocrite Natesh (*Waiting for the Mahatma*). Amongst women characters, besides Savitri, Rosie and Daisy, special mention can be made of Susila (*The English Teacher*) and Bharati (*Waiting for the Mahatma*).

While Ramani is a callous husband who refuses to see any logic in women's lib-movement, Vasu, the taxidermist marcilessly ridicules the most highly cherished ideals of the traditional Malgudi. Ramani likes to keep intact Sita-Sati-Savitri image of women of ancient India, Vasu is a modern rakshas who disturbs the quiet good old days of Malgudi, and is so much egoistic and perverse in his outlook that he does not think that the cow is necessary for milk if at all one wants to have it. Sampath, the printer of Malgudi, aspires to be the producer-director of a film with Shanti as its heroine. In the process he becomes infatuated with the heroine and runs away becoming a bankrupt in the end. Natesh, (*Waiting for the Mahatma*) is the crudest kind of opportunist whose Gandhism is only skindeep. As the Municipal Chairman he prefers Gandhian cause to serve his personal ends. In fact, his Gandhian principles are confined merely to his wearing of Khaddar and putting photographs of national leaders on the walls of his drawing room.

Both Rosie and Bharati are modern young women pursuing their profession quite independently. While Rosie becomes a famous dancer, Bharati remains confined to Gandhi's Ashram with Gandhian precepts uppermost in her mind. In the former it is Raju who has helped to fulfil her ambition in life, in the later it is the Mahatma who has guided and shaped the course of her action. The other two women Savitri (*The Dark Room*) and Susila (*The English Teacher*) are loyal, loving and simple; but their experiences are different in life. Susila is worshipped by Krishna her husband, whereas Savitri is tortured, neglected and humiliated. On the whole, Narayan's treatment of his characters is half-ironic, half-comic. Their claim of independent existence and self-assertion is held upto ridicule possibly because Narayan does not like to disturb the old cherished ideals of the Hindu society.

Rich people rolling in wealth have no fascination for Narayan, nor does the poor and the down-trodden class of workers inspire Narayan with imagination. In fact, Narayan has had a good occasion to mix with the people of non-Brahmin poor classes who were subjugated, trampled underfoot, and treated worse than animals for centuries together. To support his family Narayan was a reporter once, gathering news for a Madras paper called, *The Justice*. The Daily was intended to promote the cause of the non-Brahmin who suffered from the domination of the minority Brahmin class in public life, government service and education. The newspaper proprietors had no objection to a Brahmin reporter (Narayan belongs to a Brahmin class), indeed they relished the idea of having a Brahmin on the staff supporting non-Brahmin cause. However, for reasons best known to him, Narayan failed to do any justice to the profession as a reporter to *The Justice*. He could not take up the cause of the non-Brahmins, the poor and the down-trodden.

Besides, Narayan never involves himself with the activities of his characters. Above all beneath the veneer of the so-called comic vision for which Narayan is so highly praised one detects an extreme mistrust of life, a reluctance to accord to the average and the ordinary any kind of face saving device, a desire to put them in their place, a need somehow to prevent the average and the ordinary from triumphing.

Instead of facing the reality and doing something concrete for the betterment of caste-ridden traditional society. Narayan's characters have taken refuge in philosophy, amongst whom particular mention can be made of Krishna, *The English Teacher,* Shrinivas, the journalist (*Mr. Sampath*), and Natraj, the printer (*Man Eater of Malgudi*), Mahatma Gandhi also has been brought in by Narayan in *Waiting for the Mahatma* with some of his precepts so dear to him.

Krishna was serving as a lecturer in English at Albert Mission College. But alas, in the midst of his happy married life, he met with a profound personal loss in the death of his dear wife. Intense grief overwhelmed him during the funeral rites at the burning ghat and he did not know what to do. Krishna himself narrates the disturbed state of his mind. "I'm an imbecile, incapable of doing anything...."[14] The novel is obviously autobiographical in content. The toll that typhoid took and all the desolation that followed with a child to look after and the psychic adjustments are based on Narayan's own experience. When Narayan lost his wife Rajam, he too found no meaning in existence. "Dismal emptiness stretched before me. There were a hundred momentoes and reminders : each day that were deeply tormenting. I could not bear to stay in the room I had once shared with my wife.... I tried to cut away from every little reminder, but the event of Dettol and of burnt margosa leaf permeated the walls and haunted me night and day."[15] The person of so disturbed a mind should naturally be inclined to accept anything concerning his dead wife. In fact, Narayan as he himself said in *My Days*, had no faith in spiritualism. And before he approached Mr. Rao as suggested by his cousin, he sufficiently debated himself if he should meet Rao or not. But the 'Sanskar' he received during his childhood, and the belief in the immortality of soul that his elders had imbibed in him prompted Narayan to try Mr. Rao's spiritual experiment. The episode Narayan himself narrated in his *My Days* throws sufficient light on the psychic experiment carried out by him. He writes : "All that factual side seemed to me immaterial. Even if Mr. Rao had his own sources of enquiry and was dashing off the information at the sitting, even if Rao caught telepathically whatever went on in my or in anyone else's mind, it did not matter to me. Even if the whole thing was a grand fraud, it would not matter. What was important was the sensing of the presence in that room, which transformed my outlook."[16]

Narayan himself being psychically inclined and anxious to have psychic communion with the spirit of his dead wife, Rao found it absolutely easy in inducing the sense of his wife's presence through the so-called occult experiment. In fact, much of the writing Rao did with his pencil, was of doubtful nature or could even be rejected as sheer non-sense. And yet Narayan believed it in order to get peace of mind. That way Narayan could bring back his mental equilibrium. He could as he himself noted, survive the death of his wife.

The fact which claims attention here is that Narayan is overwhelmed with intense grief, so are other persons under similar circumstances. However, somehow one has to overcome it after a couple of days. But the case with Narayan appears different. He finds solace in spiritualism. Perhaps Narayan does lack the necessary courage to face the reality, though it has dawned upon him much later that separation is the only truth of life.

Shrinivas (*Mr. Sampath*) is a journalist by profession. Intitially he has lofty ideas to spread through his weekly *The Banner*. He is determined to remove the pigheadedness in human beings. And Mr. Sampath, the printer is available for him to render his whole-hearted invaluable service. However, in the course of time we are surprised to find him in a totally changed mood. Narayan comments: He "was filled with great wonder at the multitudinousness and vastness of the whole picture of life...which was too huge even to contemplate."[17] And it is in this total picture that Shrinivas perceived God. Now he marvelled at the invisible forces of the universe which maintained this subtle balance in all matters — things neither particularly wrong nor right. And Shrinivas philosophically told to himself. 'There is no sense in interfering in other people's lives'. Then he abruptly left to their fate the lofty ideas that thronged his mind in the beginning. The outlook that has so suddenly changed, has roots in the Hindu religion which has shaped his mind, and thus defeated the very purpose with which he began *The Banner* in high spirits.

In fact, Shrinivas has overlooked the reality that many of the evils that have plagued the Hindu society are only man-made. And hence it is only man who can remove them with strong will and sheer determination. It is absurd to think that it is unnecessary for anybody to do anything in the society. That a journalist like Shrinivas should merely sit and wait, instead of doing something concrete to eradicate the many cobwebs that have engulfed the society, explains for the social backwardness of the country.

Natraj (*The Man Eater of Malgudi*) seems to be possessed with the same philosophy that man is a mere puppet in the hands of fate, and that he has actually nothing in his hands to change his lot. When he and his friends find Vasu, the taxidermist, too strong and powerful for them, they resign to their fate in utter helplessness. When the matter goes out of their hands to the killing of the temple elephant, Natraj lets out a terrific cry which has drowned the noise of children, music everything, "Oh, Vishnu! I howled, save our elephant...."[18] There was a belief that God Krishna was really an incarnation of Vishnu who had saved Gajendra, he would again come to the rescue of the same animal. And lo, the temple elephant was miraculously saved when Vasu instantly killed himself, giving a sigh of relief to Natraj, and his bohemian circle. The belief in such things has certainly made the Indians inactive and more so, they have left making sincere efforts to fight the injustice meted out to them at the hands of the upper caste. In fact, the middle class people like Krishna, Shrinivas and Natraj particularly of the same caste to which Narayan belongs, have very little or nothing to lose by such attitude, though it has marred the onward march of progress. But the worst sufferers are the down-trodden, the people of weaker sections of the society. For all their sufferings, injustice, inhuman cruelties and exploitation at the hands of the high castes, they only blame themselves and their fate. The untouchables have separate colonies away from the mainstream of life as is realistically portrayed by Narayan in *Waiting for the Mahatma*, as if it is all pre-ordained for them to do the work of scavenging all their life and live at some distance away from the town from generations together. Does Shrinivas, the journalist mean to say that everything is right with them and that there is nothing, people can do to uplift them from that wretched lot?

Mahatma Gandhi has been brought in by Narayan in *Waiting for the Mahatma*, as a character propagating certain ideals which he held dear to him. There is no denying the fact, that the Mahatma had a lion's share in liberating the country from British domination. However, his idea of absolute faith in God appears misleading.

At one place in the novel the Mahatma speaks of God in association with the beauty around the hutments of the scavengers. He is reported to have said, "God is everywhere, and if you want to feel his presence, you will see him in a place like this with a beautiful river flowing, the sunrise with all its colours, and the air so fresh."[19] It will not be out of place here to quote what Narayan writes about the dwellings of the scavengers. "It was probably the worst area in the town, and an exaggeration even to call them huts; they were just hovels, put together with rags, tin sheets and shreds of coconut matting."[20] While one cannot doubt the idea of God being a common bond between all human beings including the wicked, since all have faith in Him, Mahatma's singling out the untouchables as being Harijans and his reported statement that God's presence can be felt only amongst the low caste people is only to hypnotise them to accept their calling as something noble. Everybody knew and even the Mahatma could not deny that the untouchables have suffered the centuries of miseries and exploitation at the hands of the high caste. Mahatma Gandhi is reported to have said: "As you all know, while we are asking for freedom from the grip of a foreign nation, we have ourselve, for centuries, trampled under-foot millions of human beings without feeling the slightest remorse for our iniquity...."[21] Placing absolute faith in God and waiting for his boons for the changes in their lot has done no good, rather it has crippled them in life.

One thing that must be noted here is that the untouchables who were denied everything in their life, had nothing more to do than to serve the high caste and believe in God and pray to Him to bless them. It is this feeling that Gandhi had exploited to the fullest extent. Whenever he went while touring the famine-stricken villages, Gandhi comforted the sufferers by talking to them about God. He met the local village men and women and spoke to them about God. The watchward with the Mahatma seemed to be to have absolute faith in God and eveything will be all right.

Mahatma Gandhi no doubt fought for the abolition of untouchability. On his visit to Malgudi, he beckoned an urchin of a sweeper to come and sit on the diwan much to the fury and anger of the Muncipal Committee Chairman. But it is all the more shocking to find that he did not touch the caste system which he felt, was not bad in itself. He wanted that the untouchables should do their scavenging ungrudgingly as assigned to them by the so-called sacred Shastras. It is absurd to think that people should serve society by filling in the station in which they happen to be placed. And Narayan's characters are possessed with the same idea that everything is pre-ordained and that there is nothing in their hands to change their lot.

Save Chandran, Raman and others of the younger generations, Narayan's characters have refused to come out of the caste barrier. Raju's mother (*The Guide*) flares up when she learns that Rosie belongs to another caste. "Are you of our caste? No, our close? No...After all, you are a dancing girl. We do not admit them in our families."[22] Even Jagan, that fanatic preserver of Gandhian principles, is reluctant to accept a non-Hindu girl as his daughter-in-law. Raman's aunt goes on pilgrimage when she knows that the girl Raman has chosen to be his wife, belongs to another religion. There is no denying the fact that the picture as portrayed by Narayan is widely seen even today; marriages are arranged within the castes, and the lower caste people are harassed some way or the other, and are looked down upon by the high caste in the society.

Narayan's individuals are a fatalistic, God fearing eccentric lot moving in the traditional society of Malgudi. Disgusted with themselves or with the life around them, they make half-hearted attempts to assert themselves, criticising some of the old soccial values, which they feel, have chocked them in life. However, they miserably fail to cope with the collective force of the traditional society. That 'they have nothing in their hands to change their lot' make their life all the more miserable. Naturally, their thoughts turn to some 'Divine Agency' to solve their problems and then follow fastings and prayings to propitiate invisible gods — the phenomenon most common in Hindu society. Many of them either run away to escape from the reality, or resign to their fate unquestioningly. While some become sanyasi, some seek refuge in spirituality. On the whole, the individuals are conservative in outlook, reluctant to accept the changes in society, although it appears that they move with the passage of time, of course passively with no will or determination on their part, treading along the predetermined mechanical track.

Notes and References

1. Ramesh Shrivastav, *What is so Great in R.K. Narayan?* from *Perspectives on R.K. Narayan*, edit Dr. Atma Ram (Ghaziabad : Vimal Prakashan, 1981), p. 206.
2. Anthony Beal, *D.H. Lawrence : Seleccted Literacy Criticism,* edit. (Heinemann, London, 1955 C.F.), p. 6.
3. R.K. Narayan, *Swami & Friends* (Mysore : Indian Thought Publication, 1971), p. 160.
4. *Ibid.*
5. R.K. Narayan, *The Vendor of Sweets* (Mysore : Indian Thought Publication, 1967), p. 179.
6. R.K. Narayan, *The Financial Expert* (Mysore : Indian Thought Publication, 1981), p. 132.
7. R.K. Narayan, *Waiting for the Mahatma* (Mysore : Indian Thought Publication, 1981), p. 124.
8. R.K. Narayan, *The Dark Room* (New Delhi : Orient paperbacks, 1978), p. 73.
9. Ram Dial, *The Anima-Animus Interaction*, From *Perspectives on R.K. Narayan*, p. 142.
10. R.K. Narayan, *The Painter of Signs* (Great Britain : Penguin, 1976), p.8.
11. R.K. Narayan, *Mr. Sampath* (Delhi : Hind Pocket Books, 1979), p. 4.
12. M.K. Naik, *The Ironic Vision* (New Delhi : Sterling Publishers Pvt. Ltd., 1983), p. 42.

13. Dr. K.C. Bhatnagar, *Realism in Major Indo-English fiction* (Bareilly: Prakash Book Depot, 1980), p. 112.

14. R.K. Narayan, *The English Teacher* (Mysore : Indian Thought Publication, 1981), p. 106.

15. R.K. Narayan, *My Days* (Mysore : Indian Thought Publication, 1979), p. 136.

16. *Ibid.*, p. 144.

17. R.K. Narayan, *Mr. Sampath*, p. 60.

18. R.K. Narayan, *The Man Eater of Malgudi* (Mysore : Indian Thought Publication, 1980), p. 183.

19. R.K. Narayan, *Waiting for the Mahatma*, p. 45.

20. *Ibid.*, p. 23.

21. Mulk Raj Anand, *Untouchable* (New Delhi : An Orient paperback, 1970), p. 160.

22. R.K. Narayan, *The Guide* (Mysore : Indian Thought Publication, 1958), p. 169.

CHAPTER 3

NARAYAN'S CONCEPTION OF SOCIETY

I. Social Values

Through the series of Malgudi novels Narayan faithfully presents the social values, norms and mores which have been in existence and still continue to play a major role in shaping the lives of Hindu people. Now that, the Indian society has undergone a considerable change under the impact of Western Civilization; the changes have been vividly noticed amongst the people. O.P. Mathur rightly observes : "Narayan does assert the validity of traditional Indian values but the wind from the West has changed much of the panorama."[1] Malgudi is seen steeped in tradition and its inhabitants are men and women with their roots in family and religion. Even today they cherish a heritage of faith and values, customs and rituals and even dogmas and superstitions.

The traditional Hindu family as the nucleus of social structure, has zealously guarded its old norms, mores and values. Its sanctity is inviolable and its violation is nothing short of a sacrilege. It causes disruption and unhappiness. Marital fidality, the most precious of the Indian values is the theme of the *Dark Room*. Savitri, the traditional Hindu wife can put up with insult and maltreatment, but her husband's infidelity is the last straw. She bursts out, "Don't touch me,...you are dirty, you are impure. Even if I burn my skin I can't cleanse myself of the impurity of your touch."[2] Similarly Sampath gets the hardest kick from life when he gets emotionally involved with Shanti, the film actress. When he tries to pursue her, she leaves him a note of warning: "If I find you pursuing me, I will shave off my head and fling away my jewelry and wear a white sari. You and people like you will run away at the sight of me. I am, after all, a widow...."[3] Margayya (*The Financial Expert*) cannot bear the sight of his graceful daughter-in-law Brinda in tears on account of his son's debauchery. Even Marco who is callous and coldblooded, disowns his wife, Rosie when he comes to know of her infidelity. "But you are not my wife, you are a woman who will go to bed with anyone that flatters your antics."[4] Raju's mother, being steeped in traditional social values, could not accommodate the idea of living with a 'tainted woman' and she left her home to go with her brother.

The husband and wife relationship in a Hindu family is more or less one-sided. For it is the man who dominates the family scene. As a matter of fact, the woman has a pivotal role to play in the Indian household. She is instrumental in keeping the family harmonious and united. And yet she is subjugated to inhuman cruelties and miseries. Her status and position in the orthodox Hindu family has been reduced to nothingness. For example, Savitri (*The Dark Room*) feels impotent in her own house. She has to greet the guests Ramani brings at odd hours, no matter if there is no food left for her. But then, there is a social custom that the guest should be received and properly fed. However, Ponni, a low caste woman we meet in *The Dark Room*, does not seem to suffer at the hands of her husband, nor does she have any pessimistic outlook, in her life. She is full of life with an independent mind of her own to face the challenges of life. The futility, the frustation and an inescapable moral weakness that has made Savitri cry and sob, does not touch Ponni who deals her husband with a firm hand. Savitri has nothing but defeat in her life. "How impotent she was, she thought; she had not the slightest power to do anything at home and that after fifteen years of married life."[5] This is the pathetic cry of a majority of orthodox Hindu women even in today's society. Rosie's predicament is all the more pathetic and miserable. Her husband Marco is callous and cruel. He does not give the slightest attention to Rosie's wishes. Raju is right when he comments: "Dead and decaying things seemed to unloosen his tongue and fire his imagination, rather than things that lived and moved and swang their limbs."[6] Even Sita who is adored as ideal woman character in *The Ramayan*, met similar cruelties and injustice at the hands of her husband. For Rama, life of Sita simply did not count, what counted was his personal name and fame, and the opinion of his subject. How cruel he was towards Sita, was evidently seen when during her pregnancy she was abandoned to her fate in the jungle in consequence of public disapprobation, for the simple reason that his honour was at stake, with a malicious gossip in the town that Sita must have conceived from Ravana while she was in Lanka. In the end she had no other alternative but to appeal to mother earth to open and bury her.

Besides marital relationship, Narayan deals with other important family themes like the father-son relationship, parental love and lack of communication between the old and the young generation. For example, Jagan, *The Vendor of Sweets* has all the cares and love for his son. But having come under the impact of Western Civilization Balu is a completely changed person. Consequently the father-son relation has been strained so much so that there is a total lack of communication between the two. It is only through the uncle that Jagan could get some information about his son's doings. As a result, in his old days Jagan has no other choice but to go out in wilderness out of frustration. Margayya, the financial expert too is very much anxious for his son's welfare and expects good many things of him. But, ironically enough, the very son, Mali becomes the cause for his total ruin in the end. The entire financial edifice that he built so laboriously collapses in no time.

Sex, even in so polite a form as arranging marriage, is the subject of much embarrassment for the young that Chandran's younger brother Seenu can not even bring himself to voice the matter to his brother. As for Chandran, it is impossible to address the girl he has fallen in love with, directly. His plight has become all the more intolerable for him when he comes to know of his mother's determined opposition to any change in social convention that initiative for marriage proposal should come only from the bride's parents.

Hindu society is divided into castes and subcastes and marriages are often arranged within the caste as is evidently seen and observed even today. Raju's mother does not accept Rosie as her daughter-in-law; Raman's aunt is opposed to his marriage with Daisy; even Jagan, the Gandhian follower is shocked to know his son's relations with a half-Korean half-American girl that he has brought from Americca. When Chandran is opposed by his parents to marry the girl he loves, he sounds rational : He wants that the watertight compartments in the society must be abolished. There are a very few persons like Marco (*The Guide*) who do not stick to their caste, as he accepts Rosie of a dancing class as his wife. But the marriage between Marco and Rosie ends on a very sad note.

In India where marriage is a sacrament, a man and a woman living together without getting married are sinners. Jagan (*The Vendor of Sweets*) the tradition respecting sweet Vendor, winces under the blow of disclosure that Mali, his Americanised son and Grace are guilty of outraging this eternal moral tenet. What breed of creatures are these? He wondered, 'they had tainted his ancient home'.

Some women characters like Swami's grandmother, Shrinivas's Granny, Raman's aunt can be cited as the representatives to uphold the old values of Hindu life. They are certainly irrational and superstitious in their outlook, and opposed to any kind of change in social conventions.

Mark Granny's feelings on Gandhi's visit to Malgudi: "For her, the Mahatma was one who preached dangerously, who tried to bring untouchables into the temples, and who involved people in difficulties with the police."[7] It is the attitude of the highcaste orthodox people, which has been largely responsible for keeping a large section of Indian population away from the mainstream of life. We have a passing reference about the life and dwellings of the sweepers in *Waiting for the Mahatma*. Mahatma Gandhi was certainly against the feeling of untouchability, and he tried to abolish it from the Indian social scene. When he saw a sweeper's urchin, he beckoned him and had him hoisted on the divan, while others in the assembly especially the Municipal Chairman of the town spurned him with "Oh, lord, all the world's gutters are on this boy and and he is going to leave a permanent stain on that Kashmir counterpane."[8]

However, instead of denouncing the prevalent chaturvarnya, he sought to perpetuate the system and thereby disillusioned the low caste people. Mahatma Gandhi belonged to the co-called higher strata of the society. And he never experienced the inhuman cruelties and exploitation as did the untouchables all their life. Had he faced himself the miseries and sufferings of the subjugated dumb race, he certainly would not resort to the mere imaginings, and play on the life of the helpless scavengers. Gandhi writes: "I do not want to attain Moksha. I do not want to be reborn. But if I have to be reborn, I should be reborn as untouchable, so that I may share their sorrows, sufferings and the affronts levelled at them, in order that I may endeavour to free myself and them from that miserable condition. I therefore prayed that if I should be born again I should do so not as Brahmin, Kshatriya, Vaishya or Shudra, but as an Atishudra."[9] To Gandhi scavenging was a noble profession, and he encouraged the scavengers that they should not be ashamed of it. Dr. Babasaheb Ambedkar is worth quoting when he remarks :

> to preach that poverty is good for the Shudra and for none else, to preach that scavenging is good for the untouchables and for none else; and to make them accept these onerous impositions as voluntary purposes of life, by appeal to their failings is an outrage and a cruel joke on the helpless classes which none but Mr. Gandhi can perpetuate with equanimity and impunity. In this connection one is reminded of the words of Voltaire who in repudiation of an 'ism' very much like Gandhism said: "Oh, mockery to say to people that the suffering of some brings joy to others and works good to

> the whole ! What solace is it to a dying man to know that from his decaying body a thousand worms will come into life."[10]

To quote Gandhi again, "The Varnas have an intimate relation to one's profession. The pursuit of one's calling is one's dharma. He who forsakes his, falls from his Varna.... When everybody discards his Varna the malorganization of society grows, chaos reigns and society perishes."[11] It is an irony that the Mahatma who tried to abolish untouchability, sought to perpetuate the Varna system by praising scavenging as the noblest service to society.

The civility which Narayan's characters display to each other does tell us something about the society in which this quality exists in everybody. It also tells something about the attitudes of the author himself who senses beneath the details of poverty and hypocrisy, the residual, enduring significance of his subjects as human beings. For exampie, Velan's civility to Raju is worth noting. The candid confession by Raju of his illegitimate love affair with Rosie and the subsequent jail for his committing forgery, could not shake Velan's absolute faith in Raju.

The attitude of civility and forebearance has roots in Hindu religious system. Except Brahmin (He is no less than Brahma Himself according to the Hindu scriptures) the people of all other castes have been taught to listen to their superiors unhesitatingly. Not only that, to fulfil their grand evil design they propound the Karma theory according to which the lot in which they are placed is pre-ordained, and that, because of sins they committed in their previous birth, they have to discharge their duties (decreed by God?) ungrudgingly. This has resulted in total submission to their fate. For fear of punishment in hell, they have got to forebear and put up with insults and cruelties the Brahmins heap upon them. It is therefore little surprising that an ordinary peasant like Velan should have unwavering faith in Raju who poses himself as Godman.

The feeling of co-operation towards fellow brethren that is seen amongst the Malgudians is most welcome. Here too, the caste creates barriers, for the social values differ from caste to caste and are fairly restricted to caste fellows, and fellow feelings never cross the boundary. A time comes in the life of man when he feels utterly helpless and miserable. It is at this juncture he needs sympathy and encouragement from his neighbours. For example, on missing of his dear and only son, Margayya (*The Financial Expert*) saw the whole house reeling in front of his eyes, the surroundings darkened and he sat down unable to bear the strain. His brother and the whole neighbourhood thronged the house with encouraging words: "You must bear it, brother; you must bear it."[12] Margayya never knew till then that he had so many wellwishers in the city. Their suggestion that Margayya must go to Madras to verify the truth himself, also bears fruit in the sense Margayya leaves for Madras and comes back with his son.

A similar incident has been presented in *The English Teacher* when the headmaster is reported dead by Krishna. His wife breaks down utterly. She collapses on the floor and the whole street crowds into the house as to what befell on the lady. Then again, when the headmaster shows his surprise presence, the whole of Anderson street is there, very few tinsmiths are at their foundary, very few blacksmiths and tailors at their work. People surround him and fire questions at him. The headmaster remarks: "I never imagined that I had such a large public." "I thought I was fairly obscure."[13]

The most prominent and enduring note in Narayan's view of life is reflected into restoration of the moral order with the liquidation of Vasu, the taxidermist, (*Man Eater of Malgudi*). His self-destruction is symbolic of the triumph of good over evil. The cosmos prevails over the powers of chaos. And everybody including Natraj heave a sigh of relief, when his problem is solved by the inexorable moral law. However, the moral law upheld by Narayan implies man's helplessness, and his utter failure to cope up with the problems of life. Natraj and his friends have miserably failed to check Vasu's nefarious activities. The only consolation in the course of their sleepless nights is the comment by Shastri, an orthodox-minded Sanskrit semischolar who says: "Every Rakshas gets swollen with his ego. He thinks he is invincible beyond every law. But sooner or later something or other will destroy him."[14]

The same moral principle that 'moral order established itself' has been echoed in *Mr. Sampath*, in which Shrinivas, the journalist marvelled at the invisible forces of the universe. It is the type of attitude that everything is right with the world, and that there is nothing in this world which a man can do or undo, that has hampered the progress of Indian society. That a journalist like Shrinivas who attempted to set the world right within twelve pages of his *The Banner* should have come to view the things in such a passive manner explains for the tremendous impact of Hindu religious attitude and the social norms and mores which have crippled the lives of Indian people.

The Hindu society being traditional and fatalistic, the social values they cherish can not be otherwise. They are a God fearing folk. For whatever, they do, they throw themselves at the mercy of God. Their success and failure, happiness and sufferings are all what they think as God's Benediction. Hindus are so dogged about the traditional ideas that they hardly come out of the social framework they have evolved from time immemorial. The social scene presents a sorry picture when we come across such examples like Margayya's going to gods on Badri Hills for the supposed infertility of his wife. Daisy (*The Painter of Signs*) has to make a strenuous fight for the eradication of such evils from the society. It is a pity that the Indians even today have miserably failed to develop scientific outlook which is the need of the hour. It is well nigh impossible for people to effectively shape their destiny, improve the quality of life and provide the basic necessities to people and an opportunity for doing creative things in life unless they are steeped in science and in the use of latest technologies. For, science awakens the urge to enquire and to search for truth. It gives one the ability to observe and sharpens one's perception. This kind of attitude would certainly help bring about a social change removing from its surface the mark of traditionality that has kept Indians in its vicious grip. Many of the social values upheld in ancient times, are now outworn and irrelevant in the changing times, and are to be discarded once for all.

Notes and References

1. O.P. Mathur, *West Wind Blows through Malgudi* : From *Perspectives on R.K. Narayan*: edited by Dr. Atma Ram (Ghaziabad : Vimal Prakashan, 1981), p. 29.
2. R.K. Narayan, *The Dark Room* (Delhi : Orient Paperback, 1981), p. 75.
3. R.K. Narayan, *Mr. Sampath* (Delhi : Hind Pocket Books, 1979), p. 274.
4. R.K. Narayan, *The Guide* (Mysore: Indian Thought Publication, 1958), p. 152.
5. R.K. Narayan, *The Dark Room*, p. 8.
6. R.K. Narayan, *The Guide*, pp. 81-82.
7. R.K. Narayan, *Waiting for the Mahatma* (Mysore : Indian Thought Publication, 1981), p.41.
8. *Ibid.*, p. 31.
9. Mahatma Gandhi, *Young India*, 27th April 1921.
10. Dr. B.R. Ambedkar, *Gandhism* (Jalandhar : Buddhist Publishing House), p. 29.
11. Mahatma Gandhi, *Harijan Bandhu*, 19-3-1933. *From The Collected Works of Mahatma Gandhi*, Publications Divisions.
12. R.K. Narayan, *The Financial Expert* (Mysore : Indian Thought Publications, 1981), p. 128.
13. R.K. Narayan, *The English Teacher* (Mysore : Indian Thought Publications, 1981), p. 191.
14. R. K. Narayan, *The Man Eater of Malgudi* (Indian Thought Publications, 1980), p. 96.

II. Economic Aspect

Narayan is castigated by leftist critics for his concentration on too narrow and unrepresentative a section of Indian society, and it is in a sense true that he prefers to write about the middle class, the class of which he is a member and which he knows intimately from the inside. Most of the protagonists of his novels are financially well settled, and though not wealthy, the pangs of poverty never touch them. The poor are nodoubt present in his novels; beggars and untouchables also appear as they do in the life and the consciousness of the middle class. They have not been given any substantial role to play in Malgudi. In fact, the so-called middle class common men Narayan presents in his novels belong to higher strata of the Indian society. It is the society of a financially middle class people of orthodox Hindu families firmly rooted in the age-old customs and traditions.

Narayan shows that in the modern society which is burdened with great stress and strain, a healthy philosophy of money merits serious consideration. Money is a mixed blessing which can become a curse if not judiciously understood and used. Pursuit of money for money's sake is frought with grave dangers both for the society and the individual. Margayya (*The Financial Expert*) in his madness to amass a huge amount of money, evolves a fantastic money circulating scheme which, through Dr. Pal, attracts hundreds of subscribers especially black-marketeers who have made stupendous fortunes through foul means during Second World War.

The entire financial world of Margayya runs on credit. Where he goes wrong is in putting away bags of currency notes in the hastily cleared rooms of his house, instead of starting productive enterprises which would have yielded him a higher interest than what he has promised to his creditors. As a result, a little quarrel with Dr. Pal who helped him build up his financial edifice, has ruined him completely making him a pauper overnight.

The issue crops up again in another novel *The Guide* in which the protagonist — Raju is possessed with greed for money. There is a phenomenal rise in the fortunes of Raju just as Rosie ascends the pinnacle of glory. He is nodoubt successful as an impressario but his motives are questionable; his eyes are always on the cheques that Rosie brings from every dance concert. In his greed for money he scarcely cares for her personal feelings. He makes her work like a machine and allows her no time for a little sight-seeing. He becomes caddish, callous, possessive and jealous. While money comes to him in cheques, he goes on leading a reckless life, drinking and gambling and squandering money till Rosie laments: "I feel like one of those parrots in a cage taken around village fairs, or a performing monkey."[1] Raju's criminal act of forging Rosie's signature with rougish intention of misappropriating her jewels and converting them into easy wealth lands him among low criminals in the lock up.

Status of man in modern society is very much linked up with his financial position. No one shows respect or even cares for a poor man however righteous and virtuous he may be in his life. He cuts a sorry figure in the company of the rich. Obviously Margayya considers the acquisition of wealth as a pre-requisite for due status and honour in the society. When he is hard-pressed for money, he feels: "If I have money, I need not dodge that spectacle dealer. I need not cringe before that stores man. I could give those medicines to my wife. The doctor would look at her with more interest, and she might look like other women. That son of mine, that Balu I could give him every thing."[2]

When insulted and threatened by the secretary of the Bank for illegally possessing the loan application forms, Margayya feels humiliated and curses himself for his low economic position. Like Beaky Sharp who is held in low esteem at Miss Pinkerton's Academy, Margayya feels that the world treats him with contempt because he has no money. Fired by insults and humiliation he undertakes prayers and fasts, befitting the Hindu religious ideas to propitiate Laxmi, the Goddess of Wealth. And lo! through a novel scheme he acquires a huge wealth. That he fails to keep it is his own fault. Dr. Pal is only an instrument for his ruin.

After becoming a big businessman, through Laxmi's grace, as Margayya himself says, he evolves a strategy of 'extra-ordinary' complexity and takes charge of the school where his own Balu has been studying. Balu who has been a failure all along, and his progress report marked zero, now shows a marked improvement in his studies. Margayya has done all this because of his influential position in the society. He wants Balu to grow up into an educated man, graduating out of a college and probably going for higher studies to Europe or America. Margayya has a fixed notion about money. He says, "Money alone is important in this world. Everything else will come to us naturally if we have money in our purse."[3]

Money works miracles and corrupts the man. In modern society corruption has become widely rampant, and Malgudi is no exception. Prior to his becoming a pseudo-saint, Raju was a man of high status in the society, of course through Nalini's dance concerts. That what Raju could do with his money is well illustrated through Raju himself. He speaks thus:

> Through my intimacy with all sorts of people, I know what was going on behind the scenes in the government, at the market, at Delhi, on the race-course, and who was going to be who in the coming week. I could get, a train reservation at a moment's notice, relieve a man summoned to jury work, reinstate a dismissed official, get a vote for a co-operative election, nominate a committee man, get a man employed, get a boy admitted to a school, and get an unpopular official shifted elsewhere, all of which seemed to me important social service, an influence worth buying at the current market price.[4]

Set against such social background, amongst the people of low economic position, there is a class labelled in Indian society as the untouchables of which we have a passing reference in *The Waiting for the Mahatma*. The picture of a sweepers' colony in the novel is most horrifying: "It was probably the worst area in the town, all crowded in anyhow, with scratchy fowls crackling about and children growing in the street dust".[5] Mahatma Gandhi called them Harijans and praised their profession (Scavenging) as the noblest service to society. He says : "God is everywhere, and if you want to feel his presence you will see him in a place like this."[6]

Indian society is divided into castes and sub-castes. Each caste tends to live in a separate part or street of the village with the sweepers' colony entirely separate from the rest as we have seen in *The Waiting for the Mahatma*. In this way a large section of the Indian population was kept away from the mainstream of life. And since the Hindu religion demanded that the untouchables should not be allowed to acquire property, it was but natural that they had to pull on somehow on begging entirely at the mercy of the so-called high caste people. Mahatma Gandhi is reported to have said: "The Shudra who only serves (the high caste) as a matter of religious duty, and who will never own anything, is deserving of thousand obeisance.... The very Gods will shower down flowers on him."[7] The religious sanctity given to the profession and ennobling it still further by no less person than Mahtma Gandhi is a conspiracy against mankind. The kind of philosophy of the Hindu religion, sought to be perpetuated by the Mahatma and the like has deprived the Shudras of the basic needs of life. They became docile and dependent, powerless and crippled all through their life. To quote C.E.M. Mathews, "The Harijans do not seem able to rebel effectively against their present position, but this seems to be due to their powerless economic position rather than to any real acceptance of the situations."[8]

Members of the middle class which Narayan presents in his novels, are also seen reduced by some fatality or family quarrel or commercial disaster like Margayya in *The Financial Expert* or Rama Rao in *Out of Business* to penury to the sale of his wife's jewels, the renting of the family house, the reduction to a diet of rice, ghee and vegetables. The way Margayya reacts to his dizzy heights, the fortune he makes and loses overnight, is typical of the average Indian. And he has no remorse for it, nor does he learn anything from his downfall, for he has a faith: "the lord gives and taketh away, praised be the lord!"[9]

The plight of peasants in general is most pathetic, for most of their time they are worried having been at the mercy of Rain God for proper nourishment of their crops. If there are heavy rains crops are submerged in flood waters destroying the entire harvest; the peasants suffer when there is scanty rain either. Since they don't have irrigation facilities and sufficient storage for rain waters, they miserably fail to utilize the waters for the growth and nourishment of crops. Having thus deprived of the chances to get enough of what they have invested, they lose their balance of mind and are engaged in petty quarrels on trivial matters. Narayan presents a realistic portrayal of drought period in Mangala during which they lose their temper and come to blows all of a sudden.

> When people asked for a measure of rice he (shopman) demanded fourteen annas for it. The man who wanted the rice lost his temper and slapped his face. The shopman came out with a chopper and attacked the customer; and those who sympathised with the man gathered in front of the shop and invaded it. The shopman's relatives and sympathisers came at night with crowbars and knives and started attacking the other group. Velan and his men also picked up axes and knives and started out for the battle. Shrieks and cries and imprecations filled the air. The little hay that was left was set on fire, and the dark night was ablaze."[10]

A realistic picture of the life of a worker is found in Narayan's short stories. For example, a worker, a male nurse in *A Breath of Lucifer* in the Volume entitled *A Horse and Two Goats* replies in answer to the question, what do you earn? "Sometimes ten rupees a day, five, two, or nothing. I have eight children, my wife, and two sisters and niece depending on me, and all of them have to be fed, clothed, sent to schools, and provided with books and medicines. We somehow carry on. God gives me enough...."[11]

Lower still, life is even more horrifying, conducted constantly on the edge of total disaster. A handful of rice, a tumbler of milk, a little coconut, can constitute the whole purpose of man's activity. Caste, poverty, family, religion and men's harshness to man are the objects of an undeflected scrutiny. The middle class boy will take advantage of the poor teacher; the employer will ruthlessly sack the servant; the blind beggar will bully his dog; the girl will be given in marriage against her will. And very cleverly and cunningly we pass the blame on to the invisible God, praying Him day in and day out for the eradication of man made sufferings. The rich and the high castes continue to exploit the poor and the low caste. And the sufferers appear so fatalistic, they hardly do anything except praying to gods. Under such circumstances how practical and full of wisdom are the words of the Buddha: "Self is the lord of Self, you are your own lord."[12]

Narayan has given interesting glimpses of Indian social life impaired by the demoralising effect of the materialistic civilization. People have sold out their souls, and do not hesitate to make money for the disposal of an unclaimed dead body. Narayan writes: "They even haggled with the grave digger and were left with so much money at the end of it all that they drank and made merry for three or four days and gave up temporarily their normal jobs."[13] Balu in *The Financial Expert,* and Mali in *The Vendor of Sweets* get completely spoiled. While Balu becomes the cause of his father's ruin, Mali makes his father, Jagan leave the home and go out in wilderness.

That a considerable part of the national income lies concealed in dark boxes, is the work of the anti-social people who have made stupendous fortunes by adopting foul means. These people include,

> the rice merchant in a certain back street who hoarded rice in a secret godown, whose frontage was stuffed with innocent looking rag and old paper collected for the papermills,...the contractor who built huts and got enormous bills passed easily by bribing the Garrison Engineer. He was a rich man because his huts meant to stand for three years would stand only for a couple of months — till the bills were passed by the friendly Garrison Engineer! It was this margin that gave him real wealth,...drug stockists who didn't show

their stock, but bargained when it was a matter of life and death to a customer.... All these people had a lot of money...the town was reeking with it.[14]

Narayan holds these persons upto mild ridicule as his intent is not to satire. He is not a progressive writer nor for that matter a moralist. "Narayan unlike Ben Johnson does not profess to write a comedy with a purpose because he has no faith in the social significance of literature."[15]

Most of Indians are blind followers of traditions, and the adherence to those irrational traditions has been largely responsible for the ruin of several families. Dowry system is one such social evil which has rocked the Indian society. In India from the days of *Atherveda* (V1-2-3)[16] "the birth of a girl, grant it elsewhere, here grant a boy..." down to the middle ages then to our modern times, has been looked upon with resignation if not with sorrow. Because the Dowry system which has come down to us, has impoverished the parents. Narayan could not overlook the evil and portrayed it realistically in *The Financial Expert*. Margayya tells his followers how his father has to face the evil while marrying his daughters. He says: "Three daughters were born to my father. Five cartloads of paddy came to us every half year, from the fields. We just heaped them upon the floors of the hall, we had five bails to our house; but where has it all gone? To the three daughters. By the time my father found husbands for them there was nothing left for us to sit at home!"[17]

Like the untouchables, womenfolk in Indian society have more or less had the same status of being slaves of their masters. That they are wholly dependent on the menfolk for their daily bread has been revealed through, Savitri in *The Dark Room*, who wails: "What despicable creations of god are we that we can't exist without a support?"[18] However, Western influence and the industrialization in modern times have considerably changed their lot and brought about a change in outlook. Thanks to the efforts by Indian social revolutionaries like Mahatma Jyotiba Fuley, which have awakened them to their rights and liberties. They have now learnt to stand on their own legs occupying position of high rank at par with menfolk in every walk of life. Shantabai in *The Dark Room* who struggles herself free from her drunkard husband, and comes all the way from Bangalore to Malgudi to work as trainee officer in the Insurance Bank, stands in complete contrast with the docile Savitri; similarly Shanti in *Mr. Sampath* who has lost her husband whom she did not know, has taken to acting in the film company established by Sampath. Rosie in *The Guide* asserts her individually, no matter she has to leave her husband

Marco to enrich her dance. But then she becomes a name to be reckoned with in the whole country. Raju's comments in this connection are worth quoting. He says: "Neither Marco nor I had any place in her life, which had its own substaining vitality and which she herself had underestimated all along."[19] Daisy in *The Painter of Signs* has revolted against her father and made her would-be-husband sign a marriage contract so that she would get ample time to fulfil her mission on family planning. Narayan held these women characters responsible for causing family disturbance, and it is true to some extent. But then, one is not necessarily to be docile and wholly submissive like Savitri at the cost of her very existence to keep the harmony of the family.

All major characters, especially the protagonists in Narayan's novels belong to middle class families. Swami the school boy; Chandran, the Bachelor of Arts; Krishna, the English Teacher; Savitri, the docile Hindu housewife; Shrinivas the Journalist; Jagan, the Vendor of Sweets; Raju, the Railway Guide; Margayya, the Financial Expert; and even Raman, the Painter of Signs...all those come under the category of average income group. They have to work to maintain their livelihood. Swami, the son of a headmaster, is of course, dependent on his parents. But Chandran has to take up the reportership of *The Messenger* as Narayan himself has done to support his family. Krishna earns his hundred a month mugging Shakespeare and Milton, and then teaching them to the students at Albert Mission college. Jagan's is a strenuous business. He wakes up at 4.00 at dawn, works on the frying pan and sells his commodities within a short period of time. Shrinivas starts *The Banner* with a view to awaken the public from its pigheadedness, and later, writing the Manuscript, *The Burning of Kama* for A Sunrise picture, a venture by Sampath, he helps his family.

Raju is the most engaging and complex character like Margayya. Both of them are obsessed with money. For them, it is money that matters. However, it is the greed that ruins them in the end. While Margayya forgets his family, loses his appetite and becomes a pauper in the end, Raju finds himself in police custody for forgery. Raman is an ordinary painter of signs moving from place to place painting the sign boards for Daisy who makes him dance to her tune. Largely, the characters portrayed by Narayan are not so wealthy as not to bother for financial problems in life, nor are they so poor as to feel the pangs of poverty as Mari is seen facing it crying in the heat of the burning sun, for umbrella repairs from every street corner of the town.

The majority of his protagonists are, however, self-complacent in their life, and are pleased with what they possess. It is only Raju the guide, Margayya, the financial expert, and Sampath, the printer of Malgudi who aspire to reach the highest peak and tumble down headlong in the end. Raju drinks and gambles and after much enjoyment ends in police lock up for his forgery. Sampath has run after Shanti, the film heroine and ended as a forlorn lover. Margayya refuses to change himself in relation to his financial position, and yet becomes a pauper for lack of proper planning and foresight to utilize the amount in some constructive purposes. Shrinivas and Natraj are portrayed as passive on-lookers and are overwhelmed by the subtle and mysterious balance in Nature. They find nothing wrong with the world, and are reluctant to bring about any change in their lot, nor do they take any initiative to improve their financial position.

Narayan's female characters especially Rosie (*The Guide*) and Daisy (*The Painter of Signs*), educated and talented as they are, are highly ambitious and missionary in their real to excel in their profession. For them, money has no fascination. While Rosie aspires to be the greatest dancer of Bharat Natyam, Daisy devotes her time and energy to check the population growth of the town. While Savitri remains docile, confined to her traditional role of a Hindu house-wife who does not stand without support; Rangi, the temple dancer ascends Vasu's attic losing her shame and honour for her bread and butter. It appears that her calling has made her what she is, rather than genuine need on her part to do so. She has no pricks of conscience about it. However, the fact that can not be denied is that it is the circumstancces that have pushed her to be a temple dancer. It is her helpless economic position that is taken advantage of by the rich and the hypocrite. The profession that has come down to her from her mother and grandmother, is nothing but the henious crime committed in the name of religion. It is the profession at the altar of which, Rangi and innumerable others surrender themselves ungrudgingly, much to the comforts of the well-to-do.

Narayan restricts his protagonists to move within the set limit. Since they are superstitious, they find themselves entirely at the mercy of the Almighty. Naturally they lack courage and determination to face the challenges of life that stand before them. They either run away or surrender themselves to their fate, praying for God's boon every now and then.

Notes and References

1. R.K. Narayan, *The Guide* (Mysore : Indian Thought Publications, 1958), p. 203.

2. R.K. Narayan, *The Financial Expert* (Mysore : Indian Thought Publications, 1981), p. 23.

3. *Ibid.*, p. 17.

4. R.K. Narayan, *The Guide*, pp. 196-197.

5. R.K. Narayan, *Waiting for the Mahatma* (Mysore : Indian Thought Publications, 1981), p. 23.

6. R.K. Narayan, *Waiting for the Mahatma*, p. 45.

7. *Varna Vyavastha*, p. 51. Quoted by Dr. B.R. Ambedkar, *Gandhism* (Jalandhar : Buddhist Publishing House), p. 27.

8. C.E.M. Mathews, *Health and Culture in a South Indian Village* (New Delhi : Sterling Publishers Pvt. Ltd., 1979), p. 74.

9. P.S. Sundaram, *Ambivalence of R.K. Narayan* edited by Dr. R.K. Dhavan, *Explorations in Modern Indo-English Fiction* (New Delhi : Bahri Publications Private Ltd., 1982), p. 147.

10. R.K. Narayan, *The Guide*, p. 96.

11. R.K. Narayan, *A Horse and Two Goats* (Mysore : Indian Thought Publications, 1982), p. 118.

12. Quoted by A.R. Kulkarni, *The Buddha, The Trimurti and Modern Hinduism* (Nagpur : Shrinivas Mudranalya, Suvichar Prakashan Building, 1980), p. 81.

13. R.K. Narayan, *The Financial Expert*, p. 22.

14. *Ibidi*, p. 158.

15. Margaret Berry, *R.K. Narayan : Lila and Literature*, Journal of Indian Writing in English IV.2 (1976).

16. Atherveda (V1-2-3).

17. R.K. Narayan, *The Financial Expert*, p. 5.

18. R.K. Narayan, *The Dark Room* (Delhi : Orient Paperbacks, 1978), p. 123.

19. R.K. Narayan, *The Guide*, p. 223.

III. Social Vision

Narayan's is an authentic portrayal of a conservative Hindu society presented through the series of Malgudi novels. Man is imitative by nature. He imitates his elders and forms an outlook which has a large bearing on him in later years of his life. The social values along with the religious faith he is being instructed to follow and inculcate, are rarely forgotten; rather they influence him in a big way. Dr. Chesnokov and V. Karpushin in their *Man and Society* rightly observe: "like a man's aptitudes his whole mental cast is influenced by his social environment."[1] It is but natural that Narayan, a product of conservative Hindu society, is committed to Hindu ideology. Despite his formal education during British Rule in India, there was no substantial change in his outlook. This was because Narayan received early training of his life under the strict supervision of an orthodox grandmother about whom Narayan writes "Grandmotherhood was a wrong vocation for her.... She had an absolute passion to teach and mould a young man."[2]

Narayan has been largely successful in projecting himself as a detached observer of life. However, his too close a proximity to the Hindu myths and legends around which he usually built his themes, and the revision of ancient epics, *The Ramayan* and *The Mahabharat* are enough for our understanding that Narayan closely followed Hindu view of life in depicting south Indian middle class society. His portrayal of the values of the south Indian society is authentic. And Narayan is all praise for his doing so. But unlike Mulk Raj Anand and Bhattacharya who are outspoken and committed, Narayan lacks conviction of purpose, and he remains fairly obscure while presenting many of the incidents that we come across. Narayan seems to shy away from the world which by its portrayal might arouse controversy or antagonism.

Narayan lacks comprehensive vision of life embracing the whole Indian society. Probably he fears risky ventures and hence sets his own limits — this far and no more. That apart, his constitutional, temperamental and social limitations account for his narrow range in characterization. Whereas Mulk Raj Anand or Raja Rao deal with the rich and the poor, the Indian and the European alike; Narayan depicts only the middle class and fumbles when he moves out of his range. The protagonists like Swami (*Swami and Friends*), Chandran (*The Bachelor of Arts*), Krishna (*The English Teacher*), Ramani (*The Dark Room*), Shrinivas (*Mr. Sampath*), Jagan (*The Vendor of Sweets*), Raju of *The Guide* and Raman of *The*

Painter of Signs all belong to the same class and the caste to which Narayan belongs. In this Traditional Hindu society revolt was practically impossible. However, Narayan has observed and drawn majority of his fellow beings especially of younger generation being frustrated and chocked up under the combined weight of customs and traditions. For example, Chandran's revolt against tallying of horoscopes, Savitri's running away from home in protest against her husband's debauchery speak volumes in this regard. Rosie has left her husband to fulfil her aspiration in life; Daisy's revolt against her father to take up a missionary work of family planning is also suggestive of the same attitude. However, they could not withstand the collective force of the traditional Malgudi and resigned to their fate. This Narayan has experienced himself as a member of the conservative Hindu society. In fact, as a travel writer and also a journalist Narayan has had a vast scope to know people of varied faiths and also of caste and categories for which India is so famous. But Narayan's Hindu mind refuses to see anything outside his class and caste.

Committed as he is to Hindu ideology, Narayan built his themes around Hindu myths and legends. *Swami and Friends*, *The Bachelor of Arts* and *The English Teacher* are more or less autobiographical in content with many of the major events being occurred in the life of Narayan himself. Narayan's psychic contact with the spirit of his dead wife, the theme Narayan developed in *The English Teacher* is more than enough to support the contention. The story of *The Guide* is evidently based on the Hindu idea of a sinner becoming a saint. Savitri in *The Dark Room* is but the projection of a *Sita-Sati-Savitri* image of India's past. Through Shrinivas (*Mr. Sampath*), and Natraj (*Man Eater of Malgudi*) Narayan depicts that the Malgudians are mere puppets in the hands of fate and that they have nothing in their hands that they can do or undo in this universe. Natraj and his bohemian circle appear so helpless before Vasu, the taxidermist that they just do what other orthodox Hindus undertake in their life, fasts and prayers to propitiate gods or goddesses and wait for their boons. They have absolute faith in the belief that the moral order establishes itself. *Waiting for the Mahatma* is replete with Hindu ideals the Mahatma represents in his life. Even the story of a modern young couple Raman and Daisy in *The Painter of Signs* has been based on the mythical king Santhanu. Narayan's revision of ancient plots *The Ramayan* and *The Mahabharat* is one more proof of the fact that the author is partial to cultural inheritance of the Hindu society.

However, Narayan has certainly seen the society fastly changing. Daisy is a remarkably modern character dedicated to the missionary work of family planning. She has to make a strenuous fight to overcome the monster of abysmal ignorance which Narayan has seen as the inherent incongruity in national life: material advancement on the one hand, and wide rampant mental impoverishment on the other, Shyam Pandharipande presents a realistic picture of Indian society thus : "....despite the spread of education and progress of science, Indian — even urban India — by and large remains superstitious; that superstition and blind faith have played and continued to play havoc with many lives."[3]

From the suffering helpless Savitri to Bharati in *Waiting for the Mahatma* and then to Daisy in *The Painter of Signs*, Narayan has shown the rise of individuality in women. Rosie in relation to this change in the social attitude towards women is the representative of a new class of women who had the opportunity to be released from the conventional confinement to join colleges and universities in order to acquire a formal education. Rosie is a master's degree holder despite the fact that she belongs to lower strata of the society. Daisy attaches no sentiments to married life. A girl's running away from the family, her bringing up and education of a missionary organization, her acceptance of a social work, and her living all by herself represent the modern trend.

The traditional Hindu family has fixed norms, mores and values which all the members have a strict understanding to follow. Marital fidelity, the most precious of the Indian values is repeated in most of his novels. Narayan's views on marriage, are in tune with the tradition and conservative atmosphere. Tallying of horoscopes still has an important role to play in Hindu marriages. They believe that marriages are made in Heaven and bride and groom meet, not by accident or design, but by the decree of fate. Boys and girls meet and love after marriage rather than before. Dr. K.C. Bhatnagar's comment: "You can only marry the girl you are destined to marry...,"[4] seems to be cyclic view of the universe adumbrated by Narayan in his novels. That Narayan himself followed all orthodox rituals is evidently seen on the eve of his daughter's marriage. Narayan noted: "In February 1956 my daughter married her cousin Chandru. In spite of house building, I had put by enough to celebrate the wedding with music, feasting, lights,...nor did I overlook the orthodox rites and rituals enjoined in our Scriptures."[5]

The division of Hindu society into four castes — Brahmin, the Kshtriya, the Vaishyas, and the Shudras — had become so rigid in the course of time that they have come to be degenerated into watertight compartments with the result that the people of one caste have no reciprocal relations with those of another caste. The people of the upper three castes could at least mix with each other. But the fourth one which includes Shudras and Untouchables, was totally alienated from the main-stream of life. That marriages are often arranged within the caste has been realistically portrayed by Narayan. Raju's mother does not approve of Raju's marriage with Rosie as she belongs to a low caste family. Jagan is reluctant to accept Grace as his daughter-in-law. Even Raman's aunt could not accommodate the idea of Raman's marriage with Daisy, a Christian girl. Narayan does not seem to be opposed to love marriage as he himself has gone through it. But even Narayan's love marriage could not have materialised, had Rajam belonged to a different caste. With rigid caste prohibitions to be followed, love marriages are a remote possibility. However it is heartening to note inter-caste marriages are being encouraged to maintain the communal harmony. Thanks to the attempts made by the social reformers such as Mahatma Jyotiba Fuley and Dr. Babasaheb Ambedkar who fought against the social stratification on the basis of caste system and brought about a remarkable change in Indian society. Chandran is unequivocal in this regard. He says, "...these watertight divisions must go. Community, Caste, Sects, Subsects and still further divisions."[6] And though Chandran's sentimentalism is disapproved Narayan's consciousness of the gradual disappearance of the caste system has been delightfully portrayed in '*Castes: Old and New.*'

As regards sex Narayan is very clear in his views. Actually there is no place for sex permissiveness in Indian ethos — as is evidently seen in most of his novels particularly in *The Vendor of Sweets* and *The Painter of Signs.* Narayan writes : "There is too much sex already, perhaps there is room for one who gives sex its proper place.... You see, it has its time...and also place."[7]

Disgusted with the present-day educational pattern dominated by materialistic considerations, Narayan appears to be in favour of 'Leave Alone' system of the ancient times. He seems to be very much helpless in the prevalent social set up. For, revolt against the social values was practically impossible. Narayan himself writes: "My outlook on education never fitted in with the accepted code at home."[8] However, Narayan went through it all without conviction, or any sort of distinction. Narayan's protagonists too have more or less the same attitude in their life. Narayan's Malgudi therefore is "utterly without hope, without glory, without any kind of magnificence.... It is supremely the world of the average and the ordinary. Even when people try to break out of the ruts they are in, they return, again and again, to the same routines, the same humdrum rounds of existence they are habituated to."[9]

Perhaps Malgudi is too proud of its cultural heritage. Life in Malgudi seems to be a rainbow of smiles, of tears, light and shade, giving a wild goose chase to each other — with the destination — status quo. After a brief escapade, his characters have a habit of returning to their original milieu, for better or for worse: Savitri to the *Dark Room*, Margayya to the Bunyan Tree, Natraj to the office. However, Narayan visualises a gradual change in the established customs and traditions. Narayan is not unaware of the fact that general trend of the modern time is to be scientific and rational. He has brought in Raman and Daisy to represent this view to its fullest extent. In spite of it, Narayan could not free himself from the clutches of age-old Hindu beliefs — which have been enjoined in the so-called sacred sastras. His belief in the immortality of soul remains unchanged. He made it clear in his autobiographical book *My Days*, that the psychic contact he narrated in *The English Teacher* was actually based on his own psychic experiment with the spirit of his dead wife. Besides, he devoted the whole, novel, *A Tiger for Malgudi* to represent the Hindu philosophy of life that made the hermit believe that he himself and the tiger were once brothers in their previous life.

The way he handled the themes, and his keeping himself detached and passive on-looker, made it abundantly clear that Narayan has no pricks of conscience about it. Narayan evidently based the story of *The Guide* on the reports he read in a leading newspaper that some Brahmin pundits had undertaken fasts and prayers to appease the rain god during drought, and that on the twelfth day it rained, much to the relief of the people anxiously waiting for it. Believing it to be true Narayan handled the theme of *The Guide* accordingly. P.S. Sundram is worth quoting when he poses a pertinent question in this regard: "Why does not Narayan write, 'The clouds were gathering fast, there was a peal of thunder, and the first drop fall?' Is he afraid that thereby he will be joining the irrational crowd asking for and getting a miracle? Why, on the other hand, does he not write, 'But there was no rain?' Would that be considered an anticlimax undercutting all that has been raised through suspense and suggestion?"[10]

Religious ideology typical of ancient Indian epics had influenced many of protagonists. Frustrated under the weight of social customs, they have run away from the problem of life; some of them have found refuge in the philosophy of life which at best be called quietism. For instance, Krishna in *The English Teacher* finds peace in the world of spirits.

Shrinivas in *Mr. Sampath* and Natraj in *The Man Eater of Malgudi* find refuge in the philosophy that the moral order establishes itself, and that, since they find nothing wrong with the world, it is absolutely unnecessary for them to do any thing in the universe. We can see some didacticism and inevitable patience, obedience, faith in reincarnation that all the hardships of this life will be compensated in the life hereafter. And it has found conscious expression in each of his novels.

There is really nothing wrong if they imitate and imbibe the good qualities of the ideal characters presented in the epics. What is really upsetting is the projection of these characters as gods and worshipping them for removal of man-made social evils which they would have certainly got rid of, had they sincerely tried themselves.

But the irony is that it was systematically and cleverly passed on to the non-existent God and they quietly slipped themselves off the scene, enjoying at the discomfiture of the subjugated dumb race. In India where so much requires to be done urgently, and those like Shrinivas who should be doing them, merely sit back and philosophise. Under such circumstances the worst sufferers are the people of the lower strata of the society, and the high caste continue to exploit them upholding at the sametime the ridiculous moral principle that the moral order establishes itself(?).

A village in the philosophy of Narayan symbolises native strength and simplicity, no doubt, but the absurdity and irrationality which mark the general mentality of the village folk are vividly noticed amongst the villagers too. Chandran, moved by the innocence, love and respect of the villagers, abandons his suffron cloth because it pricks his conscience. But it is also true that the villagers have been gullible enough to mistake him for a holy person. The same motif is developed in *The Guide* where an ex-convict Raju is mistaken for the holy person and is implored to undertake a twelve-day fast during the drought. The gullibility of the villagers has reached its peak here, for it has changed ex-jail-bird into a dying god in the end. The sylvan scenery of the surrounding area and the innocence and the simplicity have certainly encouraged Raju to play the holy man, and thus, is caught in the coils of his own self-deception, thereby deceiving the gullible masses. Krishna too initiates his psychic contact with the spirit of his dead wife in the village, while in *The Dark Room* it soothes the grief stricken Savitri to return to her still unrepentent husband accepting humiliation and total defeat in life. The general impression one gets from Narayan's portrayal is that 'there can be no such thing as evading fate', says the astrologer. reading out a sanskrit aphorism, 'but you can insulate yourself to some extent from its rigours.'

Befitting an orthodox Hindu, Narayan is primarily pre-occupied with man's filling of the life-role entrusted to him by Hindu philosophy of life. The protagonist in each of Narayan's novels is made to play his life role during the course of which he or she either matures in the process or rebels or simply drifts. He is sometimes destroyed by a characteristic inner weakness as is the case with Raju in *The Guide*. His characters have become fatalistic with little or no scope for their talents. The feeble and half-hearted attempts they make at self-assertion have been largely inadequate for the full growth of their individuality, they remain for most part of their life captives of the circumstances which have led them to believe that they are mere puppets, and that they are tossed this way and that by the caprice of fortune.

Narayan's social vision is the vision of a man visualising a conflict between the old and the new generation with gradual disappearance of old social values. However, individual efforts miserably fall short to change the collective force of the society, rather he has to accept life as it is, majority of the people around him being dipped in superstitions. Western influence has changed much of its panorama, but there is not substantial change in Narayan's outlook. The Hindu rites and rituals that have been dominating the social scene, still hold the water. However, Narayan is not unaware of the trend of the modern man of being scientific and rational. Raman and Daisy in his latest novel *The Painter of Signs* represent the trend. They are viewed with comic irony. But the fact remains that the modern young man is bent on discarding many of the rites and rituals which are merely absurd. Narayan's is a realistic portrayal of the society of which he is a member, and he presents it in a simple and lucid language with half comic-half ironic tone.

Notes and References

1. D. Chesnokov & V. Karpushin, *Man and Society* (Moscow : Progress Publishers, 1966), p. 11.
2. R.K. Narayan, *My Days* (Mysore : Indian Thought Publications, 1974), p. 11.
3. Shyam Pandharipande, *Nagpur Times : Cross Section*: Friday, 28th June 1985.
4. Dr. K.C. Bhatnagar, *Realism in Major Indo-English Fiction*, edit. R.K. Chavan (Bareilly : Prakash Book Depot, 1980), p. 109.
5. R.K. Narayan, *My Days*, p. 166.
6. R.K. Narayan, *The Bachelor of Arts* (Mysore : Indian Thought Publications, 1979), p. 56.
7. Pendurang Rao, *Tea with R.K. Narayan, Journal of Commonwealth Literature*, June 1971.

8. R.K. Narayan, *My Days*, p. 53.
9. Kripal Singh, *The Ordinary and the Average as Satiric Traps* : From *Explorations in Modern Indo-English Fiction* (New Delhi : Bahri Publications Pvt. Ltd., 1982), p. 135.
10. P.S. Sundaram, *Ambivalence of R.K. Narayan* : From *Explorations in Modern Indo-English Fiction*, p. 150.

IV. Cultural Aspect

Curiously enough, Hindu culture of which Narayan is the product, has come down to us surviving the terrible shocks in the Mugul and British empires. No wonder, poets and writers sang and wrote about its glorious past. It still has tremendous impact on the minds of Indian public. Narayan writes: "the impact of life, the material and substance of our thoughts are the same everywhere in any state. Traditionally, India is *The Ramayan*, *The Mahabharat* and *The Puranas*. The value remains the same in every village, town or city."[1] The main stories and characters are vividly real to most people young or old. It is possibly the reason why the traditional concepts like the Ashramas and Purushastras in various disguises and distortion and subterfuges have influenced Narayan in portraying many of his characters in the novels.

Generally, the middle class people of the conservative Hindu society that Narayan presents in his novels, are hardly ever ready to bring about reformative change; nor do they seem to receive with interest any alien influence. They are just complacent with what they possess and are absorbed in glorifying the culture to which they belong. And yet, under zealously guarded norms, mores and values, there appears simmering discontent amongst the people of new generation, who awakened to their rights and liberties, try their utmost to rise above the so-called pre-ordained roles they have been playing for generations together. Some have gone to the extent of revolting against the established customs and traditions. But since, they are firmly rooted in them from their very childhood, their attempts prove futile, they fall back in the end to their normal station accepting defeat in life.

Hindu culture with its norms and values which Narayan depicts in his writing discussed here in two aspects 1. Moral 2. Philosophical, practically speaking, have a far-reaching effect on the minds of Indian people.

1. MORAL ASPECT

Narayan faithfully presents in his novels Hindu beliefs and myths around which his themes are usually built. Being a product of Hindu culture he simply could not avoid the impact of the cultural surroundings around him. Conservative South Indian society that Narayan presents with all its irrational customs, induces a sense of futility amongst the people of new generation. Most of his characters believe that every thing on earth is pre-ordained and that they are helpless creatures. Chandran, *The Bachelor of Arts* who is intensely in love with Malthi at last runs away from home because he feels frustrated with the irrational and absurd custom of tallying horoscopes. *Mr. Sampath,* the cunning shark, also is impelled by the circumstances to leave Malgudi forever. Krishna, *The English Teacher*, after the death of his wife, finds solace in the world of spirits. Raju, in *The Guide*, dies a ruined man, not because he wanted to die, but circumstances so conspire that the only alternative before him was to become an unwilling martyr. Truly speaking, all his characters cherish a heritage of faith and values, customs and rituals and even dogmas and superstitions. As a result, they have all returned in the end to the original station accepting defeat and futility of action. Dr. Badal rightly observes: "His characters, mostly printers, journalists, teachers, shop-keepers, moneylenders, guides, astrologers, saints, students etc., are people oppressed with much the same sense of futility and helplessness generated by age-old social conventions within which there is no scope for their talents."[2]

Total submission largely owes to the cultural atmosphere in which they are caught. For example, Savitri in *The Dark Room* finds herself like a bamboo pole which cannot stand without any support. She has absolutely no rights in her own household. And yet she puts up with insult and maltreatment at the hands of her husband. But when she finds it all intolerable, she leaves the home to assert her individually. However, she has no courage to face the challenges of life. In the end she comes back accepting total defeat. Janamma another character in the novel, also believes that total submission to the husband leads to peace. The dictum laid down by Manu and later moralists that a woman shall have no right is so deeply embedded in the minds of both that Ramani could bluntly tell Savitri that she has no right whatsoever. Utterly helpless she repents: "In Yama's world the cauldron must be ready for me for the sin of talking back to a husband and disobeying him, but what could I do?"[3] It is very shocking that even in modern times Ramani quotes the ancient epics and scriptures which enjoin upon women the strictest identification with their husbands. Even Rosie who is highly educated, and leaves her husband for the sake of her aspirations, longs to die at her husband's doorstep. How pathetic her words are: "he may not admist me over the threshold, in which event it is for better to end one's life on his doorstep."[4]

Narayan's novels are not vehicles of mass propaganda. But they depict the breakdown of feudal society and express the changed ideas concerning the family as a unit and the conflict between the old and the new. The strains of growing individualism have not spared the age-old joint family system in India. But it is gratifying to note that, though the old system is in peril, the sense of kinship is always strong. For example,

Margayya and his brother are next door neighbours, and they are not on talking terms. But they are always ready to share each other's joys and sorrows.

However, there is a considerable change in human outlook with regard to some of the cherished ideals. Daisy in *The Painter of Signs* refuses to pay obeisance to her would-be-in-laws. And Raman considers it odd to fall at anybody's feet. Daisy rebels against her parents wishes and domestic orthodoxy. S.P. Bhardwaj rightly observes: "Narayan has certainly moved along with the times and the change in his presentation of domestic life can be clearly seen when his two novels *The Dark Room* and *The Painter of Signs* are read side by side."[5]

The perennial struggle between the young and the old has been touched in *The Vendor of Sweets.* The portrayal of Mali's character who makes his father go out in wilderness, is truly a representative of the moronic mentality of present-day youths. In spite of the changes in his surroundings, Jagan continues to live up to the traditions of his times. It appears that in Jagan Narayan depicts a Karmayogi, a disciple of Mahatma Gandhi and one who tries to live in accordance with the teachings of the Gita. He represents the timeless and unchanging values of the Hindu way of life, of course, with its obscuritanism and irrationality too. But much of Jagan's pietism is humbug. Tara Malhotra writes: "His artistic pose, his Benthemite zeal for public service, but obstensible high regard for Gandhian tenets bespeak a hypocrite."[6] Jagan renounces his home to watch a goddess to come out of stone, but he does not forget to carry a cheque book with him. It clearly shows that his renunciation is a farce.

Marital fidelity is perhaps the most precious and durable of the Indian values. Savitri, the silent suffering housewife in *The Dark Room,* puts up with insult and maltreatment at the hands of Ramani, her husband. But she could not bear her husband's infidelity with a trainee officer working under him, "Don't touch me." She cried moving away from him, "You are dirty, you are impure."[7] Sampath himself is to be blamed for the collapse of his domestic life when he gets emotionally involved with Shanti, the film actress. Margayya, unable to bear his son's debauchery, assault Dr. Pal, responsible for it, so violently that he loses his financial edifice in no time. Marco disowns his wife Rosie when he learns of her emotional attachment with Raju.

The puritanic and holistic Indian approach to sex is also reflected in Narayan's novels. A man and woman living together without getting married are regarded as sinners. Jagan is shocked when he knows that

Mali, his Americanised son and Grace are guilty of outraging this eternal tenet. However, Narayan never allows sex to become an exciting commodity in writing. Sexual passion, in fact, is not a theme which we come across anywhere in his novels. Narayan seems to think of it as something too private and holy to appear publicly. He treats the theme in *The Painter of Signs* but in a mocking manner. The morbidity in sex obsession and its ultimate dissipation comes out in Raman's frustration. Actually, there is no place for sex permissiveness in the Indian ethos. The carnal side of sex and its futility is also brought out in *The Vendor of Sweets*, when Jagan feels fatigued by all the apparatus of sex, its promises and its futility, the sadness and the sweet at the end of it all!

R.K. Narayan is evidently making use of the Indian myth of a sinner becoming a saint on the lines of Valmiki. Raju in *The Guide* is an admirable modern version of the Indian myths. That an ex-convict Raju should be mistaken for sadhu by gullible masses is not new to Indian culture. The events leading upto the death of Raju may sound fantastic to a rational mind, but in India, writes S.C. Sanyal, "whenever, there is a drought village saints are always expected to fast and work miracles and some of them like Raju may die which thousands watch with devotion studded eyes."[8] It fact, Raju has no moral discipline to guide him in his life. Shiv K. Girla rightly says: "An excess of intellectual pragmatism, coupled with a Machivellian desire to succeed, results in the total disintegration of his ethos."[9] He finds himself alienated as the vital links of traditional ethics snap one after another. He feels utterly lonely and miserable in the midst of a vast ocean of people. The anguished realisation which Krishna had after Susila's death — a profound and unmitigated loneliness is the only truth of life — is also echoed in Raju's feelings.

Unsettling impact of materialism on the traditional world of Malgudi is projected in the major novels *Mr. Sampath* and *The Financial Expert*. Both Sampath and Margayya uproot themselves from the traditional ethos to run after illusion (greed) of material success. It is not that something above them has caused their financial collapse. But it is their weakness and that unquenching greed that has ruined them in the end. Sampath gets emotionally involved with the film actress Shanti, and has to leave Malgudi abruptly. Margayya's financial edifice gets ruined by his own misdoings. Narayan rightly comments: "He was like a fanatical mountaineer who sets his heart on reaching the summit of Everest. He might be standing on the highest peak. Yet he can never feel that he has really attained the highest."[10] Margayya thus loses his way in the wilderness of materialism. His pursuit of money corrodes the very foundation of his being. The realisation of the abiding value of life 'love' dawns on him but only after his material collapse. And yet Margayya does not seem to learn anything from his experience. His fatalistic attitude has still held his mind under its firm grip. Margayya puts his arm round his son Balu and pointing to his old knobby trunk, says: "I hope the tree is still there. Go there, that is all I can say; and anything may happen thereafter".[11]

The present education system has come under severe criticism as it is completely dominated by materialistic consideration. "This education had reduced us to a nation of morons; we were strangers to our own culture, and camp followers of another culture, feeding on leaving and garbage".[12] Narayan favoured a 'Leave Alone' system adopted by the Headmaster in *The English Teacher* which he felt, would transform children into wholesome human beings. This type of education is, in fact, a revival of the old Indian tradition of open air schools run by saintly teachers with specific stress on inculcating moral principles among the students.

The most prominent note in Narayan's view of life is reflected in the restoration of moral order with the liquidation of Vasu, the taxidermist, (*The Man Eater of Malgudi*). The traditional and quiet, unruffled by social or political upheavals, Malgudi has never had such a demonic on-slaught of gross materialism. Vasu, the only villain in Narayan's fictional Malgudi is allegorically a demon on the puranic pattern. His act of self-destruction like Bhasmasura, is viewed in Malgudi as something symbolic of the triumph of good over evil. However, the belief in such triumph that 'moral order establishes itself', and that everything on earth is pre-ordained as we have seen in the case of Natraj and his friends, has robbed the people of their intellect and human potential. That they are dependent on an outside agency, implied that they are utterly helpless in the hands of the so-called Divine power. As a result, their individual will power lies crippled under the tremendous weight of cultural taboos and irrational customs and traditions leaving no scope for their talents.

Even Shrinivas, the journalist, and Krishna, *The English Teacher* come under the same category as Natraj is, totally passive onlookers at the happenings around them; giving every chance for black marketeers, drug stockists, garrison engineers, and the like to exploit the gullible masses in every possible way. Even Raman "felt abashed when he realised that he was perhaps picking his own loot in the general scramble of a money mad world! He wished he could do without it, but realised too that it was like a desire for a dry spot, while drifting along neck deep in a cesspool."[13] This being the case of a majority of persons in traditional Malgudi, one can only imagine as to what would be the lot of the subjugated dumb race. Malgudi is conservative and self-complacent, so why should they care for the miserable have-nots?

2. PHILOSOPHICAL ASPECT

R.K. Narayan owes a great deal to Hindu philosophy of life. So great is the impact that he once admitted to Ved Mehta, "...inability to write novels without Krishna, Ganesh, Hanuman, astrologers, pandit and devdasis or temple prostitutes and explained his point of view by adding in his characteristic humble way that in any case that has turned out to be my India."[14] He simply brushes aside the subject other than the Hindu myths and legends around which his novels are usually woven. With his recent books 'Gods, Demons and others' (1969), The Ramayan and the Mahabharat (1972), and also the novel '*A Tiger for Malgudi*' Narayan plunged wholeheartedly into the revival of old Hindu myths. The Hindu epics and folklores are constantly referred to in his Malgudi circle showing Narayan in his true spirit.

It would not be out of context if we peep a little into the basic assumptions that lie at the heart of Hindu religion which has largely moulded Narayan to the core of his heart.

While Hinduism has roots in the literature of the Vedic age extending from about 1500 B.C. to 600 B.C., the term Hinduism cannot be appropriately applied to the religion of the period. It can best be called, and as many scholars referred to it as 'Brahmanical' religion. The Vedic literature that has come down to us through Sanhita, Brahmnica, Aranyaka and Upnishada was mostly in the form of hymns created and memorised throughout ages by the priestly class. Hinduism is a modern term coined by him possibly because it would not then be totally confined to the Brahmin caste. To put it in a nutshell, it is 'old wine in new bottle' labelled as Hinduism so as to shrewdly hide its true nature and to accommodate a larger part of Indian population into its fold.

In fact The Veda is not a book nor the collection of books like The Bible or The Koran. It is the collection of diverse materials created over a period of a thousand years. Naturally it is bound to have several contradictions. There are a number of Hindu myths not at all consistent with each other. At times the universe is represented as having been created by God after the analogy of the work of a carpenter but at other times it is suggested that the whole of creation including the gods is the product of the process of natural generation. As regards the Upnishad it is said that

> " Over a hundred works are given the name of Upnishad but only about thirteen of these can be dated with assurance as belonging to the Vedic age. They do not present any consistent religion or philosophical system."[15]

Such contradictions in Vedic literature and even in later additions such as 'Shrutis and Smritis' have one way or the other benefited the priestly class to a considerable extent. For they have interpreted them differently at different time to suit the changing moods of the time. And that has been given legal sanction. Special provision has been made in 'Manu Smriti' to accommodate all the conflicting views. "When two sacred texts (Shruti) are conflicting, both are held to be the law, for both are pronounced by the wise to be valid law."[16]

While they proclaim rigidity in the matter of one's calling according to the station in life accorded by the so-called Divine Shastras, they allow too much flexibility and pave the way for double standard in every walk of life.

The dominating 'theme of the Upnishad is the identity of 'Brahmin' and 'Atma'. The formula 'tat tvam asi' (that art thou) has different meaning to different authors. Shankara the much acclaimed Hindu sage held that individual soul 'Atma' and the universal soul 'Brahmin' were completely identical. Brahmin being the only reality. The word 'Brahmin', the first of the four varnas was consciously used to make it synonym to Brahma, the supreme God. And the shastras have been created to show that the individual soul 'Atma' identified as being beyond change, something that is in fact, immortal, that Purush the immortal and the fearless is no other than Brahmin. "Underlying the exterior world of change there is an unchangeable reality which is identical with that which underlies the essence of man."[17]

Ramanuj, another South Indian Hindu scholar interpreted the formula 'that art thou' in a non-monistic sense believing that the human soul and the universal soul called God were distinct identities. It was this qualified non-dualism of Ramanuja that has played a very influential role in the history of Hindu religion by providing a metaphysical basis of the devotional worship.

In fact, the priestly classes have attempted every thing possible to maintain their supremacy. They have gone to the extent of making the will of God almost irrelevant while performing sacrificial ritual to win Him over; the ritual has assumed enormous significance within the whole cultural tradition. If a sacrifice were properly performed, the gods could not withhold the boons sought. Thus the sacrificer was regarded as controlling power that could bring blessings or destructions. After all, their main endeavour was to extol their supremacy and make all possible attempts to make the writings to suit the purpose. They have thus come to occupy the key position in the drama of the cosmic order. The priest is said to have controlled the secrets of the universe.

Making himself unchallenged and superior even to gods, by virtue of his being 'Brahmin', the priest has subjugated all others belonging to the lower strata of society, brainwashed them to accept the things (writings) as divinely ordained and lulled them into eternal passivity, in the fond worship of God, fasting and praying, sacrificing every thing to relieve themselves of the miseries and sufferings heaped upon by the self-proclaimed Bhu-Devs of Hindu society.

Fasting and praying to God for His blessings seem to be a common feature most popular among Hindus. Narayan's characters are no exception. Natraj and his friends (*Man Eater of Malgudi*) prayed to Vishnu to save the temple elephant from Vasu, the taxidermist. 'Oh Vishnu, save our elephant,' and lo! the temple elephant is miraculously saved when Vasu, to trap a couple of mosquitoes, bangs on his forehead with the flat of his palm and dies of concussion. We have a similar incidence of praying for the boons of goddess Laxmi in '*The Financial Expert*' where Margayya, in order to propitiate the goddess undertakes the forty day ordeal of fasting and praying till "his jaws ached, his tongue has become dry...he fell faint with hunger since he had to fast completely while praying."[18]

When there is a drought in the surrounding area of Malgudi, Raju (*The Guide*), an ex-convict who has taken refuge in the temple is mistaken for a Sadhu and is implored by Velan and others to undertake a twelve-day fast for the rains. "He went down to the river, stood facing upstream with his eyes shut and repeated the litany. It was no more than a supplication to the heavens to send down rains and save humanity."[19] It sounds incredible that a pseudo-saint like Raju should bring down rains by fast and prayers. Dr. Balram Gupta observes, "It is wrong to believe that Raju who is a selfish opportunist, a gross materialist and a voluptuous hedonist has all of a sudden become a martyr capable of making grace descend from heavens. The rains he sees (or thinks he sees) are indeed, a pathetic hallucination of a starving impostor.... For Raju life has become one stupendous hallowness and he collapses in the effusive and deceptive belief that there are rains in the hills."[20] The events leading unto the death of Raju may sound fantastic to the Western reader. But here in India it is a common phenomenon.

Absolute faith in the invisible God makes Indian masses gullible and superstitious. Narayan's is a realistic portrayal. Some elders in the village (*The Painter of Signs*) point out : God gives us children, how can we reject his gift? The chieftain argues: There is an old shrine in a cave over there where barren women can go and pray, and bear children. How would you explain it? Daisy answers, "You should ask the priest of that temple."[21] Jagan and his wife (*The Vendor of Sweets*) are taken to the temple of Santana Krishna, and very soon after this Ambika conceives. Similarly, the ritual carried out by Margayya (*The Financial Expert*) bears the fruit promised and as expected. Despite all planning and progress it is shocking to see people living in abysmal ignorance. Even long after independence the monster of illiteracy stands unvanquished and the social workers like Daisy have to face humiliation at the hands of the priest, and R.K. Narayan remains as unattached and objective, as if he has nothing to do with such things. As a result, the coming of a new child in the family is still regarded as the gift of the Almighty, and not as man's own doing. Barren women still seek the blessings paying lonely visits to the priest in the cave temple to get exercised their sterility.

God is supposed to be the infinite spirit whose presence is felt everywhere. Assuming that there exists a God outside us, the question is, would he really help us in relieving of our miseries and granting boons in life? Assuming it to be so, the God is most unjust to low caste people. In fact the so-called untouchables (a large part of the Indian population), have worshipped the God honestly and yet they have suffered untold miseries and sufferings, and also inhuman cruelties at the hands of the high-caste people. Are they free from subjugation even today? The London correspondent of *The Guardian* writes:

> " Attacks on untouchables (which is a far more candid word than the Mahatma's preposterous euphimism 'Harijans') are still regrettably common place in India, more frequent than floods, locust, plagues or incidents of sabotage on railways."

The Times of London further adds: "Various incidents are mentioned such as slicing of the ears of a harijan girl in Bihar for drawing water from a caste well. An unpleasant though specially not common mutilation is the cutting of pieces of Harijan young man with an axe by a caste Hindu mob in a village in Aurangabad,....over the renaming of Marathwada University as Dr. Ambedkar University."[22]

As a matter of fact, whether we pray to God or not, his benevolence should be alike to one and all, for we are supposed to be equal in his eyes. "If the supposed God could be won over by prayers it means that God is partial or in any case it will mean that He likes to be praised. Such a conception of God is revolting to a human mind."[23]

Man is so much accustomed to a belief in God that he finds himself amiss without Him. Therefore he creates a God to fill in the void in his mind. It is further clear that God exists in the mind only, and has no separate existence. The conception of an extraneous God is mere speculation. The theory that God is omnipotent and is all pervading, is without any basis and no rational being can accept it. A.R. Kulkarni observes: "In fact two evils flow when a man places reliance on God for the solution of the problems...firstly, he is always dependent on God and is not prepared to take any initiative himself. There is no scope for self-reliance. Faith in God and faith in one-self run counter to each other. Secondly, this belief leads to idleness and inaction."[24]

Most of Narayan's characters dependant as they are on God, appear mere puppets. To them everything on earth is pre-ordained, and that they are absolutely helpless. For most part of their life they remain captive of circumstances. As a result, they are frustrated either with their own self, or with the world around them. Sometime they run away from home in protest and take to the role of sanyasi. Sometimes they accept defeat in total submission to age-old traditional beliefs and social customs. Swami (*Swami and Friends*), Chandran (*The Bachelor of Arts*), Sampath (*Mr. Sampath*), Margayya (*The Finanical Expert*), Jagan (*The Vendor of Sweets*), Raju, the Guide and Shrinivas of the *Man Eater of Malgudi* are all helpless creatures torn this way and that by the caprice of fortune. Savitri (*The Dark Room*) is more than a bamboo pole which can not stand without support. She runs away from home in protest against her husband's illegal love affair with a trainee officer working under him. But she too accepts defeat in the end. The futility, the frustration and her own inescapable weakness made her cry and sob. "A wretched fate that wouldn't let me drown the first time...this is defeat. I accept it I am no good for this fight."[25]

Narayan consciously deals with the immortality of soul and its ultimate merger with the Divine Spirit as is evident in the second half of *The English Teacher*. The death of the wife fills the hero Krishna, the English teacher with belief that death is not the end of everything and that human personality has several other planes of existence. With this belief in mind perhaps Krishna on his wife's death undertakes psychic contact with the Spirit of his wife on the lines the writer has undergone when he too lost his dear wife. Narayan writes: "This outlook may be unscientific, but it helped me survive the death of my wife...I could somehow manage to live after her death...."[26] To the completely western-oriented persons who have no use for ghosts and planchettes, Narayan would no doubt seem to stretch their faith excessively. So far as they are concerned, Narayan's attitude in *The English Teacher* would be a puzzle. How could he, an English educated man, writing in 1945, tell us that the dead wife of his hero communicated with him regularly through a medium and referred to events and things in the house known only to her while living and found when checked, to tally? To the question whether the Tathagata exists after his death, the Buddha has a very rational and convincing reply: "That such a question is incapable of an answer as nobody can say what happens to the soul or mind after the death of the saint.... To say that the mind of the person dying with his desires unfulfilled hovers somewhere and again reborn is a baseless speculation and no rational being can accept it."[27] Death is the termination of life. The so-called soul is a combination of both life and mind. Since life and mind cannot survive without body it is meaningless to talk about an everlasting life or an immortal soul. Narayan seems to believe in an existence within a series of existence in the past and the future with spiritual and moral dividends — the result of accumulated actions leading to our present predicament and future prospects. This is evidently seen in many of his novels, and most of Narayan's characters take their present sufferings with a sense of resignation.

Varnashram Dharma

The theory that all people were divided into four classes is one of the most important aspects of the Hindu religion, laying emphasis on the performance of social duties and obligations according to carefully formulated codes of behaviour so as to keep the Brahmins on a higher plane in the society of all times. Of the four classes such as Brahmin, Kshatriya, Vaishya and Shudra, it is the two classes, the first and the last that attract attention of the scholars. For, the Brahmins controlled the religious institutions while the Shudra constituted the bulk of the composition. Literature of the Hindu religion was mostly written by the priestly class; and naturally therefore they presumably forward their own class interest. The statement such as "a Shudra is the servant of another to be slain at will, would have led to social anarchy, whereas the emphasis was always on social order."[28] The origin of the class structure was supposed to be divine and not human." No priestly class in any other civilization perhaps has made such claims for its sanctity, as did the Brahmins; but neither has any other received such willing recognition of that sanctity."[29]

Manu, the acknowleged Hindu law giver gives a graphic description as to the duties of each class and prescribes penalties for the transgression of the customary law in his *Manusmriti*.

> " To Brahmins be assigned teaching and studying (The Vedas) sacrificing for their own benefits and for others and giving, accepting (of alms).
>
> One occupation only the Lord prescribed to the Shudras to serve meekly even these (other) three castes."[30]

From the emphasis on the correct fulfillment of the proper duties of one's class, two main features come to the fore. On the one hand, it explains the high privilege accorded to Brahmins as the key stone of the social structure, on the other, it keeps Shudras entirely deprived of the basic needs required for the development of their personalities. The social order so structured and declared as divinely ordained has been maintained all through even in the great epics 'Ramayan' and 'Mahabharat'. It is interesting to note that while scholarship was confined to only one caste i.e., the Brahmin, Valmiki has been singled out for special favour and made the creator of the great epic called 'The Ramayan', possibly with the intention to show that there was no rigidity in caste barriers and that even 'Valya' the low caste, could attain the status at par with the high caste. However, we are shocked to learn therein the instance of one Shambhuk, the low caste, harassed and done to death for the alleged transgression of his Dharma he was supposed to follow, staying within the limits of the Divine social order.

"What the duties of the Shudras are", Bhisma said in Mahabharat, "The creator intended the Shudra to become the servant of the other three orders. For this the service of the other three classes is the duty of the Shudras. By such services of the three, a Shudra may attain great happiness. He should wait upon the three other classes according to their order of seniority. A Shudra should never amass wealth, lest by his wealth, he makes the members of the three superclasses obedient to him. By this he could incur sin."[31]

The religious laws so propounded and maintained all through ages have been upheld above everything else in Bhagwad Geeta also,

> " Better in one's dharma (class duties) which one may be able to fulfill but imperfectly, than the dharma of others which is more

> easily accomplished. Better is death in the fulfillment of one's own dharma. To adopt the dharma of others is perilous.... Krishna further adds : "The fourfold class system was created by Me in accordance with varying disposition and the actions (resulting from them)."[32]

From the above passage one common feature that comes out vividly is the interpretation of the system of Chaturvarna being more or less the same in all the religious books said to have been divinely ordained. We all know it that the religious books have been written by the priestly class. But to say that they have been divinely ordained and therefore eternal and perfect is to befool the gullible masses and rob them of their natural rights. They had been foolish enough so long to tolerate the unnatural social stratification in the name of religion. But to expect the same thing from new generation standing at the threshold of 21st century is an attempt at self-deception. The irreligious things perpetuated so unashamedly in one form or the other now stand openly criticised and ridiculed by educationists and scientists alike. The new generation cannot be so easily taken for granted. They accept only when they find anything natural and reasonable. When we see them revolt against the age-old social tradition, we dub them as sentimentalists. But we fail to understand the feelings that lie chocked up in their hearts. Their attempts at self-assertion simply fail to prevail. Narayan appears vehemently opposed to any kind of sentimentalism. And restoration to normalcy is widely welcome by Narayan.

It is really disgraceful that even today the system of Chaturvarnya is being upheld in one form or the other. The lower castes are looked down upon with disgust. Raju's mother (*The Guide*) is first sympathetic towards Rosie, but she changes her attitude when she learns that Rosie belongs to the dancing girls class. She flares up: "Are you of our caste? No, our class? No,... After all you are a dancing girl. We do not admit them in our families."[33] Jagan (*The Vendor of Sweets*) is reluctant to accept a non-Hindu girl as his daughter-in-law. Even Raman's aunt (*Painter of Signs*) does not favour Daisy to be Raman's wife. Narayan does really touch the pulse of the Hindu society in depicting the perverted mentality of the Hindus.

Malgudi wears a festive look on Mahatma Gandhi's visit to the town. But Shriram's Granny appears restless for the reason that he allows untouchables to touch the Hindu gods. But the crux of the matter lies elsewhere. It is not simply allowing them to enter the temples but in giving them equal rights, and treat them as human beings. From the conversation Mahatma Gandhi undertakes with an urchin of a sweeper occupying the Divan much to the chagrin of the Muncipal Committee chairman, it becomes clear that he takes immense interest in listening to him about his father's calling. The Mahatma advises him to be neat and tidy no doubt, but he hever enquires of him whether he goes to school at all. This shows how the Mahatma looks at the problem. It is a paradox that a person who thinks untouchability as a bolt on the Hindu society, should defend the system of Chaturvarnya.

Now the question remains: whether Narayan too upholds the Hindu philosophy with all his customs and traditions. Apparently it appears that Narayan's is an objective method of writing novels. And he has depicted what he has seen or observed in the society around him. But one should not overlook the fact that Narayan's writing centres round one common pattern of order disorder and return to normalcy with revival of old social order. K.R.S. Iynger interprets this theme in terms of "a flight and an uprooting, a disturbance of order followed by a return, a renewal, a restoration of normalcy."[34] However there is something arch and elusive about Narayan's treatment of Indians. In the words of H.M. Williams, "The key to the Malgudi cycle appears to me to lie in the complicated nature of Narayan's conservatism. He is typically (orthodox) Hindu in his celebration of the static: change and progress and 'future shocks' — all beat in vain upon Indian eternal passivity and on the persistence of her ageless traditions."[35]

The pattern is seen clearly revealed in the *Man Eater of Malgudi* where the peaceful life of Natraj and his friends get completely disturbed on the entry of one Mr. Vasu, the taxidermist. His self-destruction in the end is viewed as symbolic of the validity of faith in the age-old religious system. At the end of the novel Natraj and Sastri return to printing bottle labels for aerated water company and the blue curtain of printer's room is peacefully drawn upholding the moral order of traditional Malgudi. The moral order seems to be something divinely ordained rather than the one to be instinctively followed by human beings on earth. It also establishes the fact that man is a mere puppet and that he has no scope whatsoever for his talents and potentialities to develop his personality in Hindu religion.

Narayan perceived a balance of power in human relationship as is evidently seen in the philosophy of life upheld by Shrinivas, the journalist in *Mr. Sampath*. He marvelled at the invisible forces of the universe which maintained the subtle balance in all matters. The whole scheme of things "seemed so perfect that it was unnecessary for anybody to do anything...it seemed to him a futile and presumptuous occupation to analyse, criticize and attempt to set things right anywhere."[36] It is this kind of philosophy that has resulted in total inaction on the part of Hindus and hence India's social backwardness! "Shrinivas is by profession a journalist who would like to wield his paper 'The Banner' less as a flag than as a broom to sweep the many cobwebs that has taken possession of every nook and corner of our land. Is it for him to talk of the futility of action, of reform?"[37]

The doctrine of 'Karma', an important aspect of Hinduism is one of perfect justice, nor is there anything pessimistic about the scheme, since man is master of his fate; but the crux of the matter lies elsewhere. Indissolubly linked with the concept of Karma is the other great characteristic feature of the Hindu thought, the belief in transmigration of soul. The idea that the human soul in death finds lodging in another body and to link it with the doctrine of karma has given it a different turn. And all the three concepts, such as karma, rebirth and transmigration of soul, in the ultimate analysis are linked with one's calling or 'dharma' according to his station of life in the so-called divine order of Hindu society. While it is admitted that all scholarship was mostly confined to Brahmin, it must be recognised that the selfish interest of a person or the class to which he belongs always acts as an internal limitation which regulates the direction of his intellects as it happens in the case of R.K. Narayan despite the fact that he is placed in high esteem for his objective method of writing. Dr. Babasaheb Ambedkar is worth quoting when he says: "the power and position which the Brahmins possess is entirely due to Hindu civilization which treats them as supermen and subjects the lower classes to all sorts of disabilities so that they may never rise or challenge and threaten the superiority of the Brahmins over them. As is natural, every Brahmin is interested in the maintenance of Brahmin supremacy be he orthodox or unorthodox, be he a scholar or not."[38]

R.K. Narayan's portrayal is realistic and authentic. The unfounded beliefs and irrational attitudes have come down to us from generation, and there is nothing uncommon about views and philosophy of life, the Hindus follow in their life. What is surprising is that they never question the validity of the Sashtras and puranas. The Hindu philosophy upheld therein along with myths and legends are accepted as they are. And if at all any one comes forward to denounce them, his attempts beat in vain on Indian's eternal passivity. He simply fails to withstand the collective force of the society. His total submission is looked upon as something traditionally good, serene and transcendental. His outlook is considered as matured when he accepts the traditional good of the society. This is what we find in most of the novels as suggestive of Narayan's bent of mind however detached he appears to be to the readers.

Notes and References

1. *Illustrated Weekly of India* (June 23, 1963), p. 43.
2. Dr. Badal, *R.K. Nataryan : A Study* (Bareilly : Prakashan Book Depot, 1976), p. 9.
3. R.K. Narayan, *The Dark Room* (Delhi : An Orient paperbacks, 1978), p. 80.
4. R.K. Narayan, *The Guide* (Mysore : Indian Thought Publications, 1958), p. 220.
5. S.P. Bhardwaj, *The Painter of Signs : An Analysis From Perspectives on R.K. Narayan*, edit. Dr. Atma Ram (Ghaziabad : Vimal Prakashan, 1981), p. 176.
6. Tara Malhotra, *Old Times, Old Faces, Old Tunes* (Banasthali Patrika No. 13, 1969), p. 54.
7. R.K. Narayan, *The Dark Room*, p. 75.
8. S.C. Sanyal, *Indianness in Major Indo-Anglian Novels* (Bareilly Prakash Book Depot, 1984), p. 249.
9. Shiv K. Girla, *Narayan's World of Values : From Perspectives on R.K. Narayan*, p. 41.
10. R.K. Narayan, *The Financial Expert* (Mysore : Indian Thought Publications, 1981), p. 158.
11. *Ibid.*, p. 178.
12. R.K. Narayan, *The English Teacher* (Mysore : Indian Thought Publications, 1981), p. 205.
13. R.K. Narayan, *The Painter of Signs* (Great Britain : Penguin, 1976), pp. 14-15.
14. G.B. Baghmar, *R.K. Narayan : as Novelist* : Thesis submitted to Nagpur University, Nagpur, 1981.
15. A.T. Embree, *The Hindu Traditions* : Chpt. III, p. 48.
16. Manu Smriti : 11 : 6-14 *Sacred Books of the East* : XXV, pp. 30-32.
17. S.N. Dasgupta, *A History of Indian Philosophy* (Cambridge, 1922), p. 42.
18. R.K. Narayan, *The Financial Expert* (Mysore : Indian Thought Publications, 1981), p. 56.
19. R.K. Narayan, *The Guide* (Mysore : Indian Thought Publica.ions, 1958), p. 238.
20. Dr. Balram Gupta, A Sinner as a Sinner : A Study of Raju, from *Perspectives on R.K. Narayan*, Ghaziabad, Vimal Prakashan, 1981, p. 135.
21. R.K. Narayan, *The Painter of Signs* : (Great Britain, Penguin, 1976), p. 56.
22. *The Guardian* (8-8-1978).
23. A.R. Kulkarni, *The Buddha, the Trimurti and the Modern Hinduism* (Nagpur, Suvichar Prakashan, Dhantoli, 1980), p. 73.
24. *Ibid.*, p. 162.
25. R.K. Narayan, *The Dark Room* (New Delhi, Orient Paperback, 1978), p. 124.
26. R.K. Narayan, *My Days* (Mysore : Indian Thought Publications, 1979), p. 135.

27. Ref. Quotation from A.R. Kulkarni : *The Buddha, The Trimurti and the Modern Hinduism*, p. 141.

28. A.T. Embree, *The Hindu Traditions* from *Studies in Oriental Thought*, p. 75.

29. *Ibid.*

30. Manu Smriti : I and X passim : *Sacred Books of the East*, XXV, p. 24.

31. P.C. Roy, *The Mahabharat*, I and XII; 60 passim.

32. Bhagwad Geeta : III : 17-19 in *Sources of Indian Tradition*, p. 287.

33. R.K. Narayan, *The Guide*, p. 169.

34. K.R.S. Iynger, *Indian Writing in English* (New Delhi : Sterling Publishers Pvt. Ltd., 1983), p.385.

35. H.M. Williams, Precarious Innocence : Patterns in the Novels of R.K. Narayan from *Perspectives on R.K. Narayan*, p. 15.

36. R.K. Narayan, *Mr. Sampath* (Delhi : Hind Pocket Book, 1979), p. 76.

37. P.S. Sundaram, ambivalence of R.K. Narayan : from *Explorations in Modern Indo-English Fiction* edit. R.K. Dhawan (New Delhi : Bahri Publication, 1982), p. 145.

38. Dr. B.R. Ambedkar, *The Untouchables* (Jetwan Mahavihar, Shravasti, Balrampur, 1977), Preface xi.

CHAPTER 4

CONCLUSION

Comparison With Dr. Mulk Raj Anand and Dr. Bhabani Bhattacharya

The study would remain incomplete unless we compare Narayan's concept of social vision with that of Dr. Mulk Raj Anand and Dr. Bhabani Bhattacharya, the prominent contemporaries writing in the same genre as Narayan does. For the purpose, Anand's novels especially his *Untouchable,* and *Coolie,* and Bhattacharya's *He Who Rides a Tiger,* and *Music for Mohini* will be discussed. Both Dr. Mulk Raj Anand and Dr. Bhabani Bhattacharya have in their novels dealt with the social problems plaguing the country with a firm commitment and conviction of purpose which we find surprisingly lacking in Narayan who has been acclaimed as a detached observer of life.

India, inspite of her variety and complexity, seems to be a cultured unity. She has an image of her own culture. When we talk about the portrayal of the image of India, we really mean the revelation of the image of their culture, the mode of life of people, their thought process and outlook of life, social structure, values, customs, their needs, aims and aspirations; authentically presented in the novels of all the three novelists. However, since it is India divided into castes and sub-castes, caste values have a major role to play in influencing their mental make up. While Narayan and Bhattacharya belong to Brahmin caste, Mulk Raj Anand to the next lower i.e. Kshatriya caste. Naturally their childhood experiences differ widely and have largely been responsible in moulding their lives.

Narayan was born and brought up in an orthodox family of a headmaster in the heart of conservative South India, spoke Tamil at home, Kannad in the street, learnt English, by and large, from imperfect Indian teachers of English; he didn't even go to a convent or public school; and had hardly travelled beyond Madras for a good many years. Besides, Narayan's early training of his life under the orthodox supervision of his grandmother, gave him very little scope to have an independent line of thinking. Under such circumstances, it is very unlikely that Narayan could mix freely with people other than his caste brethren. On elder's advice he would begin "his exercise by reading a little bit of the puranas or Sanskrit sacred poems after which the Gaytri Mantra, a prayer to the light that illuminates the Sun to illuminate all minds".[1] It is but natural that a person whose mind is so moulded right from his childhood should develop a conservative outlook which we find consciously or subconsciously expressed in his novels. Narayan himself admitted to Ved Metha, "his inability to write novels without Krishna, Ganesh, Hanuman."[2] Natrually we come across astrologers, Pandits and Devdasis or temples prostitutes in many of his novels. And he added in his characteristic humble way, that in any case that has turned out to be his India.

Like Narayan, Bhabani Bhattacharya too belongs to the Brahmin caste. However, his close association with the humble folk and his deep understanding of their manners and his contact with people of diverse faith have enabled him to grasp the innate significance of humanity.

Born on 10th November 1906 in Bhagalpur (Bihar) Bhattacharya took his B.A. (Hons.) from Patna University in 1927. He then prosecuted his advanced studies in the University of London and was awarded Ph.D. degree on Historical Research in 1934. He worked as press Attache to the Indian Embassy in Washington D.C. He was on the staff of the Illustrated Weekly of India as Assistant Editor during 1950-52. He also acted as secretary, Tagore Commemorative Society, New Delhi in 1959-60. His worth having been recognised he was taken in as consultant in the Ministry of Education, New Delhi. He adorned the East West Centre, Honolulu, as senior specialist during 1969-70, and since 1970 he has been visiting professor in the University of Hawaii, Honolulu. All this has widened his scope and outlook and refined his sensibility. He came to regard many of the old Indian customs and traditions as totally outworn, and criticised in no uncertain terms the hyporcrisy of the Brahmin priests, the co-called upholders of Hindu religion.

Mulk Raj Anand, on the other hand, is the son of a coppersmith turned soldier. He moved with his father as his father's regiment was transferred from one place to another, which gave Mulk Raj Anand an opportunity to play with the low caste sweepers attached to his father's regiment. He could see the villagers groaning under poverty. He observed village life sucked dry by parasites and religious priests. All this had cast a spell on the mind of the novelist.

Born on December 12, 1905 in a Hindu Kshatriya family of Lal Chand, a hereditary craftsman, Ishwar Kaur, his mother nourished her son's inborn imaginative power with mythological fables and folk tales. She had a deep, though incongruous faith in such diverse gods and godmen as Krishna, Christ, Guru Nanak and the Aga Khan, each of whom she worshipped with almost equal devotion. Her observance of the rituals of two or three religions evoked amusement and ridicule in her family circle. Her religious practices did not impress Anand who after the death of his pretty cousin and playmate Kausalya at the age of nine — the first important crisis of his life — came to entertain the gravest of doubts about divinity which had turned him into an atheist undermining his faith in established institutions, religious, social or cultural.

Anand studied at Khalsa College, Amritsar and obtained his B.A. (Hons.) degree from the Panjab University. He then went to London to do research in philosophy under the guidance of a famous professor Daves Hicks. During his stay abroad Anand made friends with many celebrities. Bonamy Dobres introduced him to the great poet T.S. Eliot. Though Anand's relationship with Eliot remained cool, he wrote frequently for *Criterion* edited by Eliot. Herbert Read helped him in his creative writing with his valuable suggestions; and renowned literary figures like D.H. Lawrence, E.M. Forster, Dylan Thomas, Lowes Dickinson, Eric Gill and Anand Coomar Swamy inspired him.

Anand's frequent visits to the West and his long sojourns there, his deep knowledge of the literature of different countries, his involvement in various humanitarian activities have influenced his outlook to a large extent.

Anand was painfully shocked to notice the mendacity, ignorance and superstition of his coppersmith brotherhood. Privilege and position dominated everything in the life around him. It has forced him to sit up and think seriously. Anand was lured towards rationalism, and scientific method of enquiry. His enquiring mind did not allow him to sit quiet and accept things as they were. He attended seminars on Kant, Hegel, Bradley, Russell, and the like and also probed into the problems of God, religion, pain and immortality. Meanwhile he came across Darwin's epoch-making *The Origin of Species* which seemed to destroy the Biblical conception of genesis. His study of Eddington, Einstein, Dr. Frieud and Jung appeared to denote no close alliance between religion and science. The result of all that he obtained was that he came to become "...a ruthless critic of all that is worn out and decaying, dehumanizing and degrading customs, manners, outdated social and political institutions, reactionary thoughts and ideologies...."[3]

Literature and Society: While for Narayan, literature has no social significance, Anand and Bhattacharya have denounced purposeless art. In fact, "...Literature and society are seen to be interrelated in the sense that literary values are social values; if they are to be values, will in the last resort come to terms with the working of the imagination and the telling of the stories."[4] A work of art can hardly be judged in a vacuum. Bhabani Bhattacharya too believes in the social character and significance of art and literature. He once remarked : "I hold that a novel must have a social purpose. It must place before the reader something from the society's point of view. Art is not necessarily for art's sake. Purposelessness art and literature which is much in vogue does not appear to me a sound judgement."[5]

Anand refuses to be a literary theoretician, historical pseudo-realist or a verificalist — he is all for an integrated vision of life. For him there is no life for art's sake; real pulsating life in all its complexity and inter-relationship, is his constant source of reference, the only criterion of judgement, the only yardstick to measure the moral stature of a man. Under no circumstances can art and life be separated from each other. Anand firmly holds that the have-nots of society, like the untouchables and coolies have as great a claim to be ushered into the sacred rituals of literature as the privileged class like the Brahmin, landlords, owners of tea-estates and factories. True to his vision Anand "broke new ground and represented a departure from the tradition of previous Indian fiction, where pariahs and the bottom dogs had not been allowed to enter the sacred precints of the novels; in all their reality, it seemed to become significant and drew the attention of the critics, particularly in Europe which only knew through Ommar Khayyam, Li Po and Tagore, but very little or nothing about the sordid or colourful lives of the millions of Asia."[6] Narayan, on the other hand, has no commitment as such, nor is he an original thinker. It seems he has no philosophy of his own to give except the religious moral order which he presents in each of his novels which unmistakably reveal that "Narayan is primarily pre-occupied with man's filling of the life-role entrusted to him by tradition and environment."[7]

All the three novelists Narayan, Anand and Bhattacharya belong to the period of great upheaval in political and social life in India. India was passing through a gruelling state of affairs. The aim of the novelist under such circumstances is to render emotionally the drama of contemporary times by making the reader participate in the action. The celebrated Indian scholar Dr. Sunitikumar Chatterjee says a great deal about the duty of a writer in the former colonial countries.

> " I am fully convinced in one thing", he writes, "the most important duty of a writer who lives in a society, which during the course of centuries was in a slumberous state and did not move with the times, is to arouse his people and help them to rise on the path of progress in order to catch up with people going in the forefront. The writer in the 'backward countries' must modernise his own consciousness, and then by his books help in modernising consciousness of his people.... A true writer, in keeping with the dignity of his profession, must be a person of vision and have a kind heart."[8]

Conception of Society

Social Values : Indian Society is traditional and caste-ridden, and social values differ from caste to caste. However, Indian society as a whole is a cultural entity which is authentically presented in the novels of R.K. Narayan, Mulk Raj Anand and Bhabani Bhattacharya. The Indian society comes out vividly with all its traditions, rituals and dogmas which the individuals are seen scrupulously following. While Narayan depicts the middle class society, Anand and Bhattacharya lay emphasis on the social life of the oppressed and the exploited.

Like Narayan, Bhattacharya too refers to the various customs, traditions, superstitions and even blind beliefs. A remarkable reference is made to the perennial love and devotion of the Indians for the monumental epics *The Ramayan* and *The Mahabharat*. The Hindu's worship of the cow as 'Gomata' is evidenced by the introduction of Mangala, who is fed by Onu, Kajoli and mother *(So Many Hungers)*; she becomes human for them by long association and fondness. They have belief in the writing on one's 'forehead', fate or what is destined. It is the will of God, they believe, that rules us, says the city woman who visits Kajoli's house, and that there is a divinity that shapes ends. Fate is unscrutable and man cannot modify the will of destiny.

That the Hindus are still unable to shake off the shackles of superstitions and irrational orthodoxy is vividly depicted by Bhattacharya in his *Music for Mohini*. Mohini flares up at the old mother's objection to the modern ways of dancing and singing in public: "Why not her antiquated outlook prevail against even father's judgment? With her fixed ideas. her own prejudices against modernism, how could she expect to know, to feel, to understand the new generation?"[9]

The faith and trust in horoscope and the part played by the match-makers are graphically described. People are so dogged about the horoscopes that some girls may not get married. The life of Sudha wins our sympathy as she remains unmarried owing to the reading in her horoscope that some stars are believed to have been in malefic conjuction and the white shadow of Saturn approaches her steller line. Narayan's Chandran too leaves his home as he fails to marry the girl he loves owing to the mischief of the horoscopes.

The scriptural belief that the birth of a son is necessary for the salvation of the father from (Punnamahakarma) is pointed out with perfection, "our ancestors in heaven are joyful when a son is born to the house on earth. The family name will be carried for one more span or life on earth, and at the funeral anniversary of the departed, sacrificial water should be poured."[10]

Bhattacharya appears to have a sound knowledge of the Indian customs and rites as quoted in the scriptures: "the chanting of the Name was meant to propel the departing soul skyward. Without that and the complicated ritual which followed the departing soul would remain earthbound. The rice and coppers scattered on the street as well as the funeral feasts would earn a goodly measure of merit for the soul of this Brahmin and ensure its warm reception at the portals of heaven."[11] Similar incidence is reported by Narayan in *Waiting for the Mahatma* in which Shriram's old Granny is taken to the burning ghat for cremation; and we have seen the priest haggling for more coppers for him to carry out the rituals so that the soul of the old lady would rest in peace.

Like Narayan, Dr. Anand too touched marital fidelity, the basic tenet of Indian family. Like Savitri (*The Dark Room*), Gouri (*Anand's Old Woman and The Cow*) puts up with all sorts of insults and inhuman treatments at the hands of her husband. The moment Panchi is incensed against Gouri's chastity, as against Sita in *The Ramayan*, she is driven out of the house. However, in *The Ramayan,* the problems of the heroine are solved by the intervention of gods, that is, Sita is rescued from further humiliation by Mother Earth. But the problems of Anand's heroine Gouri are solved by herself, since there are no gods to intervene on her behalf. Unlike Narayan, Anand here suggests that man needs to rely on himself for his happiness rather than on fate or God.

Being tradition bound, Narayan's characters cherish a heritage of faith and values, customs and traditions of the past. There is no denying the fact that even the characters of Anand and Bhabani Bhattacharya are fatalistic, brought up in the same cultural surroundigns. However, the sense of futility and disappointment that has gripped Narayan's individuals in the end, could not touch the characters of Anand and Bhattacharya. They look to the future with hope and renewed vigour and are largeiy in a position to curve out their line of action. The characters of both Anand and Bhattacharya have come to realise that man is the master of his destiny.

While the religious pundits and sadhus in saffron cloth are welcome to the house and are treated with utmost reverence with their food bowls filled in to the brim, the low caste men are driven out with all kinds of abuses heaped upon them. Bakha (*Untouchable)* has a bitter experience when a caste Hindu woman flings a loaf of bread from a distance as if he is not a human being at all. Such inhuman treatment to the low caste men is not uncommon in Hindu society. In fact, the Hindu Dev-Devtas such as Bramha, Vishnu, Ram, Krishna were worshipped by them with the same devotion with which the Brahmins did worship them. The untouchables remained their devotees (as Vishwanath in *He Who Rides a Tiger*) and admirers for several centuries. Did these gods feel any sympathy towards them? Did they change their deplorable conditions under which they lived for centuries? Instead of doing any good these gods were most unjust and partial. They were trampled under the foot for no fault of theirs. Obviously, "the conditions of untouchables were very deplorable and degraded throughout India, yet particularly in South India (which Narayan represents) they were inhumanly treated by the caste Hindus."[12]

Anand presents the Hindu mind with its feeling of social and class superiority refusing to accept the fact that the so-called untouchable is also a human being like the Hindu. In the *Untouchables* : the Hindu is shown to treat the untouchable Bakha as a subhuman creature ignoring and exploiting him as occasion demands. Anand is perhaps the first novelist to venture to present in all its crude and intricate realities the disease-ridden underfed characters of Indian society. We get a miserable life presented most graphically. In the outcaste colony where they live there are : "no drains, no light, no water; of the marsh-land where people live among the latrines of the townsmen, and in the stink of their own dung scattered about here, and there and everywhere...the world where the day is dark as the night, and the night is pitch-dark."[13] Here the sweepers live for ages unmindful of the dirt and their existence too, as if that is their lot pre-ordained by the gods in heaven. And the caste Hindus think they are dirt because they clear their dirt.

In this respect E.M. Forster's observations are worth quoting: "they have evolved a hideous nightmare unknown to the West; the belief that the products are ritually unclean as well as physically unpleasant, and that those who carry them away or otherwise help to dispose off them, are outcaste from society."[14]

Like Narayan, both Anand and Bhattacharya have set their novels in rural surroundings. Indeed, it has been the misery of the poor peasants of India (the sons of the soil) to toil day and night and cultivate the lands, and it is a pity that they live in perpetual poverty and hunger only to enable the landlords to flourish. It is he that produces that has nothing to consume. The fate of the Indian farmer whose life is crushed under the wheel of grinding poverty is drawn with a breath of vision by Bhattacharya. Narayan touched the superstitious aspect of the life of peasants like Velan and others (*The Guide*) who face the natural calamity in the form of drought and then their resort to fasts and prayers to propitiate the rain god through Raju, the so-called god-man who becomes unwilling martyr in the end.

Anand and Bhattacharya have exposed the unprincipled Indians who exploit the situation for their own benefit and who are no better than vultures and jackals waiting for the flesh that dies, and sometimes not even waiting till he dies. Bhattacharya's righteous indignation, his sincerity and his compassion are in evidence all through the novel *He Who Rides a Tiger*. It is those people who drive Kalo, a blacksmith, a sincere and honest person in his life, to become a cheat, and start deceiving both people and gods. Of the two alternatives lying before him death or cheating Kalo chooses the later and wrecks his vengeance on the society and its rank indifference.

We have an ironic comment by Bhattacharya as to how the poor peasants are crushed under the debt. They fall into steep debts thereby enriching the village moneylenders who cash money even on the ashes of the poor. The interests accumulate like sins and the borrower has only to entrust his debt to the care of his children. The heartlessness and the cruelty of the moneylenders is pointed out with vehemence. "The Seth's milch cow died and he would not replace it; the jug of milk needed could come from milk woman by way of interest on the loan she had taken after her husband's sudden death by snake-bite."[15]

Bhattacharya's has a scathing attack on the inhuman and corrupt practices of the rich and apathy of the administrators. He writes in *So Many Hungers*, "Corruption had grown like an epidemic and money had become a man-made hunger. Never in the land's history had the process that made the rich richer, the poor poorer, gained such ruthless intensity. The authority took little heed and set it aside as a passing phenomenon. But the poor suffered untold misery and the end of one tale was the beginning of another."[16]

Juxtaposed with the woeful tale of man's hunger for feed, is the hateful sight of man's callous greed for wealth. While the granaries of the selfish and greedy capitalists and hoarders and black marketeers like Sir Laxminath and Surendra Bose abound in rice, the innumerable human beings die for want of it. While the restaurants of the rich city Calcutta buzz with life and music and bulge with food, destitutes in the nearby lanes and pavements lie sick and helpless and die of hunger. To the question why there is so much devilry and misery in the land of a thousand and one gods, Kalo gives a cryptic reply: "sins committed in one life may have to be expiated in another through suffering.... The real evil doers seemed untouched by 'Karma'. They ate well and spoke the name of Shia and the name of Rama and slept in beds of peace and comfort. All that you do in this life goes to make the writing on your brow in the lives to come."[17]

The callous greed for money and its demoralising effect has also unnerved Narayan. Margayya in *The Financial Export* and Raju in *The Guide* have acquired a large fortune and become influential in life. While Margayya becomes a pauper in the end, Raju lands in prison for his forgery. We also come across rice merchants, hoarders, black marketeers, garrison engineers and the drug stockists who have made stupendous fortune by adopting foul means. Narayan holds these upto mild ridicule no doubt, but his intent is not to satire. While Shrinivas, the journalist in *Mr. Sampath* thundered against municipal and social shortcoming, a voice went on asking : life and world and all this is passing — why bother about anything? The perfect and the imperfect are all the same, why really bother? This has made Malgudi fatalistic and without hope for any change in social life.

The sweep of Anand's vision reaches wider and deeper than Narayan's. Narayan selects a narrow section of the society; in its safety his art is sufficient. Anand goes to the deepest sources of the peasant's make up. He lays bare the complex elements that go to shape his characters. S. Menon comments : "The Indian background comes alive in the pattern of the lives of the peasants.... He (Anand) omits nothing, neither the crudeness of their life and outlook, nor their deep fatalism. But he sees them also as individuals and human beings coarsed by years of oppression."[18]

Anand presents an authentic picture of the black coolies who clear the forest, plant the field, toil and garner the harvest, while all the money grabbing slave driving soulless managers and directors draw their salaries and dividends and build up monopolies. He writes : "These docile, gutless, spineless coolies never raise their voices and go about the plantation with mark of gross stupidity on their faces whose habitual submission is never disturbed by an outrage of man or beast, by hunger, pestilence or slow disease."[19] Anand comes down heavily on the capitalists and the rich. He is also ruthless to the coolies for their apathy. In *Coolie* Anand expresses his feelings thus: "The rich and the powerful, the magnificient and the glorious whose opulence is built on robbery and theft and open warfare, are honoured and admired by the whole world, and by themselves.... You, the poor and the humble, you, the meek and the gentle wretched that you are, swindled of your rights and broken in body and soul. You are respected by no one and you do not respect yourself."[20]

To sum up, in the words of H.M. Williams: "where Anand is an angry protester, a satirist and revolutionary, author of the tragic, or near tragic *Coolie* and *Untouchable,* Narayan is essentially a humorous writer, interested in the lower middle classes of South India, in a world relatively free from the terrible privations and agonies, political conflicts and economic depression of Anand's India...."[21]

Moral Aspect : Ours has been a traditional and caste-ridden society. The huge mass of myths and legends that we have accumulated through centuries has become the common repository of the people of the land. These myths and legends and our religion and cultural heritage have shaped our mind and imagination, behaviour pattern and general attitude to life. Narayan, therefore, contends that all imaginative writing in India has had its origin in *The Ramayan* and *The Mahabharat*; an author would pick up an incident or a character out of one or the other and create a new work with it. And Narayan rightly does so, for it finds conscious expression in every aspect of his novel; whether it is Shrinivas, or the Financial Expert, Margayya, Natraj, or the Guide, Raju, Krishna or Ramani, all of them are dipped in Puranic traditions.

While Narayan's faith in Divine scheme has remained unshaken throughout his life with man's utter helplessness in undoing the wrongs, Anand upholds the dignity of man, and denounces the system of caste which undermines human dignity. He is a humanist because he rightly thinks that most of our problems have been created by man, they can also be solved by man. Since man is the cause for the miseries of mankind;

he should now become the powerhouse for processing his own salvation. Superstition, bigotry, class, caste, capitalism, exploitation, over-population, tyranny — man is responsible for all those, and hence man can now fight and undo them too, if he has the vision doubled with requisite will. And through Anand's writings, his preaching and example of his own life, he has been trying to awaken man's slumbering conscience so that he may acquire the true vision and develop necessary will for reconstruction of the society. Anand presents a crude picture of Indian society with all its religious hypocrisy and the injustice thriving on anachronistic practices such as untouchability, feudalism, economic exploitation of the have-nots by the haves. Anand as a novelist exposes the decayed Indian tradition and champions the cause of modernism as a cure for all the ills of Indian society.

The arrongance and hypocrisy of higher caste people is markedly portrayed even by Dr. Bhattacharya. The ritual of milk bath for the idols is not a novel feature introduced by him, but it is prevalent in many a temple in India. It is supposed that such donors of milk, will have their sins expiated and 'Punyam' or merit will accrue to them. Their so-called 'Bhakti' makes them blind to the wishes of the dying man. The cheats and sharks and the pot bellied jute merchants and rice profiteers like Sir Abalbandhu and rich stock brokers like Motichand become the upholders of religion and use it for their selfish gains. Bairagis and mendicants are bribed to create a spiritual halo round a simple girl like Lekha and popularise her as the mother of sevenfold bliss. Newspapers like *Swadesh* owned by businessmen are used to publicize widely her psychic personality, so that people in search of miracles throng before her and make liberal gifts of their earnings to her. Yogis are employed to dupe credulous lady like Radha so that she may permit her wealthy husband to have a fifth wife to save her from widowhood as ordained by gods. Such examples of corruptions and hypocrisy in the name of god and religion are widely rampant.

Dr. Bhattacharya in his *He Who Rides a Tiger* satirises the blind religious faith of ignorant masses who will grudge to feed famished destitutes but fill whole-heartedly the alms bowls of the sadhus, dressed in suffron cloth, and misguided devotees who will turn a deaf ear to the cries of children dying of hunger but donate the buckets of milk for the bath of idol in the temple. "In this society while men died of hunger, wealth grow; and while kindness dried up, religion was more in demand."[22]

Dr. Anand too has a dig at the credulous ignorant masses who are responsible for much of Lal Singh's disgust and his discomfiture and eventually for his flight from the village, despite his great love for it. It is surprising, nay shocking, that these men should be so blind to see through the greed and hypocrisy of an imposter like the Mahanta (*The Village*) who actually pleads for social inequalities in the name of religion and god. He advises the credulous folk: "God had given a place to every one in this world. You know well that a serf has not the dignity of a farmer like you (Nihal Singh). Keep your prestige, therefore, but do not set yourself in the place as other folk. For that would be sin. This is the true religion, that you should not envy your superiors, for if you did so, there would be no order in the world."[23]

In this respect Sanad Edumaruku is worth quoting when he observes: "Keeping people away from material realities and pressing them too hard around delusional beliefs like astrology, auspicious times, palmistry, demonology, reincarnation, extra-sensory perception, telepathy, prayers, pujas, mantras, pilgrimages etc., are a cunning way to ward off from social revolt. The forces representing the *status quo* want them to get addicted to such beliefs. So deliberate efforts are made towards this end. Secondly, it is a source of income for thousands of astrologers, palmists and spiritual leaders without doing any productive work."[24]

Counterfeit sainthood is a phenomenon notoriously ubiquitous in our hoary land, and it forms a recurrent theme in Indo Anglian Fiction. Narayan has dealt with it in *The Guide*. But his attitude to his hero is ambiguous. His criticism of the bogus saint is veiled and subtle. Anand's priest symbolises a kind of perfidious charlatanism and his treatment of the subject, though sporadic, is absolutely straight-forward. His Chastisement of the fraudulent gurus is acute and scathing. He views them as a positive menace to the health of the society.

Bhattacharya's is a scathing attack on so-called godman in his *He Who Rides a Tiger*. However, Kalo's purpose is mainly to avenge the cruel society which compels honest man like him to turn into impostrous masquerader. Bhattacharya's treatment is broader in the sense that he probes into the causes and consequences of assumed sainthood. Anand's priests too are hoaxes but with a difference. Pramila Paul aptly observes: "Anand's satire of these charlatans is more direct than Narayan's, and not less caustic than Bhattacharya's."[25]

Tolerance has been widely taught in Hindu society; since long it has been considered a part of Hindu religion too. This is often rooted in indifference rather than in recognition of the other man's right to be different. It rarely promotes interaction of ideas, attitudes and practices.

The traditional Hinduism within its fold insists on extreme conformism of principles to practice. When Bakha (*Untouchable*) complains of the inhuman treatment he receives from the high caste, Lakha's (Bakha's father) reaction is typical. He advises him patience for "they are our masters. We must respect them and do as they tell us."[26] Lakha's is the voice of survile humility and he cannot entertain any thought of retaliating against a high caste man. Perhaps one of the reasons for Anand choosing a young man as the protagonist seems to be that the young can feel and react to injustice whereas the old are insensitive and stoneblind to all sorts of victimization. P. Raghvendrarao observes: "The reactions of Lakha and Bakha are not of two individuals but of two generations; one the dying and the other emerging, the one reconciled to, and the other revolting against, the losses of the self-inflicted on man by historical classification of society."[27]

Complacent religious philistinism has been the bane of Indian society, and has proved positively repugnant to progress. Religious faith is bred in the bones of the Indians and it is often squeezed to yield cash. The credulity of the masses is thoroughly exploited, and astrocities are being committed in the name of religion. The fraudulence that has been allowed to creep into the religion has been ruthlessly criticized by Anand. Apart from its orthodoxy and meaningless ritualism and blind superstition, Anand criticizes Hinduism for its caste system which has proved demeaning, disintegrating and exploitative. In *Sword and The Sickle* Prof. Varma points out: "Hinduism is no religion, apart from the social organism of caste. Any one professing any belief is a Hindu so long as he is born to one of the castes! And all this ritual is a good Brahmin trick to keep people where they are and to coin money through conducting ceremonials!"[28]

Pandit Kalinath's cowardly amorous attempt to molest Sohini (*Untouchable*) appears all the more offensive because of his accusing her and her brother of defying him at the temple when the attempt is foiled. This brings into sharp focus the hypocrisy, the double standards, the perfidy underlying the facade of purity and spiritually. It is ironic that the Brahmin, the custodian of culture in India, makes unashamed attempt to violate one of the fundamental codes of culture. The innocent Bakha and Sohini become victims of the conventional moral code. Narayan too touches the Hindu caste system; but he appears to be indifferent and offers no comments. On the other hand, Bhattacharya, though of the priestly class, offers a biting criticism of the caste system in *He Who Rides a Tiger*. He makes a low caste Kalo, the blacksmith into Mangal

Adhikari, the Brahmin priest of Calcutta and proves beyond doubt how hallow our religion is. The high caste people who make his life miserable in the society, dance attendance on him; and he laughs at them exclaiming, they are praying God who is no God!

Indian saints have preached brotherhood, and the feeling is certainly noticed amongst the Indians but limited to their caste brethren. The Kshatriyas are looked down upon by the Brahmins; Vaishyas by the Kshatriyas and Brahmins. The shudras are treated worse than animals. This inhuman treatment to the lower caste people is prevalent even today in villages. Moral code of conduct is restricted to one's caste as is rightly presented in the case of low caste Bakha in *Untouchable*. Dr. Ambedkar rightly observes: "...Virtue has become caste-ridden and morality has become caste-bound. There is no sympathy to the deserving. There is no appreciation of the meritorious."[29] G.S. Ghure also supports this view when he says, "...in this caste-bound society the amount of community feeling must have been restricted and the citizens owed moral allegiance to their castes first, rather than to the community as a whole."[30]

Philosophical Aspect : Hindu philosophy owes its origin to the Vedas, Puranas, Shastras, Smritis; and even the recent additions *The Ramayan* and *The Mahabharat* have pervaded the life of Indian people, so much that the characters therein have come to be worshipped by the Hindus as gods. Not only that, they are made to believe and accept the Vedas and so-called sacred scriptures as created by God. As a result, the Hindus hardly entertain the idea to question the validity of the beliefs and mythical ideologies propounded therein. By writing fantastic things the Brahmins beguiled the entire society, and took full advantage of people's ignorance and superstitious outlook. They inserted certain cunning verses and passages in Vedas, Shastras, Upnishadas, Ramayan and Mahabharat etc., for protecting their self-interests, and subsequently such ideas were unthoughtfully eulogised by Manu, Gotam, Yajnavalkya, Narad, Vashisth and others. The philosophy incorporated in the so-called sacred Scriptures have become part and parcel of the life of Indian masses, which unconsciously find expression in the writings of Indo-Anglian novelists.

We live in the Age of Science and Scientific advancement. We cannot be called upon to accept incredible dogmas or exclusive revelations. The religion that has come to us in its present degenerated form, is filled with blind beliefs and incredible dogmas — which appear totally irrelevant in present-day society. In fact, the religion is meant for man and not man for religion. Hence its philosophy should be modifed so as to make the overall development of man's personality in its spiritual aspect. It must fit in the scientific temperament of man. The religion which does not come up to this standard should be rejected outright. Dr. Radhakrishnan comments: "Religion is not magic or witchcraft, quackery or superstition. It is not to be confused with outdated dogmas, incredible superstitions which are hindrances and barriers, which spoil the simplicity of spiritual life."[31]

The Hindu Dharma Granthas with such incredible dogmas and superstitions have come to be accepted as something created by God, and absolute conformism to the religious principles is viewed as being part and parcel of the Hindu way of life which many of the Indian novelists feel themselves proud of being faithful in its portrayal. While Narayan is authentic in its presentation, Anand is mainly in the tradition of scientific humanism. He holds that the whole of nature, the cosmas exists and operates according to natural laws. Man is part of this universe. He believes in the evolutionary conception of the universe and rejects the dualism between matter and spirit, and the body and the mind. He disallows all supernatural thoughts as mere myths, no longer tenable in the modern scientific age. Anand refuses to believe in the idea of a personal God or gods. He has made it clear in his letter to Dr. Balram Gupta : "God has been dead a long time. Men are gods or can become gods."[32]

In fact, right from his childhood Anand's occasional peeps into the inner temple led him doubt the very nature of the pot bellied priest. It has got confirmed in later years when he vehemently criticised the sharks of Hindu religion. He satirizes the fake religious leaders who exploit religion as an instrument of oppression and put an obstacle to the development of independent thought. While Kalinath of *Untouchable* forgets all about his Brahminical religion when he sees Sohini's lustrous body and attempts to have sexual intercourse with her, the Mahant of Anand's *Triology* is presented as eternal exploiter who does not want any progress of the village nor does he want any education of the people. He dislikes his authority to be questioned by others. Anand discards the idea of conventional God, and makes Dr. Mahendra (*The Old Woman and The Cow*) a living God to Gouri who regards him as her protector and the God in heaven.

While Narayan does not bring himself to expose the hypocrisy and hallowness of religious leaders, Bhattacharya, though of the same caste, does not spare the sharks and the hypocrites of the higher castes. He makes a dent in superstition the way he makes Kalo, the blacksmith into Mangal Adhikari who succeeds in taking revenge upon the society by faking a miracle and passing himself off as a Brahmin priest. It is true that Kalo reminds us of Raju who transforms himself into a Swami (Narayan's *The Guide*). In both holiness is only a convenient disguise. While Narayan does this on the line of transformation of Valmiki the sage, Bhattacharya's is a biting satire on the filmsy and meaningless rituals and blind beliefs of the people. Unlike Raju, Kalo has courage and determination to discard the flying robes of the priest thereby exposing the fact that it was all a fake invention and they were praying God who was no God. Anand Khurana is right when he observes :

> "There are lakhs of so-called 'Godmen' performing so-called 'miracles' to impress people. A magician use tricks to entertain. These Godmen also do the same — but to exploit. There are no such things as miracles. I, myself, can perform a thousand such acts ranging from producing Vibuthi (Sacred ash) to walking on fire or breaking coconuts with my head. This is B. Premanand, who with his flowing grey beard could be mistaken for a 'Godman' himself, speaking. However, he is a man out to expose all 'Godmen'." He further adds: "Guaranteeing 'instant salvation' through attractively packaged courses, these promoters of inner peace are recking in money from their burgeoning mesmerised, gullible followers. Ironically these holy men, who have renounced 'Maya' are among the richest persons in the country."[33]

That Narayan himself recites Gayatri, the first thing in the morning, and that he himself has had personal experience of psychic communion with the spirit of his dead wife, amply prove that Narayan believes in Divine scheme of things. He has firm faith in the writing of the so-called sacred Hindu scriptures. He is in favour of *status quo* in social life. C.D. Narsimhiaha rightly points out: "India's undying faith in God and goodness, holymen and miracles is here rendered quite credible by the novelist's art even to the sceptical and questioning eye."[34]

Whereas Anand's humanism does not believe in the existence of God, like the humanism of The Buddha; God is central to Vedantism. This God, says Vedanta, is realisable through intuitional experience rather than by means of intellect or reason. But how many have realised God this way? May be just a handful of mystics. Anand thinks that the mystic experience remains inexplicable to the ordinary masses. This sort of quest for God is necessarily a one way traffic, men are led to God and they do not turn back. The Vedanta philosophy which has impressed Narayan, and which sees everything as illusory except Brahmin is a ruthless monism. H.M. Williams remarks: "This non-dualistic, totally idealistic, Advaita Vedanta is blamed by Anand's poet for the other-worldliness and fatalism of Indians which have plunged their country allegedly into 'casteism' and poverty and made them easy prey for the more virile European nations."[35]

The doctrine of Karma has cast its deep imprint on the thoughts and behaviour of the people and their whole attitude to life. Geeta and the theory of Karma propounded strongly in it have remained a prime inspiration for the millions of Indians for long. It is, therefore, little surprising that Narayan too came under its spell. To Greta Garbo's question why have we been made to suffer, undergo pain, and then what is the meaning of all this? Narayan writes in his *My Dateless Diary,* "I can only view her problem from the point of view of Karma and the evolution of a being from birth to birth — I am generally reluctant to speak about my inner convictions". Later he adds "...May not be in a single birth, but after a series of them, that is why we believe in a sequence of births."[36] This proves beyond doubt that the philosophy of other worldliness is consciously expressed by Narayan through major characters like Shrinivas, the journalist (Mr. Sampath). He sees everything balanced, and it would be futile for anybody to attempt to remake the world. Narayan seems to believe that society exists as a part of universal order.

Anand rejects the concept of Karma as pernicious belief among Indians. Actually the caste system and Karma theory are complementary doctrines, both in a sense equally satanic devices to subject a part of the community to eternal subjugation and humiliation. It is monstrous to think that men like Bakha suffer in the world inevitably because of their Karma, i.e. they must have done some bad deeds in their previous births. It is equally preposterous to plead that they must endure suffering in this world patiently in order that they may merit a better deal in their next births. Dr. Balram Gupta writes: "This is all abracadabra ingeniously invented by high caste Hindus to keep untouchables from any possible revolt and to safeguard their own self-imposed exalted position...."[37] Thakur Singh....believes in Karma, for it helps him to keep his exalted position secure. We see this when he has fever, and troubled by the possible threat to his position as the head of the village implied in the coming up of untouchables. We also know that Suraj Mani's repeated talk of Karma is only designed to achieve his own end. He wants to keep the untouchables as well as caste Hindus under the strict rules of Karma so that he can keep them all humble and devoted to God and God's men Brahmins. It is a way of earning livelihood for him. The belief in Karma is so deep-rooted in the consciousness of Indians that even educated people refuse to see that it is an impediment, not a help on the road of man's progress. It is this ingrained and uncritical belief in Karma which is the chief cause of the sense of inferiority and abjectness corroding the soul of a well meaning lad like Munoo and several others like him. Since Anand believes that man is the master of his destiny, he refuses to believe in fatalism because it weakens man's faith in himself and insidiously persuades him to become a passive dependent on unseen and non-existent God.

Bhattacharya too touches the Karma theory in his *He Who Rides a Tiger*. Kalo is sarcastic when he says that sins committed in one's life may have to be expiated in another through sufferings. For, he knows that the real evil-doers seem untouched by Karma. They eat well and utter the name of Shio and the name of Rama — and sleep in beds of peace and comforts. The protest against caste system lashed out in this novel with lacerating vehemence gains a new dimension because the main symbol of this protest is himself a Brahmin. It is a telling story of a collossal hoax perpetuated by a low born blacksmith on the people of Bengal during the Last World War and offers a biting criticism of the caste system. Dr. Ram Sevak Singh observes: "Since the society has tricked Kalo into a thief, a convict, and an immoral trafficker, he has foisted a big fraud on it and thus proved how hallow our religion and its upholders are! The indignation of the novelist is all the more poignant because Kalo was forcibly wragged into the broil."[38]

Narayan touches the problems of the caste system and Karma theory. He shows in *The Waiting for the Mahatma* how a large section of the Indian population has been kept totally segregated from the mainstream of life. Marriages between people of two different castes are rarely held and Chandran feels indignant at the prevailing caste system. He also leaves his home on his failure to marry his beloved. However, Narayan denounces this kind of sentimentalism, and makes him accept the bride of his parents' choice. And since Narayan has firm faith in Karma and rebirth, many of his characters including the pious Natraj, even Shrinivas and Jagan come to believe that their's is an existence within a series of existence in the past and the future with spiritual and moral dividends, the result of accumulated actions leading to our present predicament and future prospects. That is why, Narayan's characters accept their sufferings with a sense of rare resignation, much to the enjoyment of the high caste, and lovers of *status quo* in social life.

The devilish scheme so evolved by the Brahmins has benefited none others but Brahmins alone who have monopolised the educational field keeping a large section of the population in complete dark, robbing them of their talents and legitimate rights. Edward Shill observes: "No other country can quite watch this picture of a continuing intellectual tradition carried so long by a single section of the population. In Western countries, widespread educational opportunity and social mobility have produced an educated class which is more haterogeneous in its social origin and much less hereditary related to intellectual endeavour."[39]

To both Dr. Bhattacharya and Dr. Anand there is nothing higher and more dignified than human existence. Anand is one with naturalistic humanist in discarding all the supernatural thoughts as mere myths, no longer tenable in the modern scientific age. He believes in here and now, in the flesh and blood and not in hell or heaven or rebirth. Anand is chiefly concerned with twentieth century struggle and anguish against the oppressive social system that has kept a half of her children in darkness for two thousand years. Unlike Anand who is forth-right and committed to bring about a social change, Narayan's easy and spontaneously comic expression hypnotises us into an acceptance of the *status quo* in social life. His well set pattern in his novels initial centrifugal flight, uprooting and disorder, and then return to normalcy — is a jubilant echo of the vested interest of the middle class in sterile but comforting *status quo*.

Conception of Individual : The Indian society with its myths and rituals, beliefs and superstitions is almost the same in the novels of Narayan, Anand and Bhattacharya. However, while Narayan's is the faithful presentation of the life of middle class people he is intimately familiar with, Mulk Raj Anand and Bhattacharya have in their heart genuine concern and welfare for the people crippled under the weight of social taboos and inhibitions. While Narayan holds his characters upto mild ridicule for their eccentric ways; the other two have led a scathing attack on the hypocrisy of the upper caste, exploiting the gullible masses in the name of God and religion. While Narayan, held in high esteem as a detached observer of life, looks at his characters from his 'ivory tower' without involving himself in their day-to-day affairs, Mulk Raj Anand and Bhabani Bhattacharya have a sense of commitment to eradicate the social evils. They have keenly observed the life and people around them; and cruelty, injustice and exploitation they have seen in the society prompts them to take up the cause of the underdogs who suffer the centuries of sufferings. The world of Narayan is relatively free from the terrible privations and agonies, political conflicts and economic depression of Anand's India. It is for the first-time that Anand ventures into the territory hitherto untrodden — the world of the untouchables, sweepers, coolies, the debt-ridden farmers and the like, who are not allowed to enter the sacred precints of literature. About his characters Anand writes in preface to '*Two Leaves and a Bud*':

> All these heroes, as the other men and women who had emerged in my novels...were dear to me, because they were the reflections of the real people I had known during my childhood and youth. And I was only repaying the debt of gratitude I owed them for much of the inspiration they had given me to mature into manhood, when I began to interpret their lives in my writing. They were not more phantoms.... They were the flesh of my flesh and blood of my blood and obsessed me the way in which certain human beings obsess an artist's soul. And I was doing no more than what a writer does when he seeks to interpret the truth from the realities of his life.[40]

It is not that the characters portrayed by Anand and Bhattacharya are free from blind beliefs and superstitions. Like Narayan's characters they too are traditional and fatalistic in their outlook. Moreover, being members of the unprivileged class, they are pursued by inexorable economic forces which toss them this way and that till they break to pieces. They are not able to fight these forces because they are ignorant and uneducated. It may be a tea-plantation Gangu caught in moss of civilized slavery of plantation, or it may be Ananta dying in scuffle. Permanent indebtness and eternal struggle of keeping the wolf from the door has broken their spirit. They are used to insults, they beg and cringe, and they have not the spirit to stand up and fight against injustice. Bakha (*Untouchable*) made a high resolve to assault the priest who tried to molest his sister, his fine form rising like a tiger at bay, and yet there was futility written on his face. He could not overstep the barriers which the convention of his superiors had built up to protect their weakness against him. He could not invade the magic circle which protected a priest from attack especially from a low caste man. So naturally in the highest moment of his strength the slave in him had asserted itself, and he lapsed back wild with torture, biting his lips, and ruminating his grievance.

Kalo (*He Who Rides a Tiger*) gets embittered with the society which becomes indifferent to his poverty and utter helplessness. He gets all the more wrathful and indignant against it when his daughter is caught in a crisis. In fact, Kalo is a man of accepted conventions, his roots run deep into age-old habits of mind and belief. He never doubts the Brahmin's superior status as the chosen of God. However, circumstances make him a changed man. He wrecks vengeance on the society which has pushed his lovely daughter into the harlot house. The plight of female characters is no better than the menfolk of the unprivileged classes. Gouri (Anand's *Old Woman and The Cow*), Laxmi (Bhattacharya's *Goddess named Gold*) have to face inhuman cruelties and humiliation at the hands of their husbands. So is the case with Savitri (Narayan's *The Dark Room*) who, like a bamboo pole, does not stand without support.

Whereas the work of R.K. Narayan is saturated with the classical Indian myths, Mulk Raj Anand who thinks India in her present predicament, stands in need of the creation of new myths in place of the old which have already served their purpose and are of no practical relevance or significance in the present circumstances. Hari Mohan Prasad writes: "He explodes the fairy tales afloat abroad about India of the Yogies, Sadhus and Beggars and gives an earthly presentation of human condition in our society. His novels are poems of suffering, portraying impassionedly the inequality, poverty and exploitation of characters who are a 'real individual lovable, thwarted, sometimes grand, sometimes weak and thoroughly Indian".[41] Similarly Bhattacharya through his novels, exposes the cannibalism of man, the cruel stranglehold of tradition, the blind self-deception in orthodoxy, and also the obstinate unthinking faith in industrialization. The need for a change of social outlook and re-orientation of social values is Bhattacharya's major concern.

Narayan makes his characters captive of circumstances. They move in the society rather passively with no will of their own. There are some attempts on their part at self-assertion. However, they are helpless creatures and they believe that nothing happens without the will of God. Effort or no effort, every thing will come out right in the long run, and they have to suffer what is there in store for them. It is in this light that Harish Raizada's comments are worth quoting. He says:

> the characters in the novels of R.K. Narayan always remain static and unchanging. Unlike the characters of the Jane Austine they lack the capacity to surprise us. Their weakness, their varieties, their foibles they possess from the beginning and never to lose to the end, and what actually does change is not these but our knowledge of them. Even such characters as Swami who runs away from his

> house after insulting the Headmaster; or Chandran who turns an ascetic owing to frustration in love, or Savitri who revolts against her husband and leaves her house in order to realise her personality or Margayya's son Balu who absconds from home owing to the chiding of his father, ultimately return to their own familiar surroundings.[42]

On the contrary Anand's characters are rebellious. They are not content with life as it is. They never stagnate and always try to mobilize their mental power to relate their own personalities to the realities of the world. "(He is) the first writer to have dispelled the myth built around the stereotype Indian character: the myth about 'contentment' in the midst of poverty, 'mystical silences', 'spiritual attainments'."[43] Whenever Bakha is insulted, especially when he is hit by a passer-by he is deeply hurt and he feels like hitting back. But he restrains himself, and one of the reasons for this forced restraint is that he has not yet been able to shake off the sense of servility, and meakness that weighs heavily on his shoulders as an accumulated burden of centuries of tradition. Ananta (*Big Heart*) has seen too much misery and poverty on this earth which makes him doubt — whether God will ever answer the prayers of the poor. He tells Janki sarcastically: "God works in a mysterious way, in such a heartless way that the ominous owl alone has so far taken pains to answer the peasants in the night...God seems to have deserted the world — if ever he were there, helping it along!"[44]

Like Anand, his spokesman Bhagat (*Big Heart*) believes that a revolution, an upturning of the old order and a complete removal of the cobwebs of dead customs alone can bring some happiness to the much troubled common man. He expresses his feeling thus: "So here in this country only an overturning of the old social order will bring the healing balm of love among men, only a revolution will complete the reformation and the renaissance that is going on among us and produce the new community with a new morality in which, and through which, man can live creatively...."[45]

The women characters of Dr. Anand and Dr. Bhattacharya have enough guts in them to discard the age-old customs and traditions. From the gentle cow that Gouri (*Old Woman and The Cow*) has been, she changes into a self-willed woman with her own individuality. Of course she is the same loving wife, and eagerly gets back to her husband when she is given a chance. But she is shocked beyond control when Ranchi her husband suspects her chastity, for she lives some days with the seth and

Dr. Mahendra, and hits her and orders her out. Gouri is no longer the old meek creature to accept this sort of treatment unprotestingly. Her reaction is, in fact, symbolic of modern woman, keenly conscious of her rights and potentialities. She hits back saying: "Acha if I am a curse on you, I will go away.... And if you strike me again, I will hit you back...."[46]

Characters of Bhattacharya have a more challenging role to play in the society. Kalo (*He Who Rides a Tiger*) feels oppressed by the selfish capitalistic and caste ridden society which comes in the way of his making a living and enabling him to provide a mouthful to his daughter and himself. 'Discontent is the fertile soil for a rebellion', says, Bacon, 'which, when it starts, does not end till its culmination'. Kalo, by force of circumstances, becomes a rebel. He transforms himself into Mangal Adhikari the Brahmin priest; and by a clever trick performs the miracle of making an image of Shio rise out of the soil under an old bunyan tree. He soon becomes a prosperous priest of the new temple and is idolised by the same rich and powerful people who had despised and persecuted him when he was wretchedly poor. Representatives of high caste 'aces' of society dance attendance on him. How pleased he must have been when he exclaims: "The turn of the wheel favours us beyond all reckoning! What strange things have come to pass! ...They pray to a God who is no God. What expiation could ever cleanse their soul?"[47]

Jaydeo (*Music for Mohini*) has an absolutely definite aim. He is possessed with social reform. He categorically says: "I want to make Behula a model village socially. Our political freedom is worth little without social uplift.... That means struggle. If we win, as we must, Behula will be an example for all Bengal."[48] Jaydeo stands no nonsense from his mother who, worried about the safety of her son whose longevity is predicted to be bound up with his becoming a father within specified time, takes Mohini to the temple of Virgin Goddess to offer blood from heart in the lotus leaf bowl to the Goddess to cure her of her supposed sterility. Before the fatal ceremony could be consumated, Jaydeo reaches in time to stop it and admonishes his mother in no uncertain terms. Harindra is more fore-sighted and energetic than his friends. He acts more purposefully and works out a specific programme which includes varied requirements ranging from the liquidation of caste and ban on early marriage to the improvement of sanitary conditions and medical service.

R.K. Narayan makes use of his comic genius in the presentation of Gandhi in his *Waiting for the Mahatma*. He is portrayed as a living human being possessed with a pickwikian sense of humour in keeping with the general tone and temper of Narayan's world. Anand differs from R.K. Narayan in his assessment of the Mahatma. In fact, Anand lives with Gandhi breathing the air of his Ashram at Sabarmati, discusses *Untouchables* with him; and yet there is no hero-worship of Gandhi in his novels. His heroes like Bakha, Lalu and Krishna are highly critical of Gandhi's view on celibacy, hand spinning, and passive resistance. Regarding the Mahatma, Mulk Raj Anand writes: "My conversion to truth in Sabarmati Ashram was not a conversion to Gandhi's proposition, God is Truth. I had been converted to the truth which I saw in human relations. When he said 'God is truth', I said, 'God is love'."[49]

Bhattacharya tries to find out a meeting point between Gandhian social ethics and tremendous force of science and technology. While his mind is imbued with the Gandhian way of life — simple living and high thinking —, he is not blind to the conditions of India that industrialization is equally necessary in view of the growing propulation which demands increased production.

Since Anand and Bhattacharya are modern in outlook believing in the social reform on the principles of equality, justice and liberty, their characters are full of hope, zeal and courage to bring about the expected changes in the society; Narayan, on the other hand, is traditional in his outlook. And since he has firm faith in the sacred Hindu scriptures, his characters too can not help themselves being traditional believing in the 'good old days'. Any idea of revolt on their part is viewed as sentimentalism which Narayan has denounced bringing them back to their normal station in life. They prefer *status quo* in social life.

Social Vision : Like Narayan, both Mulk Raj Anand and Bhabani Bhattacharya are the product of conservative Hindu society. However, there is a marked difference in their attitude to life. While Narayan's is a world of compromise between age-old Hindu ideals and the modern occidental civilization; Mulk Raj Anand is of the firm social commitment discarding the worn-out traditions, conventions and dasturs if they have no relevance under the changed circumstances. He could not help but condemn a society which is ridden by caste and class consciousness, which preaches piety but commits murder and survives on its pretense to holiness. Bhabani Bhattacharya too has the vision of a welfare society at heart. Unlike Narayan his concerns are clear and unambiguous. He follows the tradition of European social realism as does Mulk Raj Anand.

Both Anand and Bhattacharya believe that man is the master of his destiny. The social ailments that have plagued the society are only man-made, hence it is only man who can remove them without extraneous help of any God or supernatural power. They have absolute faith in the capacity of man to remake the world. Dr. K.C. Bhatnagar writes: "...man must have faith in his potentiality to achieve concrete results for the amelioration of mankind instead of engaging in a private battle to wrest the secret of his own existence on earth (an illusion?) from a transcendental Reality that eludes him. Social reformers right from Erasmus to Marx have, like Anand, conceded to man the capacity to rise like a phoenix from his ashes to take a hand in the regeneration of the world around him."[50]

Unlike Narayan, Anand believes in the dignity of men, hence his unwavering faith in the equality of rights, privileges and opportunities for every one in the society. That is why, he takes up the cause of the underdogs of the traditional society, who have been trampled under foot for centuries together by the orthodox caste Hindus. The very fact that Anand has chosen as the hero, an untouchable, a boy from the lowest stratum of Indian society, ignored by his predecessors as an unsuitable theme for fiction, establishes Anand's firm faith in the dignity of man irrespective of caste and social position, a doctrine central to Anand's humanism. Anand describes a waif like Munoo, an untouchable like Bakha, an undentured labour like Gangu and sets them right at the centre of the scheme of cruelty and exploitation that held Indians in its vicious grip. In writing of the pariahs and the bottom dogs rather than of the elect and the sophisticated, K.R. Shrinivas Iynger observes: "he had ventured into territory that had been largely ignored till then by Indian writers...."[51]

Mulk Raj Anand is concerned with social reforms which can not be brought about unless one rejects the caste system, the practice of which results in suppression of untouchables who are denied fundamental right, to grow into respectable citizen of society. The Hindu caste system intended originally perhaps, as an organization to facilitate mutual co-operation among different sections of society — eventually degenerated and petrified into an utterly divisive force with destructive effects particularly on untouchables — people who are considered too low and dirty to merit assumption under any of the four castes. These unfortunate men are segregated, dreaded as lepers and treated most contemptuously inspite of the enormously useful work they do in tidying up the entire village as well as cleaning the dungpots of all castemen.

That the untouchables have the segregated living away from the main-stream of life is evidenced even in R.K. Narayan's *The Waiting for the*

Mahatma. However, it appears, Narayan has left them to their fate with Mahatma Gandhi's blessings to them to have absolute faith in God that everything would be alright.

Narayan confines his writing to the people of his own caste. Malgudi that he presents through his novels appears microcosm of Hindu society. In Malgudi we find such people who pray before the image of Natraj or take coconut and camphor to a temple or call a priest for curing a man of his madness or to celebrate the completion of a religious poem by organizing functions in the temple taking a procession or consulting astrologers to study the conjunction of planets and fixing an auspicious date for the inauguration of the ceremony of a motion picture or keeping a fast for appeasing the rain-God. And though Narayan moves with the passage of time, his outlook remains substantially unchanged. He seems to prefer 'good old days' of the ancient India.

On the other hand, Mulk Raj Anand is vehemently opposed to the worn-out customs and traditions. Anand is also opposed to the formal religion. He is enraged that the religious man should entrap the superstitious folk by exploiting their gullibility. He is convinced that the institution of religion is positively detrimental to man's progress as it creates either passivity, or narrow orthodoxy and fanaticism in man. It is relevant to recall the volcanic words of Swami Vivekanand here, "Our religion is in the kitchen. Our God is in the cooking pot and our religion is: Don't touch me, I am holy."[52] Nandgir, the village Mahatma who is the custodian of sikh religion smokes charas, drinks ground heap (bhang) and leads a life of lechery and fornification and yet he is a religious guru. He takes advantage of ignorance and illiteracy of the villagers. Superstitious people look upto him for the cure of bites and ailments. Lalu Singh, who makes an attempt to break the exsiting tradition of keeping the Keshas (hair) unshaved, is punished by his parents, the Mahanta and the community in general. The village thus is the stronghold of the powerful trinity of exploiters: the landlord, the village Shaukar, and the village Mahanta. They help one another in keeping their vested interest firmly entrenched in the villages. To quote K.R. Shrinivas Iynger: 'the typical ingredients of village life — landlord and the saukar, Sarkar and numbo jumbo, convention and superstition, mass conformity and mass hysteria, the cupidity and cruelty of some and the apathy and helplessness of the many — inevitably conspire to daunt and all but crush the free and ardent spirit of Lalu Singh."[53] This has made Anand deal with the misery and wretchedness of the poor and then struggle for a better life. He has been conscious of the need to help raise the untouchables, the peasants, the serfs, the coolies and the other suppressed members of the society, to human dignity and self-awareness in view of the abjectness, apathy and despair in which they are sunk. P.P. Metha rightly observes: "Dr. Anand, in all his novels, emphasizes the fact that the nobility and dignity are not the monopoly of the rich. The poor have their greatness, honour as well as the rich. Mute inglorious Miltons and Cromwells guiltless of their country's blood are not uncommon in the ranks of the poor."[54]

Anand's delineation of his characters is double proned in the sense, while accusing the privileged people of their callousness, he also condemns the abject acceptance of inhuman treatment by the oppressed. Dr. Anand is infuriated with abject folks because once they are passively resigned, there is very little scope of salvation for them. The tragedy with us is that "...we lie about like pigs in our own sty-belching with satisfaction at our swinish state."[55] Anand would rather die without a conviction than live with a compromise. Even as a child he was referred to as an uncompromising rebel. He would either have ultimate pain or ultimate joy and would not accept a compromise of any kind. He feels that if the society exists for an individual then it must keep him to free himself from its corroding influence and educate him to be self-reliant human being.

Anand feels that the political freedom of the country should also mean freedom for others who are under-privileged. But it is unlikely that the better off sections of society who want to be more free than others will accept freedom for all, rights for all, houses and food for all. He therefore contemplates rebellion. In *Coolie* Dr. Anand tries to open the eyes of the workers to reality. "...Stand up for your rights, you roofless wretches, stand up for justice! ...and right — stand up for life, or they will crush you and destroy you altogether."[56]

Anand's is a revolutionary idea when he advocates: We need no institutionalised religion to advocate ethics like human-tenderness, service mindedness, devotion to duty, liberty, self-dependence etc., Anand calls it 'religion without religion'. He believes that there is no power transcending man who can decide things for him. Man is responsible for gaining or losing his life. So foolish faith and the resultant apathy or quarrel over the non-existent God are all in vain. The only apt solution according to Anand is to give up the old gods and follow the 'religion without religion'.

Unlike Narayan who prefers *status quo*, Bhattacharya is committed to social reform. He is opposed to outmoded customs, taboos, inhibitions, superstitions and blind beliefs, and heralds the age of science and reason.

Kalo's protest is against the arbitrary caste system, hunger and exploitation by assuming the garb of a Brahmin and by managing the fake coming of 'Shio'. He takes revenge upon the society that has ridiculed him and his daughter. He draws our attention to the pressure of circumstances responsible for the misery and suffering of the poor. What else could they have to starve off hunger or to keep the wolf from the door? They surely look more sinned against than sinning — when we see apparently decent and respectable people — wolves disguising themselves as sheep-demanding with tne money they command, gratification of their kind of hunger bestial in its lustfulness and sensuality.

Bhattacharya makes us laugh heartily at the absurdities of the old without causing any harsh feelings against them. Unlike Narayan, there is no ambiguity in Bhattacharya's treatment of such things as the comparing of horoscopes or looking at the signs of the bride's hand before the marriage is finalised, or the offering of the blood by a woman from her bosom to the deity to secure the boon of pregnancy. And unlike Anand, without resorting to an explicit commentary, Bhattacharya disapproves of these things by means of gentle irony and humour, never through open denunciation as Anand does in his novels.

Unlike Narayan whose characters are mere puppets in the hands of fate, Bhattacharya has great faith in man's ability to change the world and reminds the reader of the inexhaustible fund of surging creative energy latent in ordinary folk.

With the vision of freedom to the country from the alien rule in view, Bhattacharya wants his countrymen to awake to the need of bringing about social freedom if the former is to be made effective and the country has to advance to the forefront of the fast developing world. How can a country which is caught in the deadly mire of obscurantism, superstition, rituals and obsolete customs make progress even though it may be free. Jaydeo (*Music for Mohini*) remarks: "India was on the verge of freedom; a new page of world history was writing itself. The political implications were visible to all but not the social problems. What was political freedom worth to the common man if it was not part of a renaissance in social life?"[57] In this respect Dr. Ambedkar's observations are worth quoting when he says: "We must make our political democracy a social democracy as well, political democracy can not last unless there lies at the base of it social democracy."[58] The freedom of a country does not usually mean the freedom of the people of that country. Moreover, Bhattacharya is conscious of the social and economic inequalities which corrode social reform on the principles of equality and justice.

Advocting the liquidation of barriers of caste, he openly attacks religion and feudal prejudices. Born as a Brahmin, he is deadly against the hypocrisy of the cunning sharks of his caste who exploit the gullible masses in the name of God and religion. He laments that religion has become an instrument of oppression in the hands of a cunning few who are more than wolves in sheep's clothings. Bhattacharya also denounces 'Karma' theory of the Hindus. Because he has seen the real evil doers remaining untouched by Karma. They eat well and utter the name of 'Shio' and the name of 'Rama' and sleep in beds of peace and comforts. And the innumerable destitutes cry and die for food. It is foolish to think that all those born in low caste families have done bad deeds in their past life. Rejecting all that is irrational, outdated wornout customs and traditions, Bhattacharya wants to make Bahula a model village where all people would breathe freely irrespective of caste and class, with equal opportunities to one and all in the society.

All the three novelists, Narayan, Anand and Bhattacharya have expressed dissatisfactions with the present-day education system prevalent in the country. It has failed to make allround development of man's personality so as to enable him to face realities of life. While Narayan favours 'Leave Alone' system of the ancient times, which he hopes, will transform children into 'Wholesome human beings' by providing them with an opportunity for the natural growth of the 'original vision'. This type of education is, in fact, a revival of the old Indian tradition of 'open air school' run by saintly teachers in ancient India. Narayan himself writes about present education "...I am not averse to enlightenment, but I feel convinced that the entire organization, system, outlook, and aims of education are hopelessly wrong from beginning to end."[59] Dr. Anand and Bhattacharya believe that education is a powerful instrument for social reconstruction. They have absolute faith in man's capacity to transform the society with the aid of advancing science and technology and with the practice of love and compassion for the weak and the lowly. Both Anand and Bhattacharya being rational and of scientific temper, feel that in a society riven by superstitions fossilized traditions and beliefs in the miraculous, the promotion of a new outlook is essential. The tendency to subject everything to close scrutiny and criticism with 'intolerant tolerance'[60] results in catholicism in outlook. They feel that science and scientific advancement would only enhance man's understanding and would awaken him from centuries of slumber of superstitions and blind beliefs. Unfortunately, the scientific temperament one requires to develop through education is surprisingly lacking in Indian educationists. They have failed to take up the task of liberating the illiterate mass from prejudices and superstitions. Their limited pre-occupation with their professional works and their shying away from social responsibility has created the present situation. Not only have they failed in taking up the challenge of transforming the outlook of the people but also in creating a faith in them that science and technology would help solve their problems. In an Address to the Indian Science Congress Association in 1969, Mrs. Indira Gandhi expressed her feelings :

> Silently and inexorably, a revolution is taking place in our towns and villages. Our people are changing, yearning for the economic progress which could deliver them from the poverty of centuries. They are ready to learn new skills and to take to new methods. Yet the old pulls of tradition and the familiarity of dead habit remain strong. India is not governed by a small elite. The people are sovereign, and if their outlook is superstitious and tradition-bound, it will surely be reflected in the country's administration and politics. Thus, the inculcation of a scientific temper among our people — and this includes politicians, administrators, managers, farmers, workers, students and of course, scientists themselves — is of primary importance. It is not enough for this temper to be cultivated in our laboratories, class rooms and offices, it must permeate our homes, the market place and the village square.[61]

However, it is a pity that the trditional pulls are as deep-rooted in our educated people even today that the scientific temper so essential to bring about a social change appears a remote possibility. This is so because the so-called religious leaders with ulterior motives in them try their utmost to keep up *status quo* in social life so that they may continue to enjoy their exalted position in the society. Dr. Anand and Bhattacharya have observed this hypocrisy in the society and led a scathing attack on the hypocrites eating into the vitals of social life. Hence their genuine concern for social reforms; Narayan on the other hand, tries all along to maintain the religious moral order, upholding the old social values.

Notes and References

1. Ved Mehta, *John is Easy to Please.* (New York : Farrer Straus distributed by Secker and Warburg, 1971).
2. Quoted by Dr. G.P. Bhagmar in his Thesis entitled *R.K. Narayan : The Novelist*, 1981, p.67.
3. S. Laxman Shastry, *A Few Words about this Issue (Editorial)*, *Contemporary Indian Literature*, Nov., Dec., 1965, p. 10.
4. Robert Weimann: *Structure And Society in Literary History* (Lawrence and Wishart, London, 1979), p.234.

5. Sudhakar Joshi, *An Evening with Bhabani : Sunday Standard*, April 27, 1969.
6. Mulk Raj Anand, *Two Leaves And a Bud*, preface (Delhi : Hind Pocket Books), p. 2.
7. M.K. Naik, *The Ironic Vision* (New Delhi : Sterling Publishers Pvt. Ltd., 1983), p. 1.
8. (Dr. Sunitikumar Chatterjee) Quoted by Elena J. Kalinnikov, *Indian English Literature : A Perspective* (Ghaziabad : Vimal Prakashan, 1982), pp. 110-111.
9. Bhabani Bhattacharya, *Music for Mohini* (New Delhi : An Orient paperbacks, 1952), p. 44.
10. *Ibid.*, p. 140 (Jaico).
11. Bhabani Bhattacharya, *He Who Rides a Tiger* (Delhi : Hind, Pocket Books, 1955), p. 53.
12. S.L. Sagar, *Hindu Culture and Caste System in India* (Delhi Uppal Book Store, 1975), p. 95.
13. Mulk Raj Anand, *Untouchable* (Now Delhi : An Orient paperbacks, 1970), p. 92.
14. E.M. Forster, preface to *Untouchable*, A Novel by Mulk Raj Anand (New Delhi : Orient Paperbacks, 1970), p. 6.
15. Quoted by D. Shyamla Rao, *Bhattacharya and his Fiction* (Bareilly : Student's Store), p. 129.
16. Bhabani Bhattacharya, *So Many Hungers* (Jaico, 1964), p. 109.
17. Bhabani Bhattacharya, *He Who Rides a Tiger*, pp. 116-117.
18. S. Menon Marath, *Three Indian Novelists : Life and Letters*, Vol. 59, 1948, p. 16.
19. Mulk Raj Anand, *Two Leaves and a Bud*, p. 198.
20. Mulk Raj Anand, *Coolie*, (Bombay), pp. 265-266.
21. H.M. Williams, *Indo Anglian Literature : A Survey* (New Delhi : Orient Longmans Ltd., 1976), p. 49.
22. Hari Mohan Prasad, *Response : Recent Revelation of Indian Fiction in English* (Bareilly : Prakash Book Depot, 1983), p. 136.
23. Dr. Mulk Raj Anand, *The Village* (Bombay, 1960), p. 43.
24. An article, *Hoax* by Sanad Edumaruku, *Illustrated Weekly of India*, Sept. 1, 1985.
25. Promila Paul, *The Novels of Mulk Raj Anand : A Thematic Study*. (New Delhi : Sterling Publishers Pvt. Ltd., 1983), pp. 63-64.
26. P. Raghvendra Rao, Mulk Raj Anand, *The Two Fold Voice :* Essays on Indian Writing in English, Edit. O.V.K. Reghavacharulu (Guntur, Navodaya Publishers, 1971), pp. 90-91.
27. *Ibid.*, p. 91.
28. Mulk Raj Anand, *Sword and the Sickle* (Bombay, 1951), pp. 166-167.
29. Dr. B.R. Ambedkar, *Annihilation of Caste* (Bheem Patrika Publications, Jalandhar, 1936), p. 23.
30. G.S. Ghure, *Caste and Race in India* (Kegan Paul, Trench Trunber & Co. Ltd., Hertford, Great Britain, 1932), p. 4.
31. Dr. S. Radhakrishnan, *Indian Religions* (Delhi : Orient paperbacks, 1983), pp. 9-10.
32. Anand's letter to Dr. Balaram Gupta, July 12th, 1967.
33. Anand Khurana, *Godmen Or Conmen? Nagpur Times: Sunday Magazine*, Jan. 26, 1986.

34. C.D. Narsimhiaha, *R.K. Narayan's The Guide : Literary Criterion*, Vol. IV.
35. H.M. Williams, *Indo-Anglian Literature* : A Survey, p. 38.
36. R.K. Narayan, *My Dateless Diary* (Delhi : An Orient paperbacks, 1969), pp. 189-190.
37. Dr. Balram Gupta, *Mulk Raj Anand* (Bareilly : Prakash Book Depot, 1974), p. 29.
38. Dr. Ram Sevak Singh, *Bhabani Bhattacharya : A Novelist of Dreamy Wisdom* (Banasthali Patrika, July 1969), p. 67.
39. Edward Shill, *The Intellectual between Tradition and Modernity* : The Indian Situation (The Hague Mount & Co., 1961), p. 22.
40. Mulk Raj Anand, *Two Leaves and a Bud* (Preface to the 1951 IInd edition).
41. Hari Mohan Prasad, *Response : Recent Revelations of Indian Fiction in English*, p. 15.
42. Harish Raizada, *R.K. Narayan : A Critical Study of His Works* (New Delhi : Young Asia Publications, 1969), p. 165.
43. Saros Cowasjee, Vasant A. Sahane : *Modern Indian Fiction* (New Delhi : Vikas Publishing House, 1981), p. 1.
44. Mulk Raj Anand, *Big Heart* (Bombay), p. 166.
45. *Ibid.*, pp. 143-144.
46. Mulk Raj Anand, *Old Woman and The Cow* (Bombay, 1960), p. 283.
47. Bhabani Bhattacharya, *He Who Rides a Tiger* (Jaico), p. 243.
48. Bhabani Bhattacharya, *Music for Mohini* (New York : Crown Publishers, 1952), p. 170.
49. Mulk Raj Anand, *Why I Write? Indian Writing in English* edit. K.N. Sinha (New Delhi: Heritage Publishers, 1979), p. 67.
50. Dr. K.C. Bhatnagar, *Realism in Major Indo-English Fiction* (Bareilly : Prakash Book Depot, 1980), p. 99.
51. K.R. Shrinivas Iynger : *Indian Writing in English* (New Delhi : Sterling Publishers Pvt. Ltd., 1983), p. 333.
52. Quoted by M. Tarinayya, *Mulk Raj Anand's Untouchable : An Analysis* (Journal of Mysore University, March 30, 1969).
53. K.R. Shrinivas Iynger, *Indian Writing in English*, p. 347.
54. P.P. Metha, *Indo-Anglian Fiction : An Assessment* (Bareilly : Prakash Book Depot, 1968), p. 166.
55. Mulk Raj Anand, *The Old Woman and The Cow*, p. 259.
56. Mulk Raj Anand, *Coolie*, p. 252.
57. Bhabani Bhattacharya, *Music for Mohini* (New Delhi : Orient paperback, 1952), p. 67.
58. *Constituent Assembly Debates* (25-11-1949), Vol. XI, p. 972.
59. R.K. Narayan : *My Outlook on Education : Reluctant Guru* (New Delhi : An Orient Paperbacks, 1974), p. 17.
60. In answer to a questionnaire submitted to Dr. Balram Gupta, Anand defines 'Intolerant tolerance' as non-acceptance of fanatical par'san assertions with a kind of good humour without fighting back with ones own assertions.
61. Address by Mrs. Indira Gandhi, Prime Miniser of India at Indian Science Congress Association in 1969. (*Sccience Today : A Times of India Publication*, March 1985), p. 51.

SELECT BIBLIOGRAPHY

Primary Sources

(A) Novels

Narayan, R.K., *Swami and Friends* (Mysore : Indian Thought Publications, 1971)

——, *The Bachelor of Arts* (Mysore : Indian Thought Publications, 1979)

——, *The Dark Room* (New Delhi : An Orient Paperbacks, 1978)

——, *The English Teacher* (Mysore : Indian Thought Publications, 1981)

——, *Mr. Sampath* (Delhi : Hind Pocket Books, 1979)

——, *The The Financial Expert* (Mysore : Indian Thought Publications, 1981)

——, *Waiting For The Mahatma* (Mysore : Indian Thought Publications, 1981)

——, *The Guide* (Mysore : Indian Thought Publications, 1958)

——, *The Man Eater of Malgudi* (Mysore : Indian Thought Publications, 1980)

——, *The Vendor of Sweets* (Mysore : Indian Thought Publications, 1967)

——, *The Painter of Signs* (Great Britain : Penguin Books, 1982)

——, *A Tiger For Malgudi* (New Delhi : Allied Publishers Pvt. Ltd., 1983)

(B) Other Works

Narayan, R.K., *An Astrologer's Day And Other Stories* (Mysore: Indian Thought Publications, 1964)

——, *Fifteen Years, Next Sunday* (Delhi : Hind Pocket Books, 1972)

1967)

——, *A Horse And Two Goats* (Mysore : Indian Thought Publications, 1982)

——, *The Ramayan* (Delhi : Hind Pocket Books, 1972)

——, *My Days* (Mysore : Indian Thought Publications, 1979)

——, *My Outlook On Education, Reluctant Guru* (New Delhi : An Orient Paperbacks, 1974)

——, *The Mahabharat* (Delhi : Hind Pocket Books, 1978)

Secondary Sources

(A) Books

Ambedkar, B.R., *Gandhism* (Jalandhar : Buddhist Publishing House)

——, *Annihilation of Caste* (Bheem Patrika Publications, Jalandhar, 1936)

Allan Walter : *The English Novel* (A Penguin International Edition)

Anand, Mulk Raj, *Untouchable* (New Delhi : An Orient Paperback, 1970)

——, *The Village* (Bombay, 1960)

——, *Sword And the Sickle* (Bombay, 1951)

——, *Two Leaves and a Bud* (Delhi : Hind Pocket Books)

——, *Big Heart* (Bombay)

——, *Old Woman And The Cow* (Bombay, 1960)

Badal, R.K., *R.K. Narayan, A Study* (Bareilly : Prakash Book Depot, 1976)

Baghmar, G.B., *R.K. Narayan : The Novelist* (The Ph.D. Thesis submitted to Nagpur University, Nagpur, 1981)

Beal, Anthony, *D.H. Lawrence ; Selected Literary Criticism*, edit. (Heinemann, London, 1953)

Bhatnagar, K.C., *Realism in Major Indo-English Fiction* (Bareilly: Prakash Book Depot, 1980)

Bhattacharya, Bhabani, *He Who Rides a Tiger* (Bombay, Jaico Publishing House, 1953)

——, *So Many Hungers* (New Hind Pocket Book, 1978)

——, *Music for Mohini* (New Delhi : An Orient Paperback, 1952)

Chesnokov, D. and Korpushin, V., *Man And Society* (Moscow : Progress Publisher, 1966)

——, *So Many Hungers* (New Hind Pocket Book, 1978)

——, *Music for Mohini* (New Delhi : An Orient Paperback, 1952)

Chesnokov, D. and Korpushin, V., *Man And Society* (Moscow : Progress Publisher, 1966)

Cawajee Saros & Sahane Vasant, *A Modern Indian Fiction* (New Delhi: Vikas Publishing House Pvt. Ltd., 1981).

Dhavan, R.K., *Explorations in Modern Indo-English Fiction* (New Delhi : Bahri Publications Pvt. Ltd., 1987).

Dev, Som, *The Guide : A Critical Appreciation* (Bareilly : Prakash Book Depot, 1982)

Embree, Ainslie T., *The Hindu Tradition.* From *Readings in Oriental Thought*, edit. William Therdore De Bary (New York: Modern Library Book, 1966)

Forster, E.M., Preface to *Untouchable*, A Novel by Mulk Raj Anand (New Delhi : Orient Paperbacks, 1970)

Frye, Northrop, *The Critical Path* (Bloomington : Indian University Press, 1971)

Ghure, G.S., *Caste And Race In India* (Kegan Paul. Trench Trubner and Co. Ltd., Hertford, Great Britain, 1932)

Girla, Shiv K., *R.K. Narayan : His World and His Art* (Meerut: Suru Publishing House, 1984)

Gupta, Balram, *Mulk Raj Anand* (Bareilly : Prakash Book Depot, 1974)

Iynger, K.R. Shrinivas, *Indian Writing in English*

Joshi, K.N. and B. Shymla Rao, *Studies in Indo-Anglian Literature*, (Bareilly : Prakash Book Depot, 1979)

Kalinnikov, Elena, J., *Indian English Literature : A Perspective*, (Ghaziabad : Vimal Prakashan, 1982)

Kovoor, Abraham, *Begone Godman* (Bombay : Jaico Press Pvt. Ltd., 1977)

Kulkarni, A.R., *The Buddha The Trimurti and Modern Hinduism* (Nagpur : Shrinivas Mudranalya, Suvichar Prakashan Building, 1980)

Kumar, Raj, *The Modern Novel* (Bhopal : Lyall Book Depot, 1967)

Mathews, C.M., *Health and Culture in a South Indian Village* (New Delhi : Sterling Publishers Pvt. Ltd., 1979)

Mehta, P.P., *Indo-Anglian Fiction : An Assessment* (Bareilly : Prakash Book Depot, 1968)

Mehta, Ved, *John is Easy to Please* (New York : Farrer Straus, distributed by Secker and Werburg, 1971)

Muche, D.C., *The Compass of Irony* (London, 1969)

Mukharjee, Meenakshi, *The Twice Born Fiction* (New Delhi : Arnold Hainemann, 1971)

Naik, M.K., *The Ironic Vision* (New Delhi : Sterling Publishers Pvt. Ltd., 1983)

Pandeya, Shiv M., *Studies in Modern Fiction* (New Delhi : Vikas Publishing House Pvt. Ltd., 1983)

Paul, Promila, *The Novels of Mulk Raj Anand : A Thematic Study* (New Delhi : Sterling Publishers Pvt. Ltd., 1983)

Prasad, Hari Mohan, *Recent Revelation of Indian Fiction* (Bareilly: Prakash Book Depot, 1983)

Radhakrishnan, S., *Indian Religions* (Delhi : Orient Paperback, 1983)

Raizada, Harish, *R.K. Narayan : A Critical Study* (New Delhi: Young Asia Publications, 1969)

Ram, Atma, *Perspectives on R.K. Narayan*, (Ghaziabad : Vimal Prakashan, 1981)

Rao, B. Shymla, *Bhattacharya And His Fiction* (Bareilly : Students Store)

Rao, P. Raghavendra, *Mulk Raj Anand, The Twofold Voice* : Essays on Indian writing in English Ed. D.V.K. Raghavacharyulu, (Guntur: Navodaya Publishers, 1971)

Reddy, C.R. Foreword to K.R.S. Iynger's, *Indo-Anglian Literature*, 1943

Sagar, S.L., *Hindu Culture And Caste System in India* (Delhi : Uppal Book Store, 1975)

Sanyal, S.C., *Indianness in Major Indo-English Novels* (Bareilly: Prakash Book Depot, 1984)

Shirwadkar, Meena, *Image of Women in Indo-Anglian Novel* (New Delhi : Sterling Publishers Pvt. Ltd., 1979)

Shill, Edward, *The Intellectual Between Tradition and Modernity The Indian Situation*. (Hague : Mount Co., 1961)

Walsh, William, *R.K. Narayan : A Critical Appreciation* (New Delhi : Allied Publishers Pvt. Ltd., 1963)

Weimann, Robert, *Structure And Society in Literary History* (London: Laurence and Wishart, 1979)

Williams, H.M., *Indo-Anglian Literature* (New Delhi : Orient Longmans Ltd., 1976)

(B) Articles/Journals/Periodicals

Amur, G.S., *R.K. Narayan in his Own Culture : An approach to The Vendor of Sweets.* From *Explorations in Modern Indo-English Fiction.* Edit. R.K. Dhavan (New Delhi : Bahri Publications Pvt. Ltd., 1982)

Berry, Margaret, *R.K. Narayan : Lila and Literature : Journal of Indian Writing in English*, IV, 2 July 1976

Bhardwaj, S.P., *The Painter of Signs : An Analysis,* From *Perspectives on R.K. Narayan*, edit. Atma Ram (Ghaziabad : Vimal Prakashan, 1981)

Constituent Assembly Debates, (25-11-1949), Vol. XI

Dial, Ram, *The Anima Animus : Interaction in The Guide* (From *Perspectives on R.K. Narayan,* edit. Atma Ram

Edumaruku, Sanad, *Hoax*, *Illustrated Weekly of India*, Sept. 1, 1983

Gandhi, Mahatma, *Young India*, 27th April, 1921

——, *Harijan-Bandhu*, 19-3-1933. From *The Collected Works of Mahatma Gandhi Publications Division* (Volume 54, April 1973)

Girla, Shiv K., *Narayan's World of Values.* From *Perspectives on R.K. Narayan,* edit. Atma Ram

Ref. *Guardian, The* (8-8-1978)

Gupta, Balram, *A Sinner is a Sinner : A Study of Raju.* From *Perspectives on R.K. Narayan*, edit. Atma Ram

Gupta, Balram, *The Journal of Indian Writing in English*, Vol. 12, Jan. 1984, No. 1

Harrex, S.C., *The Fire And The Offerings* (Calcutta : Writers Work Shop, 1977)

Illustrated Weekly of India, June 23, 1963

Joshi, Sudhakar, *An Evening with Bhabani : Sunday Standard,* April 27, 1969

Khurana, Anand, *Godmen or Conmen? Nagpur Times : Sunday Magazine*,

Gupta, Balram, *The Journal of Indian Writing in English*, Vol. 12, Jan. 1984, No. 1

Harrex, S.C., *The Fire And The Offerings* (Calcutta : Writers Work Shop, 1977)

Illustrated Weekly of India, June 23, 1963

Joshi, Sudhakar, *An Evening with Bhabani : Sunday Standard*, April 27, 1969

Khurana, Anand, *Godmen or Conmen? Nagpur Times : Sunday Magazine*, Jan. 26, 1986

Krishna, S., *A Day With Narayan : Span* (Vol. XVI, No. 4, April 1975)

Literary Criterion, Vol. IV, 1961

Malhotra, Tara, *Old Places, Old Faces and Old Times : A critical Study of R.K. Narayan's latest Fiction, Banasthali Patrika* (Supplement), July 1969

Mathur, O.P., *West Wind Blows Through Malgudi.* From *Perspectives on R.K. Narayan*, edit. Atma Ram

Marath, S. Menon, *Three Indian Novelists : Life and Letters*, Vol. 56, Dec. 1948

Narsimhiaha, C.D., *R.K. Narayan's The Guide, Literary Criterion*, Vol. IV

Pandharipande, Shyam, *Nagpur Times : Cross Section*, Friday, 28th June 1985

Prasad, Hari Mohan, *Shades in the Prism : An Analysis of The Dark Room.* From *Perspectives on R.K. Narayan*, edit. Atma Ram.

Rao, Pandurang, *Tea with R.K. Narayan : Journal of Common-wealth Literature*, June 1971

Science Today, A Times of India Publication, March 1985 (Address by Mrs. Indira Gandhi, Prime Minister of India, At Indian Science Congress Association in 1969)

Shastry, S. Laxman, *A Few Words about this Issue, Editorial Contemporary Indian Literature*, Nov./Dec. 1965

Shrivastav, Ramesh, *What is so Great in R.K. Narayan?*

Singh, Ram Sevak, *Bhabani Bhattacharya : A Novelist of Dreamy Wisdom.* (*Banasthali Patrika*, July 1969)

Singh, Kirpal, *The Ordinary and the Average as Satiric Traps.* From *Explorations in Modern Indo-English fiction*, edit R.K. Dhavan

Sundaram, P.S., *The Ambivalence of R.K. Narayan*, From *Explorations in Modern Indo-English Fiction*

Tarinayya, M., *Mulk Raj Anand's Untouchable : An Analysis* (Journal of Mysore University : March 30, 1969)

Walsh, William, *Literature and Humanity : A Human Idiom* (London, 1964)

Williams, N.M., *Precarious Innocence : Patterns in the Novels of R.K. Narayan.* From *Perspectives on R.K. Narayan.*

Vattam, Krishna, *Interview with R.K. Narayan, The Deccan Harold,* 19 June 1980.

INDEX

A

Abu Lane, 93

Albert Mission School, 2, 93

Albert Mission College, 21, 104, 123

Allahabad, 89

Almighty, 51, 60, 61, 82, 124

Altruism, 71, 74

Ambedkar, Dr. Babasaheb, 40, 49, 113, 129, 148, 164, 178

Ambika, 76

America, 112, 118, xx

Amritsar, 153

Amur, G.S., 73

Anand, Mulk Raj, Dr., xi, xiii, xviii, xxii, 17, 100, 126, 151-161, 163, 166-172, 174-180

  Big Heart, 172

  Coolie, 151, 160, 177

  Old Woman & the cow, The, 17, 156, 165, 171, 172

  Sword and The Sickle, 163

  Two Leaves and a Bud, 170

  Village, The, 162, 165

  Untouchable, 151, 157, 160, 163, 164

Anderson, 115

Aranyaka, 139

Asia, 154

Atherveda, 122

Atta Deep Bhav, 91

Austin, Jane, xviii, 43, 171

Aurangabad, 142

B

Babu, 12, 13

Bacon, 173

Badal, Dr., 15, 135

Badri Hills, 76, 97, 116

Bakha, 157, 163, 164, 167, 170, 172, 174, 175

Balu, 17, 42-44, 97, 112, 118, 121, 172, xvi, xx

Bahula, 173, 179

Banglore, 122

Begone Godmen, 23

Bengal, 168, 173

Benaras, 49, 85, 98

Bhagwat Geeta, 54, 71, 73, 145

Bhagwantam, Dr., 81

Bhardwaj, S.P., 83, 136

Bharti, xix, 47, 48, 51, 52, 83, 102, 103, 128

Bhattacharya, Bhabani, xi, xv, xxii, 58, 126, 151, 152, 154-158, 160, 163, 165, 168-175, 177-180

  Goddess named Gold, 171

  He Who Rides a Tiger, 58, 151, 157, 158, 161-163, 168, 170

  Music for Mohini, 151, 155, 173, 178

  So Many Hungers, 155, 158

Bhatnagar, K.C., 17, 35, 102, 128, 175

Bhu-Gods, 70, 142

Bibal, 140

Bihar, 142, 152
Birla House, 50
Bradley, A.C., 153
Brahmnica, 139
Brahma, 157
Brunton, Paul, Dr., 20
Bose, Subhash Chandra, 48
Bose, Surendra, 159
Buddha, 59, 121, 144, 166

C

Calcutta, 50, 159, 164
Cambridge, xiii
Chandran, xv, xvi, xvii, xx, 5-11, 17, 78, 100, 107, 112, 123, 126, 129, 134, 143, 156, 168, 172
Chand Lal, 153
Chaturvarna, 50, 146
Chatterjee, Sunitikumar, Dr., 155
Chesnokov, Dr., 126
Chidambaram Temple, 34
Chinna Dorai, 77
Christ, 153
Church, Rechard, 39
Coleridge, 26
Columbia University, 64

D

Daisy, xix, xx, 80-87, 96, 99, 102, 112, 116, 123, 124, 127-130, 132, 136, 142, 146
De Mello, 36, 37
Defoe, xi
Delhi, 62
Delhi University, xiii
Detached Observer, xviii, 35, 36
Dev, Som, 55, 57
Devdasi, 70, 139, 152, xiv
Dial, Ram, 99
Dickinson, 153
Dobree, Bonamy, 153

E

Ebenezar, Mr., 2
Eddington, 153
Edinaruku, Sanad, 162
Eliot, T.S., 153
Einstein, 153
Erasmus, 175
Europe, 118, 154
Eyre and Spottiswoode, 28

F

Fatalistic, 31, 35, 64, 65, 132, 138
Feudal society, 18
Forster, E.M., 153, 158
Frieud, Dr., 153
Fyre Northrop, xxii

G

Gandhi, 47, 48, 50-52, 73-75, 101, 102, 104, 106, 107, 113, 114, 119, 136, 146, 147, 173, 174, 176
Gandhi, Mrs. Indira, 180
Gandhism, 73, 103, 113
Ganges, The, 49, 98
Ganga-Yamuna-Saraswati, 89
Garrison Engineer, 44, 121, 138
Gauri, 17, 156, 165, 171, 172, 173
Gill, Erik, 153
Girla, Shiva K., 137
Grace, 75, 77, 78, 112, 129, 137
Greene, Graham, 1, 6, 20, 39
Greta Garbo, 167
Guardian, The, 142
Gupta, 86
Gupta, Balram, Dr., 141, 165, 167
Guindy, 81

Guru Nanak, 153

H

Half-American, 77, 112
Half-Korean, 77, 112
Hamilton Harish, 1
Harijan, 47, 107, 119, 142
Harrex, S.C., 86
Hawaii, 152
Hegel, 149
Heinemann, William, 89
Hema, 20
Herbert, 153
Hetero Hypnosis, 23, 26
Hicks, Daves, 153
Himalaya, 93
Hindu Ethos, 10
Hinduism, 67
Hiroshima, 65
Hollywood, 36
Horoscopes, xiv, xx, 7, 42, 46, 99, 128

I

Indian Freedom Struggle, 47
Indian Institute of Technology, 81
Indo-Anglian, 162, 164
Indoctrination, 23
Inferiority Complex, 40, 43
Invisible Force, xviii, 31
Iyer, Krishna, D.W., 7, 9
Iynger, Shrinivas, K.R., xiii, 7, 85, 147, 175, 176

J

Jagdish, 47, 48
Jagan, xv, xx, 73-78, 93, 97, 101, 107, 111, 112, 121, 123, 126, 129, 136, 142, 143, 146, 168
Japan, 65
Jaydeo, 173, 178
Jayraj, 91, 93
Johnson, Ben, 122
Joseph, 55
Journal, The, 29
Joyce, James, xi
Jung, 153
Justice, The, xii

K

Kailas, 32, 35
Kalinath, 165
Kalo, 58, 158, 159, 163, 168, 170, 171, 173
Kannad, xiii, 151
Kant, 153
Karma, xiii, 17, 45, 92, 114, 148, 167, 168, 179
Karpushin, V., 126
Karmayogi, 136
Kashi, 83
Kashmir, 52, 113
Kattiadiyas, 22
Kaur, Ishwar, 153
Kausalya, 153
Kaveri, 54
Khayyam, 14, 154
Khurana, Anand, 166
Krishan, S., 17, 78
Krishna, xiv, xvi, xxi, 20-26, 65, 71, 100, 103, 104, 106, 115, 123, 126, 130, 131, 135, 137, 138, 139, 143, 146, 152, 153, 157, 160, 174
Krishnaraja Sagar, 54
Koran, 139
Kovoor, Abraham, Dr., 23, 25, 26, 81, 90, 91
Kovoor, Eipe Thomma Kattanar, 24-25
Kulkarni, A.R., 144

Kumbha Mela, 67, 89, 91

L

Lakha, 163

Lalu, 174

Lancashire, xiii

Lanka, 111

Lawley, Sir Frederic, 80

Lawrence, D.H., 67, 153

Laxminath, Sir, 159

Leave Alone System, xxi, 129, 138

Leela, 20

Lib-Movement, xx, 85, 99

Life after death, 25

London, xiii, 28, 39, 47, 142, 153

Lord Shiva, 32

Lord of Tirupati, 4

M

Machavellian, 34, 137

Macmillan, 12

Madras, xii, 7, 23, 35, 103, 115, 151

Malabar, 24

Mahanata, Dr., 17

Mahisha, 68

Mali, xv, 5, 75-78, 97, 112, 121, 137,

Malgudi, xi, xii, xiv, xvii, xviii, 1-4, 6, 18, 20, 26, 28, 29, 30, 35, 36, 47, 50, 56, 64, 65, 70, 77, 78, 81, 84, 85, 94, 96, 102, 103, 107, 108, 110, 113, 117, 119, 122, 124, 126, 127, 129, 130, 135, 137-139, 141, 143, 146-147, 159, 176

Malthi, xvi, 6, 7, 10, 134

Malhotra, Tara, 73, 136

Maharaja college, xii, xxi

Man and society, 126

Mangal Adhikari, 163, 166, 173

Mangala, 59, 61, 102, 120, 155

Manu, 13, 135, 146, 168, 175

Manusmriti, 16, 140, 145

Margayya, xvi, xviii, xx, 5, 39, 40-46, 97, 98, 100, 110, 112, 114, 115, 117, 118, 120, 122, 123, 124, 130, 136, 137, 138, 141, 142, 143, 159, 160

Marco, xix, xxi, 45, 55, 56, 59, 60, 62, 99, 102, 123, 136

Markandaya, 45

Mary, xv, 16-18, 100, 123

Mathews, C.E.M., 120

Mathur, O.P., 110

Mehta, P.P., 177

Mehta, Ved, 23, 139, 152

Mempi Hills, 39, 81

Michigan University, 77

Milton, 26, 123, 177

Mohammad of Gazni, 2

Mohini, 67, 173

Moksha, xiii

Mount Everest, 39

Mukherjee, Meenakshi, 58

Muthu, 69, 70

Mystic, 22, 40

Mysore, 52

N

Narayan Rushipuram Krishnaswami
Novels

Bachelor of Arts, The, xiii, xv, xvi, xvii, xx, 5, 6, 8, 10, 17, 20, 99, 100, 123, 126, 127, 134, 143

Dark Room, The, xii, xvi, xvii, 5, 12, 14, 15, 17, 18, 37, 84, 85, 99, 100, 102, 110, 111, 122, 126, 127, 130, 131, 135, 136, 143, 156, 171

English Teacher, The, (Grateful to Life & Death), xiii, xvi, xix, xxi, 20, 21, 22, 23, 26, 102-104, 115, 123, 126, 127, 130, 135, 138, 143, 144

Financial Expert, The, xiii, xx, 5, 39, 40, 42, 97, 100, 101, 110, 112, 114, 117, 120, 121-124, 137, 141-143, 159

Guide, The, xiii, xv, xvi, xviii, xix, xx, 15, 54, 85, 100, 101, 107, 112, 117, 122, 124, 126, 127, 130, 131, 132, 135, 137, 141, 146, 157, 159, 162, 166

Man Eater of Malgudi, xvii, 34, 44, 64, 66, 69, 71, 85, 100, 101, 102, 104, 106, 127, 131, 138, 147

Sampath, Mr., xiii, xv, xvi, xvii, xviii, 15, 28, 39, 85, 100, 105, 115, 122, 126, 127, 135, 137, 143, 147, 159, 169

Swami & Friends, xiii, xvii, xviii, xix, 1, 2, 5, 17, 126, 127, 143

Painter of Signs, The, xiii, xiv, xix, xx, 37, 80, 85, 86, 87, 96, 99, 100, 102, 116, 123, 124, 127-129, 132, 136, 137, 142, 146

Tiger for Malgudi, A., 89, 90, 91, 100

Vendor of Sweets, The, xx, 5, 17, 73, 85, 97, 100, 101, 111, 112, 121, 123, 126, 129, 136, 137, 142, 143, 146

Waiting for the Mahatma, xiii, xix, 5, 47, 52, 83, 98, 102, 103, 106, 113, 119, 127, 128, 168, 173, 175

Astrologer's Day & Lawlay Road, xiii

God, Demons and Others, xiii, 37, 140

Horse & Two Goats, A, xiii

Mahabharat, The, xiii, 33, 126, 127, 134, 139, 145, 155, 156, 160, 164

My Dateless Dairy, xiii, 167

My Days : A Memoir, xiii, 17, 20, 22, 104, 130

Next Sunday, xiii

Ramayan, The, xiii, 33, 66, 111, 126, 127, 134, 139, 145, 155, 156, 160, 164

Nagasaki, 65

Naloppa's Grove, 50

Nalini, 60

Naik, M.K., 26, 41, 102

Nandgir, 176

Narad, 164

Narsimhiaha, C.D., 166

Natesh, 50, 52, 102, 103

Natraj, xvi, xvii, 32, 34, 64, 65, 66, 67, 68, 69, 70, 71, 97, 101, 102, 104, 106, 115, 124, 127, 130, 131, 138, 141, 147, 160, 168, 176

New York, 64

O

Objectivity, 1

Occult Message, 23, 24

Oddities and Angularities, xviii

Open Window, 28, 101

Origin of Species, 153

Orthodox, xx, 1, 2, 4, 7, 8, 12, 16, 18, 32, 60, 61, 74, 76, 78, 85, 96, 98, 99, 111, 113, 117, 126, 127, 128, 132, 151, 175

Ovure, 1

P

Pal, Dr., 41, 42, 43, 44, 45, 101, 117, 118, 136

Palmist, 65

Pandey, Shiv, M., 51

Pandhari Pandey, Shyam, 128

Parvati, 30, 35

Patna University, 152

Paul, Pramila, 162

Phule, Mahatma, 49

Poltergeist phenomena, 42

Ponni, 16-18, 100, 111

Prasad, Harimohan, 171

Presence of Mars, 7

Pre-ordained, 31

Previous Birth, 21

Priest, 8, 22, 41, 43, 45, 48, 49, 50, 52, 80, 82, 84, 98, 141, 142, 162, 163, 165, 166, 170, 173, 176

Primitivism, 18

Protagonist, 4, 5, 11, 20, 21, 23, 39, 58, 62, 98, 100, 117, 123, 124, 129, 132

Panjab University, 153

Puranas, 69, 134, 152, 164

Purushastra, 134

R

Radha-Krishna, 65. 67, 68

Radha Krishnan, Dr., 165

Raja, 90

Rajam, xii, xiv, 4, 5, 20, 22, 104, 129

Raju, xv, xvi, xvii, xx, 54-62, 99-101, 103, 110, 111, 114, 117-119, 123, 124, 126, 131, 132, 135, 135-137, 141, 143, 158-160, 166

Rakshas, 64, 69, 102, 115

Raman, xv, 80, 81-83, 85-87, 96, 99, 107, 108, 123, 126, 127, 130, 132, 136, 138

Ramani, xvii, 12, 13, 15, 16, 37, 78, 102, 111, 126, 135, 136, 160

Ramanuj, 140

Ram, 111, 120, 156, 159, 168, 179

Rangi, 124

Rao, Raja, xxii, 100, 104, 126

Rao, Mr., 104

Rao, Raghvendra P., 153

Ravana, 3, 67, 111

Ravi, 15, 30, 34-36

Rebirth, 89, 92

Religious taboos, 12

Richardson, xi

Rita, 93

Rolls Royce, 69

Rosie, xv, xix, xx, xxi, 15, 54-62, 99, 102, 103, 107, 110-112, 114, 117, 118, 122, 124, 126, 128, 129, 135

Russell, 153

Russians, 32

S

Sabarmati, 174

Sacred, 37

Sahitya Academy Award, 54

Sampath, xvi, 30, 34-37, 102, 103, 110

Sanyal, S.C., 18, 32, 137

Sanyas Ashram, 25

Sanhita, 141

Sanjivani Vidhya, 67

Santana Krishna, 76, 143

Sarayu River, 80

Satya Sai Baba, 81

Satyagrah, 52

Saturn, 81, 156

Satyavan, 13

Savitri of ancient legend, 13

Savitri, xvii, xix, 5, 12, 13, 14, 16-19, 37, 84, 99, 100, 102, 103, 110, 111, 122, 123, 124, 127, 128, 130, 135-137, 143, 156, 171, 172

Sen, Mr., 64, 70

Seances, 24

Sentimentalism, 5

Shakespeare, 123

Shastri, 65, 68, 70, 71, 102, 115

Shambhuk, 145

Shantabai, 12, 14-16, 18, 37, 122

Shanti, 15, 30, 35-37, 103, 110, 122, 124, 136, 137

Shirwadkar, Meena, 16

Shriram, xv, xviii, 3, 5, 47, 48, 49, 51, 98, 102

Shrinivas, xv, xvi, 21, 28, 29, 30

Shruti, 141

Shrivastav, Ramesh, 65, 66

Siddharth, 90

Sita, 111, 156

Singh, Kirpal, 75, 92

Smruti, 140, 164

Spiritual Cripple, 14, 16

Spiritualism, 24, 26

Split Personality, 18

St. Thomas Syrian Church, 24

Status quo, xxii, 5, 11, 130, 166, 169, 174, 177, 180

Sunrise Pictures, 30, 33, 34, 35

Sundaram, P.S., 31, 92, 130

Sukracharya, 67

Susila, xvi, 10, 20, 21, 22, 100, 102, 103

Swami, xvii, xx, 1-4, 17, 54, 61

Swaminathan, 1-4

T

Tagore, 26, 152, 154

Taranath, Rajiv, xvi

Tat Twan Asi, 140

Tathagat, 144

Taxidermist, 64, 65, 101, 102, 106, 111, 138

T. Checkov, 1, 39

Temple Prostitute, xiv

Thackery, xxii

Thought Provoking, 7

Thomas Dylan, 153

Tirupathi Hills, 9, 21, 42, 97

Truth Printing Works, 34, 36

U

Upanishada, 28, 36, 139, 164

Underdogs, xviii

University of Leeds, xiii

United States, 77

Union Jack, 93

Untouchability, 32, 33, 47, 50

Unmitigated loneliness, 20

V

Vale of Tears, xviii

Valya, 146

Valmiki, 146, 166

Varna-Vyevastha, 51, xiv

Varnashram Dharma, xiii, 33, 144

Vasu, 44, 45, 64, 65, 67, 68, 69, 70, 71, 97, 101, 102, 106, 115, 131, 146

Velan, 55, 57, 58, 59, 60, 61, 101, 120, 141

Veerswami, 10

Viking Press, 64

Vishnu, 65, 66, 67, 97, 106, 141, 157

W

Walsh, William, 2, 32, 36, 40, 45, 61, 66, 81

Washington, D.C., 152

Western Civilization, 110, 112

Williams, H.M., 148, 160, 167

Willing Suspension of disbelief, 42

World War II, 65